AI, Without the Anxiety

A Plain-English, Deep-Dive Guide to Using ChatGPT for Business, Productivity, and Modern Work

by Matthew J. Shively, MSc

PROMETHEAN
— LITERARY PRESS —

San Antonio, Texas – First Edition

Permissions: For permission requests, contact afshively@yahoo.com.

Disclaimer: No part of this book may be reproduced, stored in a retrieval system, or transmitted in any form or by any means (electronic, mechanical, photocopying, recording, or otherwise) without prior written permission of the publisher, except for brief quotations used in reviews or scholarly works.

This book is provided for educational purposes only. While the author has made every effort to ensure the information is accurate and practical, the author and publisher make no representations or warranties with respect to the completeness or suitability of the content for any particular purpose. The examples, prompts, and workflows in this book are offered as general guidance and may require adaptation to your role, organization, policies, and applicable laws.

This book does not provide legal, medical, financial, or HR advice. If you need such advice, consult a qualified professional.

Trademarks: All product names, logos, and brands are the property of their respective owners. Use of these names does not imply endorsement.

AI Assistance Acknowledgment

This book was developed with support from OpenAI's ChatGPT. ChatGPT was used to assist with early-stage outlining and the generation of preliminary draft text and figure briefs based on author-directed prompts. All AI-generated material was treated as a starting point only and was subsequently reviewed, validated, and substantially edited to ensure clarity, accuracy, and alignment with the professional standards and intent of this publication. The prompting methods and workflow practices described in this book were also applied during development to structure inputs, guide revisions, and support an efficient drafting process.

Why This Book Exists

Most people do not need "more AI." They need less pressure.

If you're reading this, you've probably felt it: the steady drumbeat of headlines, the anxious conversations in meetings, the vague expectation that you should "use AI" to keep up, even if no one has clearly defined what "using AI" means in your job.

For working professionals, that pressure creates a specific kind of stress. It isn't fear of technology. It's fear of waste: wasted time, wasted effort, wasted credibility. You don't want to look careless. You don't want to produce nonsense. You don't want to accidentally share something sensitive. You don't want to add another tool to an already overloaded day.

And yet, under pressure, there's a quieter truth: knowledge work has become heavier than it used to be. Not because people are less capable, but because the environment demands more:

More writing. More coordination. More stakeholders. More context switching. More decisions made faster, with less clarity.

This book exists to reduce that weight.

ChatGPT can be useful, not as a hype machine, and not as an authority, but as an assistant that helps you think, plan, write, and revise with less friction. Used well, it can reduce cognitive load, which is defined as the mental strain of holding too many moving parts in your head at once.

But "used well" is not automatic.

To benefit from ChatGPT without increasing risk or anxiety, you need three things:

1. A plain-English understanding of what it does and doesn't do
2. A professional method for getting reliable work output
3. Guardrails for accuracy, confidentiality, ethics, and judgment

This is a business and productivity textbook because that's what most people actually need: not inspiration, not slogans, but skills.

You will learn how to turn vague work into clear inputs, how to get drafts you can trust, how to verify what matters, and how to build repeatable workflows you can use daily. The goal is not to "be good at AI." The goal is to do better work with less strain and to feel calm and confident while doing it.

How to Use This Book

This book is designed to be used, not admired.

A few important notes before you start:

1. You will see prompts you can copy and paste.
    Prompts are not magic spells. They are professional instructions. When you reuse them, adjust the context (your role, your audience, your goal, your constraints). That adjustment is the difference between a generic answer and a useful one.

2. This book assumes you are non-technical.
    You will not need to code. When technical terms appear, they will be explained in plain English. The goal is practical skills, not jargon.

3. You will learn a repeatable method, not a bag of tricks.
    Many people get stuck because they use ChatGPT randomly: sometimes it's helpful, sometimes it isn't, and they can't predict which. This book teaches a method so you can produce more consistent results.

4. Use the "Practice" sections seriously.
    Each chapter includes exercises that mirror real workplace scenarios. If you do only the reading, you'll understand the ideas. If you do the exercises, you'll build the skill.

5. Take accuracy seriously and calmly.
    ChatGPT can be wrong. That fact doesn't make it useless. It means you must treat it like an assistant: helpful for drafts, structure, options, and reasoning support, while you remain responsible for verification and final decisions.

Suggested reading paths:

If you want immediate day-to-day productivity:

- Prompting Fundamentals for Professionals
- Writing at Work - Emails, Reports, Proposals
- Productivity Systems Powered by AI
- ChatGPT for Business Operations & SOPs

If you feel anxious or uncertain:

- A Calm Reframing of AI Anxiety (Business-Focused)
- How ChatGPT Actually Thinks (Plain English)
- Ethical Use, Accuracy, and Trust in AI Outputs

If you are building long-term capability:

- Thinking, Planning, and Decision-Making with ChatGPT
- Advanced Prompting Frameworks for Professionals
- Personal Knowledge Management With AI
- Building Long-Term Confidence and Judgment With AI

One more important instruction: do not attempt to "use AI everywhere" all at once. Start with one or two safe, high-value workflows. Build confidence. Expand gradually.

Contents

A Calm Reframing of AI Anxiety (Business-Focused)

AI anxiety usually has a reasonable cause.

In business settings, "new tool" rarely means "new benefit." It often means:

- Another system to learn
- Another place for errors to hide
- Another expectation without clear training
- Another risk to manage with limited time

So if you've felt tense about ChatGPT, that is not a personal failure. It is a rational response to unclear standards.

Let's replace uncertainty with a stable frame.

1. ChatGPT is not a coworker. It is not accountable.
   In business, accountability matters. When a human coworker contributes, they can be questioned. They can explain their reasoning. They can be trained. ChatGPT cannot be accountable in the same way. That means you must treat it as a tool, not a decision-maker.

2. The goal is not automation. The goal is cognitive relief.
   Many people hear "AI productivity" and imagine replacing large parts of their work. That framing increases anxiety because it implies risk, disruption, and identity threat.

A calmer framing is this: ChatGPT can help you reduce the mental effort required to start, organize, draft, and revise. It can help you get from "blank page" to "workable draft," from "messy thoughts" to "clear plan," from "too much input" to "structured summary." You still decide. You still verify. You still own the result.

3. Most business value comes from mundane improvements.
   You do not need dramatic transformations. You need:

- Faster first drafts
- Clearer meeting notes
- Better-structured plans
- Stronger emails with fewer revisions
- More consistent processes
- Less time staring at a screen wondering where to begin

Those are quiet wins, and they add up.

4. Safety and professionalism are skills, not personality traits.
   Some people seem fearless with new tools. Often, they are simply less aware of risk. Your caution can be a strength if you pair it with a method.

5. You are allowed to start small.

This book will teach you how to:

- Keep sensitive data out of prompts
- Ask for sources or uncertainty where relevant
- Use verification steps that match the risk level
- Build a personal "trust workflow" that keeps you calm

If you adopt only one practice from this book at first, adopt this: **Use ChatGPT as a drafting assistant, not a final answer machine.**

Drafting is where ChatGPT shines. Drafts can be reviewed, edited, and verified. Drafts reduce anxiety because you remain in control.

As we move into the chapters, you will gain a clear working understanding of what ChatGPT is doing under the hood (in plain English), how to instruct it like a professional, and how to build a reliable system you can use daily.

Chapter 1: The New Reality of Knowledge Work

Knowledge work didn't get harder because people got weaker. It got harder because the job quietly changed.

If you work in operations, management, marketing, professional services, HR, project delivery, customer communication, or any role where your primary output is decisions, writing, plans, or coordination, your work is increasingly shaped by three forces:

1. **Volume:** more inputs than you can fully process
2. **Speed:** shorter time between "question" and "answer"
3. **Complexity:** more stakeholders, constraints, and downstream consequences

This chapter will do three things:

1. Name what has changed in modern work (so you feel less "it's just me")
2. Define the hidden cost of that change: cognitive load
3. Establish a practical role for ChatGPT: reducing friction without sacrificing judgment

We will stay grounded. No hype. No fear. Just the reality you are living in and a method for working with it.

Section 1.1: What "Knowledge Work" Really Means Now

Knowledge work used to be described as "thinking for a living." That phrase is true but incomplete. Today, knowledge work is also "communicating your thinking" in systems that require constant translation.

A typical professional day includes tasks like:

- Translating a messy situation into a clear problem statement
- Translating a decision into a written rationale others can accept
- Translating technical details into stakeholder language
- Translating meetings into tasks, owners, and timelines
- Translating a strategy into a plan that survives real constraints
- Translating a plan into updates that maintain trust and alignment

Notice what's missing from that list: deep uninterrupted time to think.

The work isn't only thinking. It is packaging thinking into formats that move other people.

That packaging is the real work product in many roles:

- An email that prevents confusion
- A brief that makes a decision possible
- A proposal that earns trust
- A process document that reduces errors
- A summary that prevents a project from drifting
- A set of options that turns conflict into choice

In other words, your output is often clarity. And clarity has become more expensive.

Section 1.2: Why Clarity is More Expensive Than It Used to Be

Figure 1.1 – The modern knowledge work loop

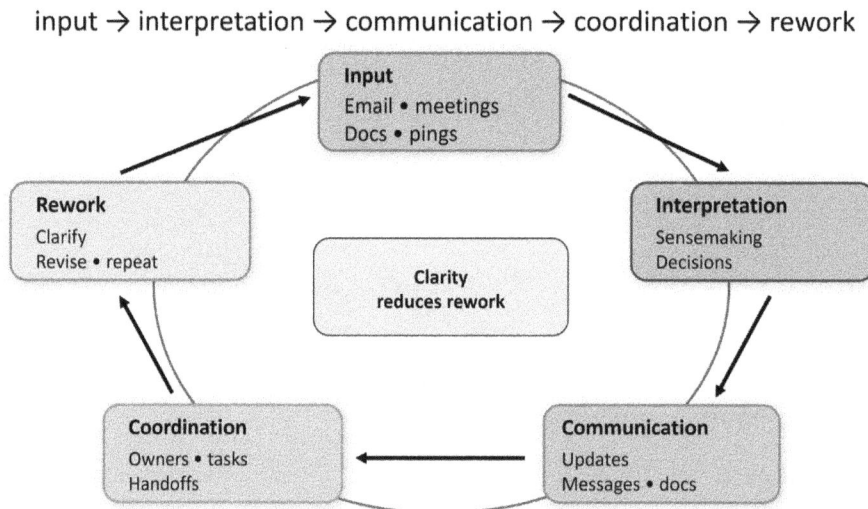

input → interpretation → communication → coordination → rework

Input
Email • meetings
Docs • pings

Interpretation
Sensemaking
Decisions

Rework
Clarify
Revise • repeat

Clarity
reduces rework

Coordination
Owners • tasks
Handoffs

Communication
Updates
Messages • docs

When meaning is missing, the loop tightens into rework.

Clarity costs more now for a simple reason: the number of "edges" around each task has increased.

In business, the edge of a task is anything you must consider beyond the core action. For example, "write an email" sounds simple until you include the edges:

- Who is the audience, and what do they care about?
- What is the political context?
- What is the risk of misinterpretation?
- What is the required tone: firm, warm, neutral, urgent?
- What must be documented for compliance or accountability?
- What details are sensitive and should not be included?
- What is the next action you want the reader to take?
- What attachments, links, or data support your point?

Those edges are not "extra." They are the difference between professional communication and costly confusion.

The problem is that modern work increases edges while reducing time.

More stakeholders mean more perspectives to anticipate. More tools mean more places for information to hide. More speed means less time to slow down and write clearly.

This is why many professionals feel tired even when they "didn't do anything physical." The exhaustion is often mental: sustained attention, decision-making, and constant context switching.

That brings us to the concept that explains the strain.

Section 1.3: Cognitive Load - The Invisible Weight in Your Day

Cognitive load is the amount of mental effort you are using at a given time.

Think of your attention as a backpack. A few items are fine. But if you keep adding items like deadlines, messages, decisions, open loops, and half-finished drafts, the backpack becomes heavy. You can still walk, but everything costs more energy.

Cognitive load increases when you must hold many things in your mind at once, such as:

- The current task plus its dependencies
- The history of a project plus its politics
- What you promised to someone, plus what has changed since then
- The details of a process plus its exceptions
- Multiple "next steps" without clear prioritization

Cognitive load also increases with uncertainty. When you don't know what "good" looks like, your brain keeps searching. That search consumes energy, even if you are sitting still.

In business, cognitive load shows up as:

- Staring at a blank document longer than you want to admit
- Overthinking a short email because the stakes feel unclear
- Re-reading the same paragraph without absorbing it
- Putting off a task you normally could do easily
- Feeling "busy all day" but not satisfied with output
- Making avoidable mistakes because your attention is fragmented

This matters because productivity is not only about time management. It is attention management.

And attention is finite.

Figure 1.2 – Cognitive load as a backpack

Tasks, open loops, decisions, and interruptions compete for your attention.

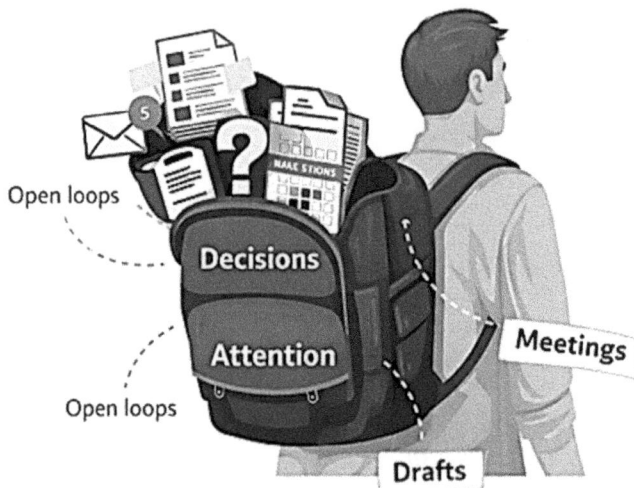

Your "Attention" backpack fills up throughout the day — then feels heavy when you try to focus.

Section 1.4: The Real Bottleneck - Starting, Structuring, and Revising

Many professionals assume their bottleneck is "not enough time."

Often, the real bottleneck is one of these:

1. **Starting:** turning vague intent into a first draft
2. **Structuring:** organizing messy information into a coherent form
3. **Revising:** improving clarity without burning hours

These bottlenecks feel like personal weakness because they happen quietly. You can't point to them like a broken tool. But they consume a surprising amount of your day.

Starting is expensive because it requires decisions:

- What is the point?
- What is the angle?
- What belongs in, and what stays out?
- What does the audience already know?
- What tone is safe?

Structuring is expensive because it requires judgment:

- What is the main idea versus supporting detail?
- What order helps the reader?
- What does the reader need first to understand the rest?

Revising is expensive because it requires both:

- You must see what is unclear and also know how to fix it
- You must keep the goal in mind while changing the text
- You must avoid introducing new errors while correcting old ones

This is where ChatGPT can help if we define its role correctly.

Section 1.5: The Calm, Professional Role for ChatGPT

Here is the role we will use throughout this book: **ChatGPT is a thinking-and-writing assistant that helps you reduce friction in drafting, structuring, and revising while you keep responsibility for accuracy, judgment, and final decisions.**

That sentence contains the boundaries that reduce anxiety:

1. **Assistant:** supports you; does not replace your judgment
2. **Reduce friction:** helps you move faster and clearer, not magically "know"
3. **Drafting/structuring/revising:** focuses on process, not authority
4. **You keep responsibility:** you verify, you decide, you own outcomes

This is similar to how professionals use other tools:

- A spreadsheet can calculate, but you choose the model.
- A template can format, but you choose the content.
- A search engine can retrieve, but you choose what to trust.

ChatGPT fits best when you want:

- A first draft you can improve
- A clearer structure for messy notes
- Options for phrasing, tone, or framing
- A summary that helps you see the shape of information
- A checklist that ensures you didn't miss key points
- A set of questions that sharpen your thinking

Used this way, ChatGPT reduces cognitive load because it externalizes part of the mental work. Instead of holding everything in your head, you can place a draft on the table and react to it.

Reacting is often easier than creating from scratch.

Section 1.6: What ChatGPT is Not (And Why That's Okay)

A major source of anxiety is expecting the wrong thing.

ChatGPT is not:

- A guaranteed source of truth
- A database with perfect facts

- A mind reader that knows your context
- A replacement for expertise in high-stakes decisions
- A secure vault for sensitive information by default

If you expect those things, you will either distrust the tool entirely or use it recklessly.

The calm alternative is to treat ChatGPT as strong at language and structure and limited in certainty.

A practical rule you will use repeatedly: **If the task is about wording, structure, options, or reasoning support, ChatGPT can be helpful quickly.**

If the task is about precise facts, legal compliance, or sensitive decisions, you must add verification and guardrails.

We will not treat this as a moral lecture. We will treat it as a professional craft.

Section 1.7: A Simple Model of Work: Input → Draft → Judgment → Output

To use ChatGPT without anxiety, you need a workflow that keeps you in control.

Figure 1.3 – Drafting assistant workflow

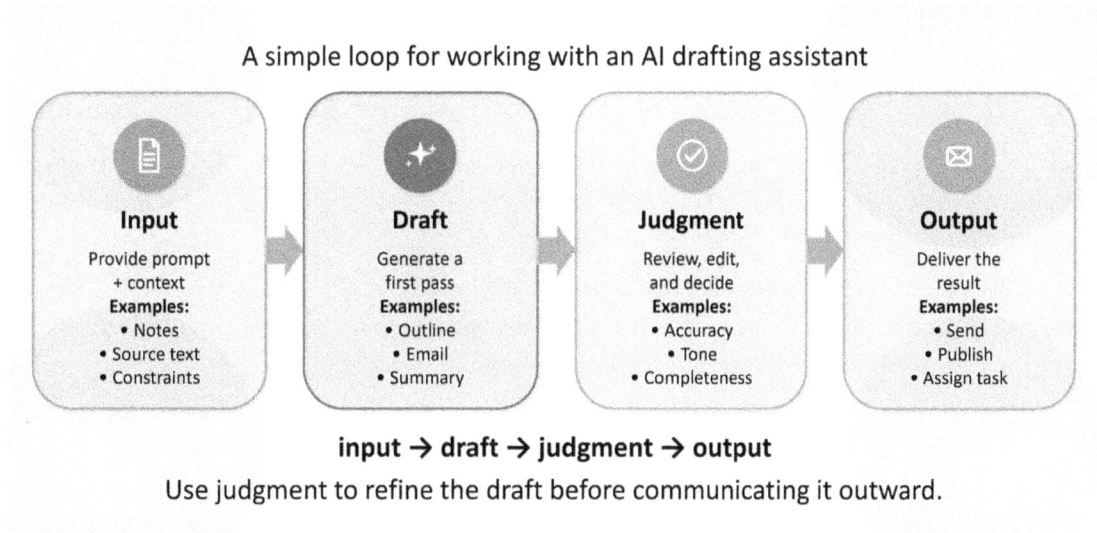

A simple loop for working with an AI drafting assistant

Input	Draft	Judgment	Output
Provide prompt + context	Generate a first pass	Review, edit, and decide	Deliver the result
Examples:	**Examples:**	**Examples:**	**Examples:**
• Notes	• Outline	• Accuracy	• Send
• Source text	• Email	• Tone	• Publish
• Constraints	• Summary	• Completeness	• Assign task

input → draft → judgment → output

Use judgment to refine the draft before communicating it outward.

Here is the simplest version:

1. **Input:** you provide goal, context, constraints, and any necessary source material
2. **Draft:** ChatGPT produces a structured response (draft, plan, summary, options)
3. **Judgment:** you evaluate, edit, verify, and align with reality
4. **Output:** you deliver the final work product (email, plan, memo, SOP, etc.)

This model matters because it defines a professional boundary: ChatGPT generates drafts. You provide judgment.

The anxiety drops when you stop asking, "Can I trust it?" and start asking a better question: "What parts of this task am I using it for, and what verification is appropriate for those parts?"

That question turns vague fear into concrete practice.

Section 1.8: Levels Of Risk - Match Your Verification to The Stakes

Not every task needs the same level of caution.

A friendly internal email about scheduling has lower stakes than a policy memo, a customer commitment, or a financial analysis.

In this book, we will often classify tasks into three levels:

Level 1: Low-risk drafts
Examples: brainstorming, outlining an agenda, rewriting for tone, creating a checklist, summarizing your own notes.
Verification: basic review for clarity and fit.

Level 2: Medium-risk work products
Examples: client emails, proposals, performance communications, operational plans, and internal documentation that will be reused.
Verification: review for accuracy, alignment with policy, and unintended implications; confirm any factual claims.

Level 3: High-risk outputs
Examples: legal/HR decisions, medical/financial guidance, compliance-sensitive statements, public claims, safety-critical instructions.

Verification: do not rely on ChatGPT as a source of truth; use authoritative sources and professional review.

Figure 1.4 – Risk levels and verification

As risk rises, verification needs to get more rigorous.

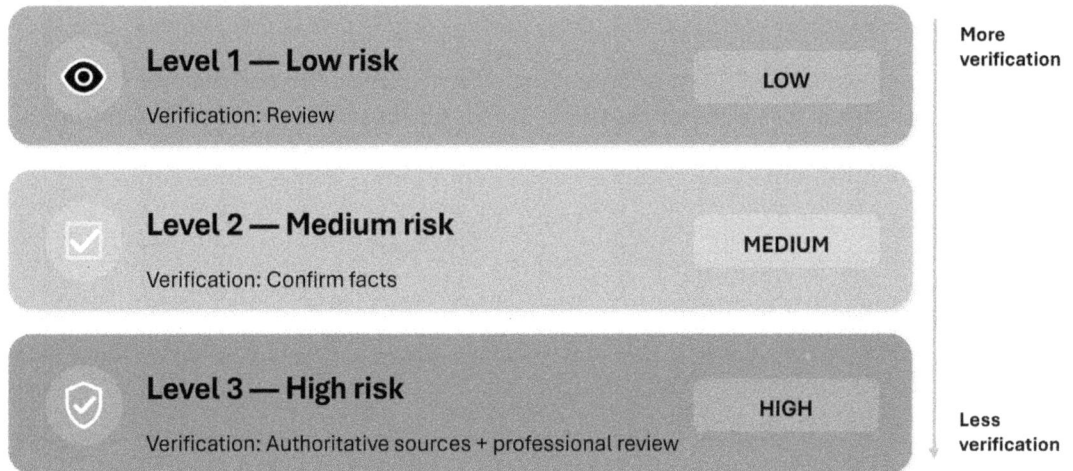

This is not meant to scare you. It's meant to give you a calm, stable standard.

Professionals already work this way:

- You proofread a casual email quickly.
- You review a contract carefully.
- You don't treat a draft like a final answer.

ChatGPT simply makes the distinction more important.

Section 1.9: What Productivity Really Means in Modern Work

In knowledge work, productivity is not "doing more tasks." It is producing more clarity per unit of attention.

A productive professional is often someone who can:

- Turn ambiguity into a clear problem statement
- Turn conflict into options and tradeoffs
- Turn complexity into a simple plan others can execute
- Turn a messy situation into a coherent message
- Reduce rework by communicating clearly the first time

ChatGPT can support all of those when instructed well.

But before we get to prompting, we need one more foundation: the difference between "thinking" and "writing," and why writing is often where people get stuck.

Section 1.10: Why Writing Feels Like Thinking (And Why That Drains You)

Many professionals say, "I'm not a strong writer," when the real issue is that writing at work is not a literary activity. It is a thinking activity performed in public.

Work writing forces you to:

- Choose what matters
- Commit to a position
- Anticipate objections
- Define terms
- Make requests clearly
- Clarify accountability

That is why writing drains you. It is decision-making in text form.

This is also why a drafting assistant is useful: it lowers the cost of externalizing your thinking.

When you can quickly generate a draft, you can move from "internal confusion" to "visible material." Once material is visible, you can improve it.

This is the core psychological advantage of a good assistant:

- It helps you begin
- It helps you see
- It helps you revise

But it doesn't remove responsibility.

Section 1.11: A Realistic Before-And-After - Where the Gains Come From

Let's make this concrete.

Consider a common scenario: you need to send an update email to a mixed audience (leaders, peers, and a partner team). You have notes in your head, a few data points, and a vague sense of urgency.

Figure 1.5 – "Before vs. after" time map of a work email task

Compare how an assistant reduces delay, uncertainty, and follow-ups by structuring input and accelerating drafting.

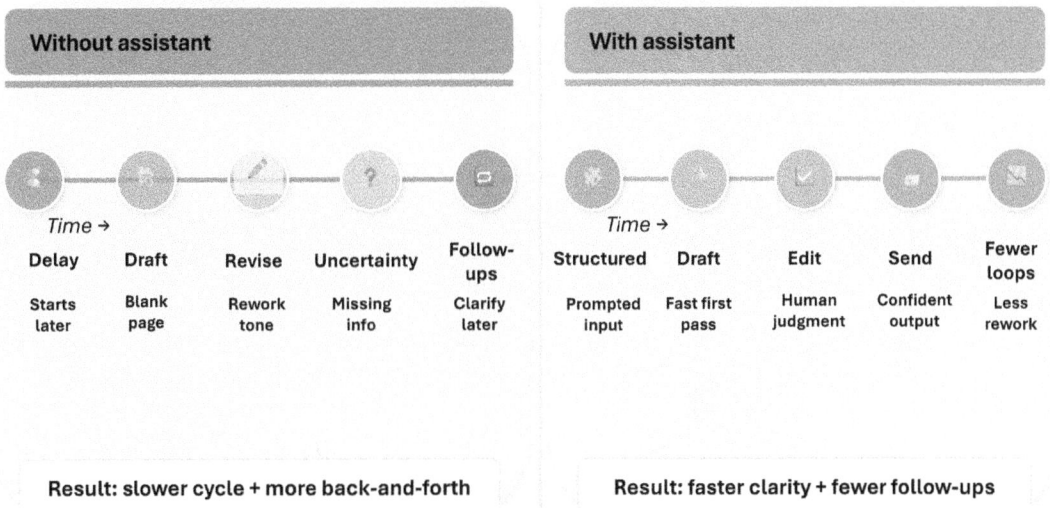

Without assistant					With assistant				
Time →					Time →				
Delay	Draft	Revise	Uncertainty	Follow-ups	Structured	Draft	Edit	Send	Fewer loops
Starts later	Blank page	Rework tone	Missing info	Clarify later	Prompted input	Fast first pass	Human judgment	Confident output	Less rework

Result: slower cycle + more back-and-forth   **Result: faster clarity + fewer follow-ups**

Tip: Missing context early tends to reappear later as "rework" and extra clarification cycles.

Without an assistant, the process often looks like:

- Delay starting because it feels risky
- Write a draft that's too long or too vague
- Revise repeatedly because the tone feels off
- Hit send while still uncertain
- Receive follow-up questions because key details weren't clear
- Spend more time clarifying than the email saved

With a drafting assistant, the process can change:

- You provide context, audience, tone, and the specific ask
- You get a structured draft with headings and clear next steps
- You edit for accuracy and strength

- You send a clearer message
- You reduce follow-up questions and rework

The gain is not "AI wrote the email." The gain is "you reached clarity faster."

That is the standard we will use throughout this book.

Section 1.12: The Professional Mindset That Makes This Work

Before we move into how ChatGPT works (in plain English), adopt three professional mindsets.

Mindset 1: Treat prompts as instructions, not wishes.
If you want reliable output, you must specify:

- What you want
- Who it's for
- What constraints apply
- What success looks like

Mindset 2: Treat outputs as drafts, not authority.
A draft is useful even if imperfect. Your job is to shape it.

Mindset 3: Treat verification as part of the workflow, not a sign of distrust.
Professionals verify because they care about quality. Verification is a skill.

These mindsets reduce anxiety because they place you back in the driver's seat.

You are not "trusting AI." You are managing a tool.

Practice Exercises

Instructions: For each exercise, copy the prompt into ChatGPT and replace bracketed fields with your context. Keep your responses professional and avoid sensitive information. Treat outputs as drafts.

Exercise 1 — Identify your cognitive load triggers (reflection + action)

> *Prompt:*
> "I want to reduce cognitive load at work. Ask me 12 diagnostic questions to identify what is currently overloading me (inputs, meetings, unclear priorities, writing, decision volume, interruptions, open loops). After I answer, summarize the top 3

load drivers and propose 5 practical interventions I can
implement this week. Keep it calm and businesslike."

Exercise 2 — Turn "vague work" into a clear task statement

Prompt:
"Help me turn this vague task into a clear work request with
success criteria.
Vague task: [paste your vague task].
My role: [your role].
Audience: [who it's for].
Deadline: [when].
Constraints: [tone, length, policy considerations].
Output format: Write (1) a one-sentence goal, (2) a definition of
done, (3) 5 clarifying questions you need from me, and (4) a
first-draft outline."

Exercise 3 — Map your daily "clarity outputs"

Prompt:
"Based on my role, help me list the top 10 'clarity outputs' I
produce (emails, updates, plans, summaries, SOPs, decision notes,
stakeholder messages).
My role: [your role].
My industry/context: [context].
Then help me choose the top 2 outputs where better drafts would
reduce the most rework."

Exercise 4 — Build your personal risk ladder (Level 1–3)

Prompt:
"Help me create a personal risk ladder for using ChatGPT at work.
List 8 tasks I might use ChatGPT for. For each, label it Level 1,
2, or 3 risk and explain why in plain English. Then recommend the
verification step I should use for each.
My work context: [brief context]."

Exercise 5 — Drafting assistant test: rewrite for clarity without changing meaning

Prompt:
"Rewrite the message below for clarity and professional tone
without changing the meaning. Provide three versions: (A) neutral
and direct, (B) warm and collaborative, (C) concise executive
style.

```
Message: [paste your message].
Audience: [who].
Purpose: [what you need].
Keep it under [word limit]."
```

Exercise 6 — From messy notes to structured summary (your notes only)

```
Prompt:
"Turn the notes below into a structured summary with: Key points,
Decisions made, Open questions, Next steps (with owners and
dates). If information is missing, leave a placeholder labeled
'Missing.'
Notes: [paste your notes].
Tone: calm, professional."
```

Exercise 7 — Debug-the-prompt: why the output was generic

```
Step 1 prompt (intentionally vague):
"Write an update email about my project."
```

```
Step 2 prompt (debug):
"The output was too generic. Explain exactly what information you
lacked. Then ask me the 8 most important questions you need to
write a useful update email in my context. After I answer,
rewrite the email."
```

Exercise 8 — Reduce rework by adding "definition of done"

```
Prompt:
"I want to prevent rework on a task. Here is the task: [task].
Create a 'definition of done' checklist with 10 items, written in
plain English, including quality checks and stakeholder alignment
checks. Keep it role-appropriate for a professional environment."
```

Exercise 9 — Create a "starting script" for hard writing tasks

```
Prompt:
"I often delay starting [type of document]. Create a reusable
'starting script' I can paste into ChatGPT that collects the
context you need and produces a strong first draft.
Document type: [email/proposal/report/SOP/etc.].
My audience: [audience].
My goal: [goal].
Constraints: [length/tone/policy].
```

> *Include a short instruction that reminds me to remove sensitive*
> *information."*

Exercise 10 — Personal baseline: measure your current friction

> *Prompt:*
> *"Help me measure where my time goes when I produce a work draft.*
> *Ask me to estimate: time to start, time to structure, time to*
> *revise, time spent on follow-ups after sending. Then propose a*
> *simple experiment for the next week to reduce total cycle time by*
> *20% using ChatGPT as a drafting assistant."*

Skill Check

After completing this chapter, you should be able to:

- Describe what has changed in modern knowledge work and why clarity is more expensive
- Explain cognitive load in plain English and recognize how it shows up in your day
- Use a stable role definition for ChatGPT: drafting/structuring/revising support, not authority
- Classify tasks by risk level and match verification effort to the stakes
- Apply the input → draft → judgment → output workflow to a real workplace task
- Identify one or two high-value, low-risk starting points for daily use

Chapter 2: How ChatGPT Actually Thinks (Plain English)

If you've ever felt uncertain about ChatGPT, the uncertainty usually comes from one hidden question: "What is it doing when it answers me?"

People imagine one of two extremes:

- It's "searching the internet" and pulling facts like a super Google.
- Or it's "making things up" like a random text generator.

Neither picture is accurate enough to help you work confidently.

This chapter will give you a plain-English mental model of how ChatGPT produces responses, why it can sound confident even when it's wrong, and how professionals can use it responsibly without becoming technical.

You will learn:

- What ChatGPT is trained to do (and what it is not trained to do)
- Why it feels like "thinking" even though it doesn't reason like a person
- How to reduce errors by changing how you ask and how you check
- A practical "reliability routine" you can use daily

We are not aiming for computer-science depth. We are aiming for professional clarity.

Section 2.1: A Calm Definition - What ChatGPT Is

ChatGPT is a language model: software trained to generate and transform text.

At a practical level, it does three kinds of work extremely well:

1. It recognizes patterns in language.
2. It predicts what text is likely to come next.
3. It follows instructions in conversation form (within limits).

That phrase "predicts what comes next" can sound dismissive, like a fancy autocomplete. But the scale matters.

Imagine reading millions of pages of writing and learning the patterns:

- How business emails typically flow
- How arguments are structured
- How project plans are phrased

- How summaries compress information
- How a polite refusal is worded
- How different tones feel (firm, warm, cautious, executive)

Now imagine that, when you ask a question, the system produces a response by assembling likely text patterns that fit:

- Your prompt
- The conversational context
- The kind of answer you seem to want
- The style you've requested

That's the basic mechanism.

The key professional insight is this: **ChatGPT is optimized to produce a plausible, coherent response, not to guarantee truth.**

Figure 2.1 – Plain-English model of ChatGPT: "pattern-based drafting"

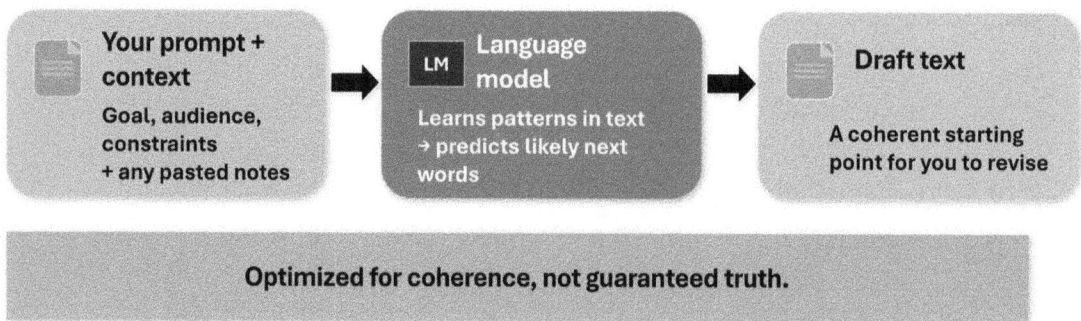

Your prompt + context
Goal, audience, constraints
+ any pasted notes

LM **Language model**
Learns patterns in text
→ predicts likely next words

Draft text
A coherent starting point for you to revise

Optimized for coherence, not guaranteed truth.

Plain-English mental model: treat outputs as drafts you verify and refine.

That is why it can be so helpful for drafting and structure. And that is why you must manage accuracy for facts and decisions.

Section 2.2: Why it Feels Like "Thinking" When it's Really "Text Generation"

When you talk with ChatGPT, it can:

- Explain tradeoffs
- Offer step-by-step reasoning
- Ask clarifying questions
- Identify risks
- Suggest options and improvements
- Write in a calm, competent voice

This can feel like you're talking to a thinking partner.

But the "thinking" is not the same as human thinking.

A person has experiences, goals, emotions, and a model of the world built through living. A person can also choose to pause, consult sources, and deliberately verify.

ChatGPT has none of that lived experience. It produces text based on learned patterns.

So why can it reason at all?

Because a lot of reasoning is expressed through language patterns:

- "If X is true, then Y follows…"
- "Option A is better when you value speed; option B is better when you value accuracy…"
- "The risk here is…"
- "A sensible next step would be…"

It has seen countless examples of people reasoning in writing and conversation. It can reproduce those structures convincingly.

That's useful. But it also creates a risk. If the system doesn't have enough context, it will still try to complete the task by producing the most plausible-sounding answer. That's where you get confident nonsense.

Professionals reduce this risk by doing two things:

1. Give better constraints and source material
2. Use verification appropriate to the task's risk level

We'll make that concrete soon.

Section 2.3: A Simple Metaphor - ChatGPT as a Very Fast Drafter

Here's a metaphor you can hold onto. Imagine you have an assistant who can draft extremely quickly, in many styles, and can reorganize your text instantly. But this assistant has a specific limitation: they are not allowed to leave the room to look things up.

They can help you:

- Turn your notes into a structured memo
- Create a plan template
- Rewrite an email so it's clearer
- Generate options and phrasing choices
- Create checklists and frameworks
- Summarize the content you provide

But if you ask:

"What is the exact policy requirement?"
"What does the law say?"
"What are the precise numbers?"
"What happened on a specific date?"

They might guess because they can't verify by default.

This metaphor removes both hype and fear.

You can trust the assistant to draft. You cannot treat the assistant as a source of truth without checks.

Section 2.4: What "Training" Means in Plain English

ChatGPT is trained on large amounts of text, so it learns language patterns and relationships between concepts.

For non-technical professionals, you only need three training ideas:

1. **It learns from examples, not from understanding like a human.**
   If it sees many examples of professional memos, it becomes good at writing memos. That doesn't mean it "knows" your company's memo policy unless you tell it.

2. **It generalizes.**
   It can apply patterns from one situation to another. This is why it can help in many domains.

3. **It does not have your context unless you provide it.**
   Your company's priorities, your team's history, your audience's sensitivity; none of that is automatically available.

This is why "prompting" matters. Prompting is simply the act of supplying the missing context and constraints.

Section 2.5: Why it Can Be Wrong - The Three Most Common Failure Modes

ChatGPT can produce incorrect outputs in several ways. Knowing the failure modes helps you prevent them calmly.

Figure 2.2 – Failure modes map

Common ways outputs go wrong when inputs or verification are weak

Missing context → generic filler	Confident formatting → polish hides uncertainty	Fabrication under pressure → made-up specifics
When key details are absent (audience, tone, examples, constraints), the model fills gaps with safe, vague language that sounds right but helps little.	Clean structure, bullets, and strong tone can make uncertain content feel certain. Formatting improves readability—not accuracy.	If asked for exact names, numbers, or citations without sources, it may generate plausible-sounding details instead of admitting uncertainty.
What to do: add missing details	**What to do: add missing details**	**What to do: add missing details**

Tip: Ask for assumptions, request citations/sources, and verify high-stakes outputs.

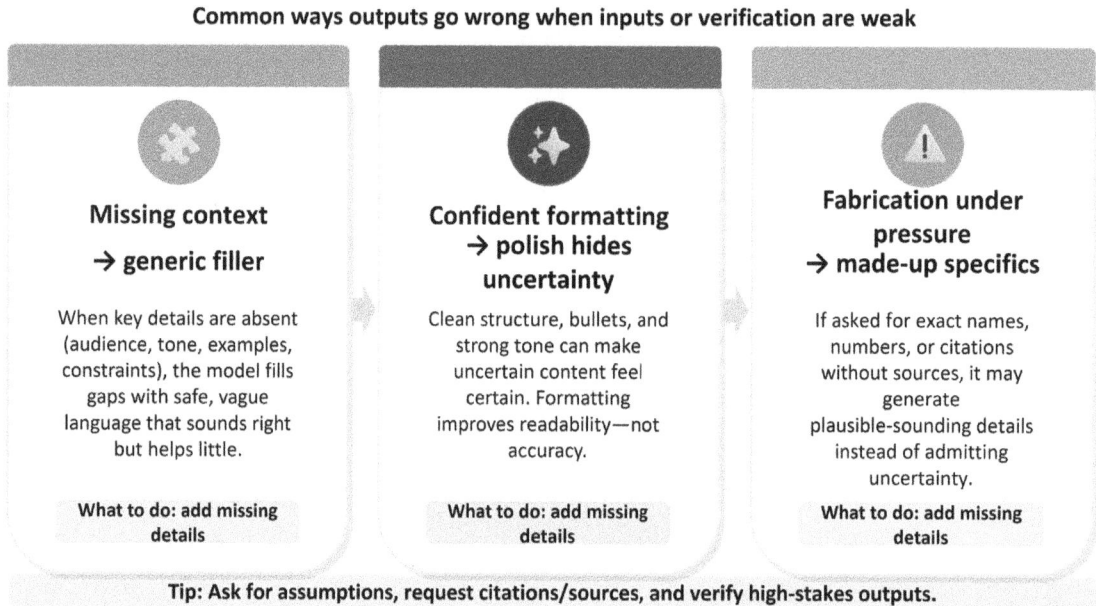

Failure Mode 1: Missing context → plausible filler

When you don't provide key details, it fills gaps with generic assumptions.

Example: You ask for "a project update email" but don't specify:

- Audience (leaders vs peers vs customers)
- Project status (on track vs behind)
- Risks and asks
- What decisions are needed

You'll get a generic email. It may be "well-written" but not useful.

Failure Mode 2: Confident formatting hides uncertainty

ChatGPT can produce a neat-looking answer with headings, bullet points, and a professional tone. That formatting can make the content feel more trustworthy than it is.

This matters in business. We often equate "polished" with "correct." ChatGPT can be polished even when it's wrong.

Failure Mode 3: Fabrication under pressure (hallucination)

When asked for specific facts it can't reliably produce, it may generate details that sound right.

Professionals call this a hallucination: The model produces invented information presented as if it's true.

You do not need to fear this. You need to manage it.

A practical rule: **The more specific the factual claim, the more you should either provide the source material or require verification.**

Section 2.6: How To Make ChatGPT More Reliable - The Professional Input Triad

Most improvements come from better input.

Use this simple triad whenever you want better outputs:

1. **Goal:** what you want and why
2. **Context:** what the assistant must know to do it correctly
3. **Constraints:** tone, length, format, boundaries, and what not to do

Figure 2.3 – The professional input triad

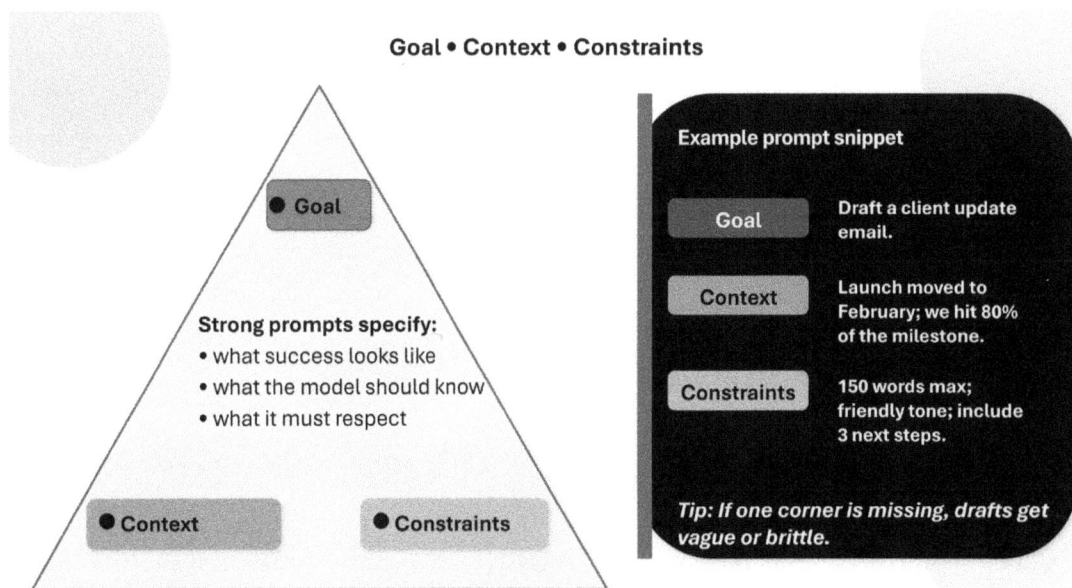

Goal • Context • Constraints

Goal

Strong prompts specify:
• what success looks like
• what the model should know
• what it must respect

Context   Constraints

Example prompt snippet

Goal	Draft a client update email.
Context	Launch moved to February; we hit 80% of the milestone.
Constraints	150 words max; friendly tone; include 3 next steps.

Tip: If one corner is missing, drafts get vague or brittle.

Here is what this looks like in practice.

> *Weak prompt:*
> "Write a policy memo about remote work."
>
> *Stronger prompt using the triad:*
> "Write a 1-page internal memo proposing an updated remote work policy for a 20-person professional services team.
> Goal: Clarify expectations while maintaining flexibility and

> *fairness.*
> *Context: Current policy is inconsistent; managers interpret it differently; we've had confusion about in-office days and availability.*
> *Constraints: Calm tone, no legal claims, include 5 policy principles, define eligibility, include a simple exception process, and end with next steps for feedback."*

Notice what you did. You moved from vague to instructed. That shift reduces anxiety because it reduces randomness.

Section 2.7: The "Source-First" Habit - When You Should Feed It Material

If you want accuracy about specific content (e.g., your meeting notes, your process steps, your policy draft) give ChatGPT that content.

Professionals often misuse ChatGPT by asking it to invent what they could provide.

> *Instead of:*
> *"Summarize our meeting."*
>
> *Do:*
> *"Here are my notes. Turn them into a structured summary with decisions, owners, and next steps."*
>
> *Instead of:*
> *"Write an SOP for our onboarding."*
>
> *Do:*
> *"Here is our current onboarding checklist and pain points. Create a draft SOP."*

ChatGPT becomes more reliable when it transforms your information rather than guessing unknown information.

This is one of the most calming ways to use it at work:

- You are not asking it to "know" your business
- You are asking it to structure what you already know

Section 2.8: ChatGPT's "Memory" in a Conversation - Why Context Drifts

In a conversation, ChatGPT uses the text you've provided to maintain context. But context can drift for three reasons:

1. You assume it remembers details you didn't actually state.
2. The conversation gets long and earlier details become less prominent.
3. You change goals midstream without restating constraints.

The professional fix is simple: Restate the essentials when the output matters.

For important work products, include a short "context recap" in your prompt: "Reminder: audience is executives, tone is concise, we do not promise dates we can't guarantee, and we must avoid naming specific vendors."

This takes ten seconds and can save twenty minutes of revision.

Section 2.9: A Practical "Reliability Routine" You Can Use Daily

Here is a reliability routine you can apply to almost any business output:

Step 1: Define the role
"Act as a [role] writing for [audience]."

Step 2: Provide the facts you want included
Paste your notes, numbers, constraints, and policies; sanitized for confidentiality.

Step 3: Ask for a draft in a specific format
"Write a 6-sentence email with a subject line and 3 bullet next steps."

Step 4: Require uncertainty labeling for unknowns
"If you are unsure, label it 'Unverified' and ask me a question instead of guessing."

Step 5: Add a verification checklist
"After the draft, list 5 things I should verify before sending."

Figure 2.4 – Reliability routine

role → facts → format → uncertainty labeling → verification checklist

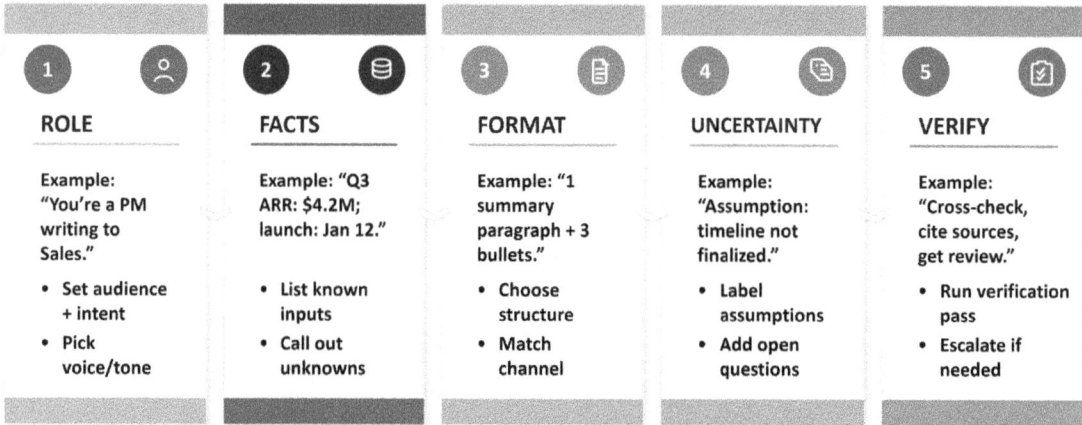

ROLE	FACTS	FORMAT	UNCERTAINTY	VERIFY
1	2	3	4	5
Example: "You're a PM writing to Sales."	Example: "Q3 ARR: $4.2M; launch: Jan 12."	Example: "1 summary paragraph + 3 bullets."	Example: "Assumption: timeline not finalized."	Example: "Cross-check, cite sources, get review."
• Set audience + intent • Pick voice/tone	• List known inputs • Call out unknowns	• Choose structure • Match channel	• Label assumptions • Add open questions	• Run verification pass • Escalate if needed

Tip: Use this routine every time stakes rise — legal, medical, finance, policy, or high-visibility comms.

This routine does something important for anxiety: It turns "trust" into a process.

You are no longer relying on hope. You are using a method.

Section 2.10: Why ChatGPT Sometimes "Argues" Or "Agrees" Too Much

Some users notice that ChatGPT can sound overly agreeable. Others notice it can sound overly confident.

This is not a personality. It is a product of how it is designed to be helpful and conversational.

In professional use, you can manage this with direct instructions:

> *"Challenge my assumptions."*
>
> *"Offer a counterargument."*
>
> *"List risks and failure modes."*

> *"Give me three options with tradeoffs."*
>
> *"Do not flatter; be concise and practical."*

The assistant is sensitive to instructions about tone and posture.

A powerful prompt line for business users is: "Be useful, not polite."

That doesn't mean rude. It means direct, structured, and focused.

Section 2.11: The Most Important Limit - Confidentiality and Data You Should Not Share

This chapter is about how ChatGPT works, so we must address a central professional issue: what you put into prompts.

A calm baseline rule: **Do not paste sensitive personal data, confidential company information, or regulated information into a general AI chat unless your organization has approved it and you are using an approved environment.**

This includes, for example:

- Personally identifiable information (like full names tied to sensitive context, addresses, IDs)
- Customer records
- Internal financials not meant to be shared
- Legal strategies or privileged information
- HR performance details
- Passwords, access codes, or security procedures

You can still use ChatGPT effectively without sharing sensitive details.

Use sanitization:

- Replace names with roles ("Client A," "Manager," "Vendor")
- Remove identifying numbers
- Summarize sensitive parts instead of pasting raw text
- Focus on structure and language rather than proprietary detail

We will return to this with depth in the ethics chapter. For now, the practical point is: Safe inputs lead to safe outputs.

Section 2.12: A Working Definition Of "Good Output" For Professionals

Before we move into GPT-5-specific capabilities in the next chapter, establish what "good output" means at work.

Good output is not "impressive writing." Good output is:

- **Clear:** the reader understands the point on the first pass
- **Correct:** facts and commitments are accurate
- **Appropriate:** tone matches the relationship and context
- **Actionable:** next steps and owners are clear
- **Efficient:** minimal rework and follow-up questions
- **Aligned:** fits policy, strategy, and professional norms

ChatGPT can help with clarity, structure, tone, and actionability. You must ensure correctness and alignment.

This division of labor is the foundation of confident use.

Practice Exercises

Exercise 1 — Rewrite a weak prompt using the Input Triad

> *Prompt:*
> *"Here is a weak prompt I used: [paste it].*
> *Rewrite it using Goal, Context, and Constraints. Create two versions: (A) quick version I can type in 30 seconds, (B) detailed version for high-importance work. Explain in plain English what you added and why."*

Exercise 2 — Force uncertainty labeling (anti-hallucination practice)

> *Prompt:*
> *"I want you to answer the question below, but do not guess. If you are unsure, label the statement 'Unverified' and ask me for the missing information instead.*
> *Question: [your question].*
> *After answering, list what you would need to verify for a Level 2 professional deliverable."*

Exercise 3 — Transform your own notes into a structured output

> **Prompt:**
> "Turn the notes below into a structured work product:
> Format: [choose one: executive summary / meeting minutes /
> project update / decision memo].
> Include headings, decisions, risks, and next steps.
> Notes: [paste notes]."

Exercise 4 — Debug-the-output: identify missing context

> **Prompt:**
> "Your previous draft felt generic. Diagnose why by listing the
> top 10 pieces of context you did not have. Then ask me the 8 most
> important questions to improve the draft. After I answer, rewrite
> it."

Exercise 5 — Create a verification checklist for a real deliverable

> **Prompt:**
> "I'm using ChatGPT to draft a [email/memo/proposal].
> Create a verification checklist with two sections:
> (1) Accuracy checks (facts, dates, numbers, commitments)
> (2) Professional alignment checks (tone, policy, stakeholder
> sensitivity, confidentiality).
> Keep it short and practical (max 12 checklist items)."

Exercise 6 — Practice "source-first" prompting

> **Prompt:**
> "I will paste source material. Your job is to transform it
> without adding new facts.
> Rules: Do not invent details. If something is missing, label it
> 'Missing.'
> Source material: [paste text].
> Task: [summarize / outline / rewrite / extract action items]."

Exercise 7 — Tone control drill (same content, three audiences)

> **Prompt:**
> "Rewrite the message below for three audiences:
> (A) my manager, (B) a peer partner team, (C) a customer.
> Keep the facts identical. Adjust tone and structure
> appropriately.
> Message: [paste message]."

Exercise 8 — Build your personal "safe prompt template" (confidentiality-aware)

> *Prompt:*
> *"Help me design a reusable prompt template I can use at work that avoids sensitive information.*
> *It should include placeholders for: goal, audience, context (sanitized), constraints, and 'do not include' items.*
> *Then show me an example filled out for a common workplace task like an update email."*

Exercise 9 — Create a "challenge mode" prompt

> *Prompt:*
> *"I want you to challenge my thinking instead of agreeing.*
> *Topic: [decision or plan].*
> *Ask me 10 tough questions, list 5 risks, and propose 3 alternative approaches with tradeoffs. Keep it calm and professional."*

Exercise 10 — Identify which tasks in your week are best suited for drafting support

> *Prompt:*
> *"Here is my typical weekly task list: [paste list].*
> *Classify each task into one of three categories:*
> *(1) Great for ChatGPT drafting/structuring,*
> *(2) Use with caution and verification,*
> *(3) Not appropriate for ChatGPT.*
> *Explain your reasoning in plain English and suggest safer adaptations where possible."*

Skill Check

After completing this chapter, you should be able to:

- Explain what ChatGPT does in plain English without hype or fear
- Describe why it can sound confident even when it is wrong
- Recognize the three common failure modes and respond calmly
- Use the Goal–Context–Constraints triad to get more reliable outputs
- Apply a daily reliability routine that includes uncertainty labeling and verification steps

- Use "source-first" prompting to transform your material instead of forcing guesses
- Create a confidentiality-aware prompt template for professional use

Chapter 3: What GPT-5 Changes for Business Users

If Chapters 1 and 2 gave you the calm foundation of what modern work demands are and what ChatGPT is actually doing, this chapter answers the practical question professionals ask next: "Okay. So what's different now?"

You do not need to track model versions like a hobby. But you do need to understand the handful of changes that directly affect your daily workflow: reliability, instruction-following, longer work sessions, better handling of complex tasks, and more consistent behavior when you ask for professional structure.

This chapter is written for non-technical business users. We will not focus on benchmarks or engineering language. We will focus on what you can do differently at work because GPT-5 behaves differently and how to capture those gains without increasing risk.

A note about stability (a calm assumption): model capabilities and product features change over time. This chapter describes GPT-5 as documented by OpenAI in 2026, and it distinguishes between the model's core behavior and optional features (like browsing or file handling) that may depend on your plan, your organization, or your settings.

Section 3.1: The Most Important Shift - GPT-5 is a "System," Not One Static Thing

Earlier generations often felt like "one model answering you." GPT-5 is described as a unified system with multiple model variants and a router that chooses which one to use based on the task and your intent.

Plain English translation:

- Sometimes you need speed: a clean email rewrite, a quick agenda, a concise summary.
- Sometimes you need depth: a decision memo with tradeoffs, a process redesign, a risk analysis.

GPT-5 is designed to handle both by routing work to a fast model for most questions and a deeper reasoning model for harder problems, with the router deciding based on complexity, tool needs, and cues like "think hard about this."

Why this matters for business users:

1. You can stop treating every prompt like a high-stakes exam.
   You don't need to squeeze every detail into one request, "or else it will fail."
   GPT-5 is better at handling multi-step work when you collaborate with it
   like a drafting partner.

2. You can deliberately choose "quick" versus "deep" behavior.
   Even if the system routes automatically, your words influence the posture of
   the response. If you need speed, you can ask for a short draft. If you need
   depth, you can explicitly request rigorous reasoning, risks, and verification
   steps.

Figure 3.1 – GPT-5 as a routed system

Two lanes: "Fast Draft Mode" vs "Deep Reasoning Mode" (selected by a simple router)

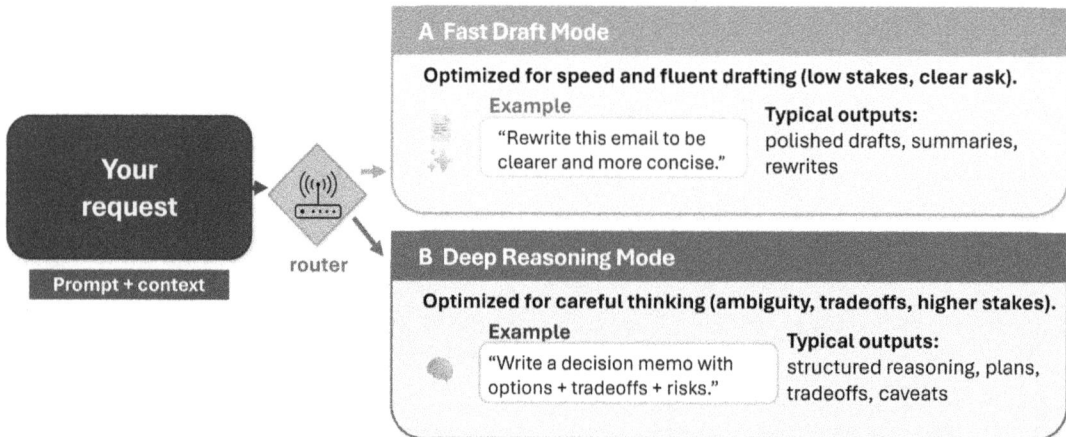

Your request

Prompt + context

router

A Fast Draft Mode

Optimized for speed and fluent drafting (low stakes, clear ask).

Example
"Rewrite this email to be clearer and more concise."

Typical outputs:
polished drafts, summaries, rewrites

B Deep Reasoning Mode

Optimized for careful thinking (ambiguity, tradeoffs, higher stakes).

Example
"Write a decision memo with options + tradeoffs + risks."

Typical outputs:
structured reasoning, plans, tradeoffs, caveats

Router chooses a lane based on task type, stakes, and uncertainty.

3. You can reduce cognitive load by separating phases.
   Instead of doing everything in one pass, you can use a two-pass workflow:

   - **Pass 1:** generate structure quickly
   - **Pass 2:** refine with deeper reasoning and checks

That workflow fits modern knowledge work: it externalizes thinking into a draft
you can improve, which is exactly the "input → draft → judgment → output" model
from Chapter 1.

Section 3.2: What Improved in Practice - Instruction Following, Steerability, and Less "People-Pleasing"

Business users care less about "raw intelligence" and more about a simple question: "Did it follow my instructions?"

OpenAI describes GPT-5 as improving instruction-following and reducing sycophancy (a tendency to agree too readily or mirror the user).

In plain English:

- Better instruction-following means fewer rounds of "No, not like that."
- Better steerability means you can shape tone, structure, and format more consistently.
- Reduced sycophancy means it is more willing to disagree, flag issues, or challenge assumptions when asked, rather than simply affirming.

This changes how you should prompt.

In older habits, professionals often wrote overly long prompts because they expected the assistant to "wander." With GPT-5, you can often get better results by being clear and directive rather than verbose. For example, a directive prompt that works well for professionals:

```
"Draft a 10-sentence project update for executives.
Constraints: neutral tone, no excuses, include status, risks,
decisions needed, and next steps with owners.
If any information is missing, ask me questions instead of
guessing."
```

This is not magic. It's management. You are telling a capable drafting assistant what "good" looks like.

But there is a caution here and it's important for anxiety reduction.

Section 3.3: A Calm Warning - Stronger Instruction Following Can Create New Types of Mistakes

When a system gets better at following instructions, it may sometimes prioritize strict formatting over "stopping when it should stop."

OpenAI's GPT-5.2 system card describes cases where, under strict output requirements (for example, "Only output an integer"), the model may try to produce an answer even when it lacks necessary information, because the instruction is strict.

You do not need to be alarmed by this. You simply need one professional habit: Always give the model permission to say "Missing," "Unverified," or "I need more information."

If you want fewer hallucinations (fabricated facts), you must make abstention acceptable. In practice, that means adding lines like:

- "If you are unsure, label it Unverified."
- "If information is missing, ask me questions."
- "Do not invent names, dates, or numbers."

This aligns with Chapter 2's reliability routine, especially Step 4 (require uncertainty labeling).

In business terms, you are implementing a quality control rule: **it's better to ask one clarifying question than to ship a confident error.**

Section 3.4: Longer Context - Why GPT-5 Feels More Useful in Real Projects

One of the biggest practical improvements for professionals is long-context handling, meaning the model can work with longer documents and longer conversations more effectively. OpenAI highlights long-context understanding and complex multi-step project handling as key strengths in the GPT-5.2 series, and GPT-5 is positioned for long chains of tool calls and agentic tasks.

"Context" in plain English means: the information available inside the conversation at the time you ask.

Longer context supports several work realities:

1. **Real work comes in packets, not single questions.**
   You don't have just one email. You have a thread. You don't have one requirement. You have a policy plus exceptions plus stakeholder preferences.

2. **Real work requires consistency.**
   If you're writing a proposal, you want terminology, tone, and priorities to stay stable across sections. If you're building an SOP, you want steps and definitions to stay consistent.

3. **Real work includes reference material.**
   Meeting notes, customer feedback, and existing process docs. These are the "source material" that makes outputs accurate.

Longer context does not remove the need for good prompting. It changes what "good prompting" looks like.

Instead of repeatedly re-explaining everything, you can create a context packet at the start of a project.

A context packet is a clean, sanitized summary you provide once and maintain as the "source of truth" inside the chat.

Example: a context packet (work-safe version)

> *"Context packet for this project (use as source of truth):*
>
> *Purpose: Update our customer onboarding process to reduce delays and improve clarity.*
>
> *Audience: Operations team + Sales leadership.*
>
> *Current pain points: handoff gaps, unclear ownership, inconsistent timelines.*
>
> *Constraints: Keep it simple; no new tools this quarter; must fit current staffing.*
>
> *Deliverables: (1) Draft SOP, (2) onboarding checklist, (3) customer-facing welcome email.*
>
> *Tone: calm, practical, no hype.*
>
> *Do not include: customer names, contract terms, internal financial numbers."*

Figure 3.2 – Context packet workspace

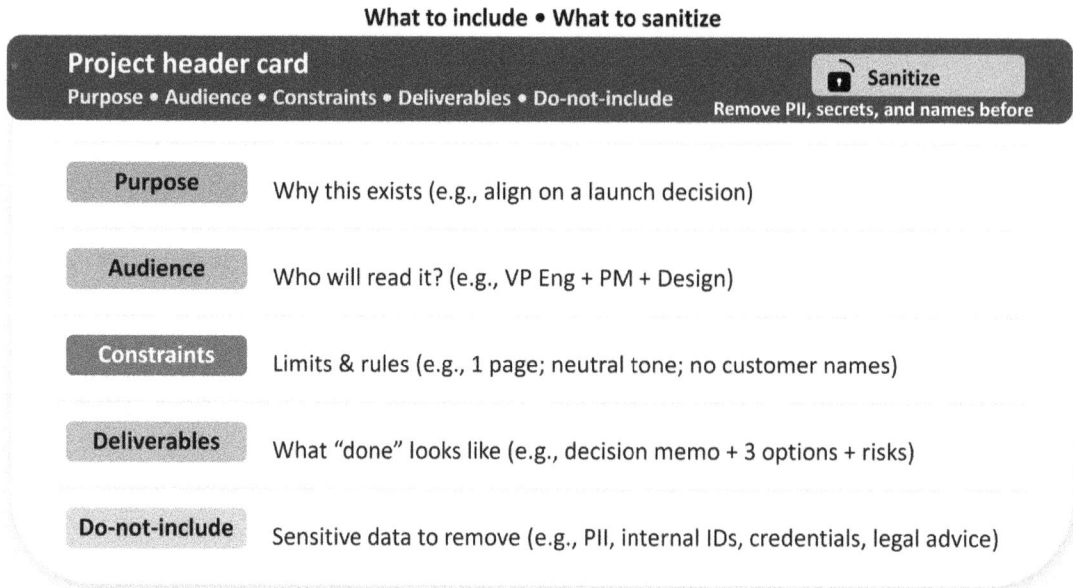

What to include • What to sanitize

Project header card
Purpose • Audience • Constraints • Deliverables • Do-not-include

🔓 **Sanitize**
Remove PII, secrets, and names before

Purpose — Why this exists (e.g., align on a launch decision)

Audience — Who will read it? (e.g., VP Eng + PM + Design)

Constraints — Limits & rules (e.g., 1 page; neutral tone; no customer names)

Deliverables — What "done" looks like (e.g., decision memo + 3 options + risks)

Do-not-include — Sensitive data to remove (e.g., PII, internal IDs, credentials, legal advice)

Then you do the work in phases: SOP draft, checklist extraction, email drafting, review prompts.

This is how professionals get compounding value: you build a stable "workspace" for the project rather than treating every prompt as isolated.

Section 3.5: Tool Use and "Agentic" Work - What This Means Without Any Coding

You will hear phrases like "tool use" and "agentic tasks." In business settings, those phrases can sound technical, so let's translate them.

Tool use means the model can use built-in capabilities or connected tools to complete work, such as working with files, generating structured artifacts (like spreadsheets or slides), interpreting images, or executing multi-step tasks that involve external actions in supported environments. OpenAI positions GPT-5 as improved at executing long chains of tool calls and agentic tasks, and GPT-5.2 as better at creating spreadsheets and presentations and handling complex multi-step projects.

Agentic work (in plain English) means it can plan and execute a sequence of steps rather than answering a single question.

For non-technical professionals, you can think of "agentic" as a project manager inside the chat:

- It can propose a plan
- Break the plan into steps
- Generate drafts for each step
- Check for missing information
- Iterate based on your feedback

You are still the decision-maker. You still approve. But the assistant reduces friction by coordinating the drafting and checking.

This changes what you should ask for.

> **Instead of:**
> "Write an SOP."
>
> **Try:**
> "Create a 5-step plan to draft an SOP. Start by asking me the minimum questions you need. After I answer, draft the SOP and include a checklist for verification."

When you prompt this way, you are taking advantage of two improvements at once:

- Better instruction following
- Better multi-step task handling

Section 3.6: The Business Payoff - Fewer "Rewrite Loops," More "Review Loops"

In older workflows, many people used ChatGPT like this: **Prompt → output → disappointment → rewrite prompt → output → disappointment → repeat**

That pattern increases anxiety because it creates uncertainty and wasted time.

GPT-5's practical advantage is that it supports a healthier loop: **Prompt → output → review → targeted edits → improved output**

In other words, you spend less time wrestling with the assistant and more time doing what professionals do best: applying judgment.

Here is a concrete pattern you can adopt today:

- The Two-Pass Drafting Pattern

> **Pass 1 (Structure Pass):**
> *"Give me a structured outline / draft skeleton. Keep it short. Ask questions where needed."*
>
> **Pass 2 (Quality Pass):**
> *"Now refine for clarity, tone, and actionability. Add risks, tradeoffs, and a verification checklist."*

Figure 3.3 – Two-pass drafting pattern

structure pass → quality pass

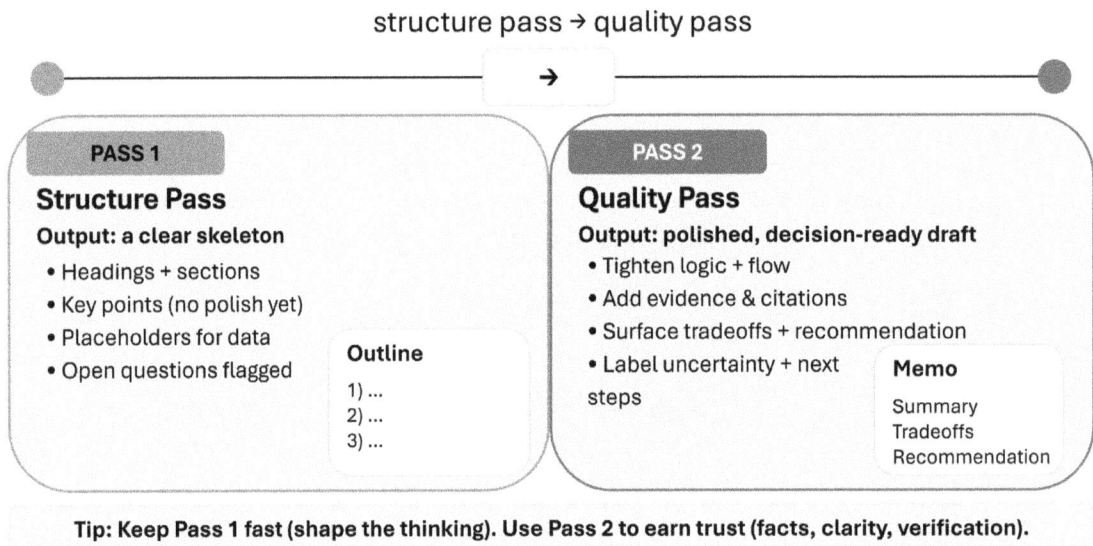

PASS 1

Structure Pass

Output: a clear skeleton
- Headings + sections
- Key points (no polish yet)
- Placeholders for data
- Open questions flagged

Outline
1) ...
2) ...
3) ...

PASS 2

Quality Pass

Output: polished, decision-ready draft
- Tighten logic + flow
- Add evidence & citations
- Surface tradeoffs + recommendation
- Label uncertainty + next steps

Memo
Summary
Tradeoffs
Recommendation

Tip: Keep Pass 1 fast (shape the thinking). Use Pass 2 to earn trust (facts, clarity, verification).

This pattern reduces cognitive load because it separates:

- Generating content (creative load)
  from
- Evaluating and improving (judgment load)

Most professionals find evaluation easier than creation. Two-pass drafting uses that fact.

Section 3.7: What Did Not Change - You Still Own Accuracy, Ethics, and Final Decisions

It is tempting when a model feels more capable to relax your standards. That's not professional.

OpenAI continues to emphasize that hallucinations remain a challenge for language models, even as they are reduced.

So the business rule remains: **Use ChatGPT to draft and structure. Verify what matters.**

In Chapter 1, we introduced risk levels. GPT-5 changes how quickly you can produce drafts. It does not eliminate the need to match verification effort to stakes.

A quick re-anchor:

- **Level 1 (low risk):** drafting, rewriting, summarizing your own notes
- **Level 2 (medium risk):** customer communication, proposals, internal documents that become reusable
- **Level 3 (high risk):** legal/HR/financial/regulatory claims, safety-critical instructions

Figure 3.4 – Risk level x verification effort grid

Rows = Risk Level (1–3). Columns = Verification intensity.

Risk Level ↓ × → Verification	Review	Confirm facts	Authoritative sources + peer review
Level 1 Low risk	✓ Required Quick skim for clarity	△ As needed Names, dates, numbers	△ As needed External claims/citations
Level 2 Medium risk	✓ Required Structure & tone check	✓ Required Validate key facts	△ If high impact Use trusted sources
Level 3 High risk	✓ Required Line-by-line review	✓ Required Evidence for each claim	✓ Required Authoritative sources + peer/pro review

Rule of thumb: higher risk → more verification steps.

GPT-5 helps at all levels if used responsibly, but the verification burden increases as risk increases.

A calm professional stance is not "trust" or "distrust." It is governance: you decide what must be true, and you check it.

Section 3.8: The Most Practical New Skill - Intent Signaling

Because GPT-5 is routed and responsive to cues about complexity, you can "signal intent" in plain language.

Intent signaling means you explicitly tell the assistant what kind of work you want.

Examples:

> "Quick draft, minimal detail, I'll refine."
>
> "Think hard: list risks, counterarguments, and tradeoffs."
>
> "Be conservative: do not invent facts, ask questions instead."
>
> "Executive style: concise, structured, decision-ready."
>
> "Workshop mode: propose options and ask me to choose."

This is not fancy prompting. It is professional directing.

Intent signaling reduces anxiety because it makes the interaction predictable. You get fewer surprises.

Section 3.9: Using GPT-5 for Decision Support without Turning it into An Authority

Professionals often want help with thinking, not just writing. GPT-5 is especially useful here, but framing matters.

Safe framing: Use GPT-5 to generate options, questions, and structured reasoning, then use your expertise and real-world constraints to decide.

Here are three decision-support patterns that work well in business:

> **Pattern A: Options with tradeoffs**
> *"Given this situation, propose 3 options. For each, list benefits, risks, and likely stakeholder reactions. End with what you'd recommend if we prioritize speed vs accuracy."*
>
> **Pattern B: Pre-mortem (risk rehearsal)**
> *"Assume this plan fails in 90 days. List the top 10 reasons it failed and the early warning signs we would have seen. Then propose mitigations."*
>
> **Pattern C: Assumption audit**
> *"List the assumptions in this plan. For each, tell me how to test it quickly, cheaply, and ethically."*

These patterns reduce cognitive load because they externalize structured thinking. You are still responsible for truth and action, but you no longer have to generate every angle from scratch.

Section 3.10: The Workplace Practice That Makes Gpt-5 Feel "Safer" - Output Contracts

An output contract is a small set of rules you put in your prompt that define acceptable behavior.

Think of it like acceptance criteria for an assistant's draft.

Example output contract (copy-paste):

> *"Output contract:*
>
> *If you don't know something, say 'Unverified' or 'Missing' (do not guess).*
>
> *Do not include sensitive data or personal identifiers.*
>
> *Use short paragraphs and headings.*
>
> *End with a verification checklist and 3 clarifying questions."*

Output contracts work especially well with models that follow instructions more reliably.

They also reduce anxiety because they give you a consistent "quality bar." You are not improvising safety every time. You are applying a standard.

Section 3.11: What GPT-5 Means for Your Daily Routine - A Realistic Upgrade Path

You do not need to rebuild your entire workday around AI.

A realistic upgrade path looks like this:

Week 1: Drafting support
- Rewrite emails
- Turn notes into summaries
- Create checklists and agendas

Week 2: Planning support
- Convert goals into plans
- Create meeting structures
- Build SOP skeletons

Week 3: Decision support
- Options + tradeoffs
- Risk analysis
- Assumption audits

Week 4: Systems
- Reusable templates
- Prompt library
- Weekly review workflow

This progression builds mastery and reduces anxiety because you are stacking safe wins before you attempt more complex use.

Practice Exercises

Exercise 1 — Intent signaling drill (quick vs deep)

> *Prompt:*
> *"I'm going to give you a task. Produce two outputs:*
> *(A) Quick Draft: fastest useful version, minimal detail.*
> *(B) Deep Draft: think hard, include risks, tradeoffs, and a verification checklist.*
> *Task: [paste task].*
> *Audience: [who].*
> *Constraints: [tone/length].*
> *If anything is missing, ask clarifying questions instead of guessing."*

Exercise 2 — Build a context packet for a real project

> *Prompt:*
> *"Help me create a sanitized context packet for this project.*
> *Project description: [paste].*
> *Identify what should be included (purpose, audience, constraints, deliverables, definitions), and what should be removed or generalized for confidentiality.*
> *Then produce a final context packet I can paste into a new chat."*

Exercise 3 — Create an output contract you will reuse

> *Prompt:*
> *"Create an 'output contract' I can paste at the end of any prompt.*
> *It must (1) reduce hallucinations, (2) protect confidentiality, and (3) enforce business-ready formatting.*
> *Keep it to 7 rules max.*
> *Then show it applied to an example: drafting a project update email."*

Exercise 4 — Two-Pass Drafting Pattern on a workplace document

> *Pass 1 prompt:*
> *"Structure pass: Create an outline and a draft skeleton for a [email/memo/proposal] using headings and placeholders marked 'Missing.' Ask me 5 clarifying questions."*

Pass 2 prompt (after you answer):
"Quality pass: Fill in what you can from my answers. Improve clarity and tone. Add a verification checklist. Do not invent facts."

Exercise 5 — Reduce "strict formatting errors" by allowing abstention

Prompt:
"I want a structured output, but I want you to abstain when information is missing.
Task: [task].
Output format: [format requirements].
Rule: If you do not have enough information, write 'Missing' in the output field and ask me a question. Do not guess."

Exercise 6 — Decision support without authority (options + tradeoffs)

Prompt:
"I need decision support. Do not decide for me.
Situation: [describe].
Constraints: [budget/time/policy].
Stakeholders: [who].
Generate 3 options. For each, list benefits, risks, tradeoffs, and what would make the option fail.
End with 6 questions I should answer before choosing."

Exercise 7 — Pre-mortem (plan failure rehearsal)

Prompt:
"Run a pre-mortem. Assume this plan fails in 90 days: [plan].
List the top 10 reasons it failed, early warning signs, and mitigations.
Keep it calm and practical. Label any assumptions you make."

Exercise 8 — Build a "review loop" checklist for medium-risk work (Level 2)

Prompt:
"Create a Level 2 review checklist for a draft before I send it. It must include: accuracy checks, tone checks, confidentiality checks, and 'unintended promise' checks.
Keep it to 12 items max and written in plain English."

Exercise 9 — Consistency pass across multiple sections (long-context use)

> *Prompt:*
> *"I will paste three sections of a document.*
> *Task: Make terminology and tone consistent across all sections*
> *without changing meaning.*
> *Rules: Do not add new claims. If you detect contradictions, list*
> *them.*
> *Text: [paste sections]."*

Exercise 10 — Build a "weekly upgrade path" for your job

> *Prompt:*
> *"Design a 4-week adoption plan for using ChatGPT in my role*
> *without overwhelm.*
> *My role: [role].*
> *My common tasks: [list].*
> *Constraints: [privacy/policy/time].*
> *Output: Week-by-week focus, 3 workflows per week, and how to*
> *measure success (time saved, fewer revisions, fewer follow-ups)."*

Skill Check

After completing this chapter, you should be able to:

- Explain why GPT-5 behaves like a routed system (fast vs deep) in plain English
- Use intent signaling to reliably request quick drafts or deeper, decision-ready analysis
- Build and use a context packet to maintain consistency across a multi-step work project
- Apply the Two-Pass Drafting Pattern to reduce rework and anxiety
- Prevent strict-format errors by explicitly allowing "Missing/Unverified" outputs
- Create and reuse an output contract that improves reliability and protects confidentiality
  Match verification effort to risk level, keeping human judgment central

Chapter 4: Prompting Fundamentals for Professionals

Prompting is not a dark art. It is management.

In a business setting, "prompting" simply means giving clear instructions to a drafting assistant so the output is useful, safe, and aligned with your goal. When people feel anxious using ChatGPT, it's often because prompting feels unpredictable, like sometimes it works, sometimes it doesn't.

This chapter makes it predictable.

You will learn how to:

- Write prompts that reliably produce business-ready drafts
- Reduce "generic" output by supplying the right context (without oversharing)
- Control tone, length, and structure
- Debug bad outputs calmly and quickly
- Use repeatable templates so you're not reinventing the wheel every time
- We will build from the core method already established: **Input → Draft → Judgment → Output**

Prompting is the "Input" part. If you improve the input, you reduce rework and cognitive load downstream.

Section 4.1: Why Most Prompts Fail (And Why That's Normal)

Most prompts fail for one of three ordinary reasons:

1. **The prompt describes a task, not an outcome.**
   "Write an email about the project" describes an activity, not what success looks like.

2. **The prompt lacks professional context.**
   Who is the audience? What is the situation? What tone is appropriate? What constraints apply? Without this, ChatGPT fills the gaps with generic assumptions.

3. **The prompt demands certainty where uncertainty exists.**
   If you request strict formatting and do not allow "Missing" or "Unverified," the model may attempt to satisfy the format by guessing.

None of these mistakes means you're bad at AI. They mean you're doing what humans always do with assistants at first: you speak in shorthand. In real life, a human assistant could ask follow-up questions naturally. ChatGPT can ask questions too, but only if you instruct it to.

Professional prompting is the act of reducing ambiguity, especially around:

- Audience and purpose
- Tone and stakes
- Format and length
- Boundaries (what not to include)
- Source material (what to use as truth)

Section 4.2: The Prompt is a Brief, Not A Question

A common shift for business users is moving from "asking a question" to "writing a brief."

> Questions are fine for quick help:
> "What are three meeting agenda items for a weekly sync?"
>
> But professional work products require a brief:
> "Create a weekly sync agenda for a cross-functional team, including status, blockers, risks, and decision needs. Keep it to 20 minutes."

If you remember nothing else, remember this: A prompt is a short brief that tells a drafting assistant what you need, who it's for, and what constraints matter.

You don't need perfect prompts. You need brief prompts that contain the right ingredients.

Figure 4.1 – Prompting as a brief, not a question

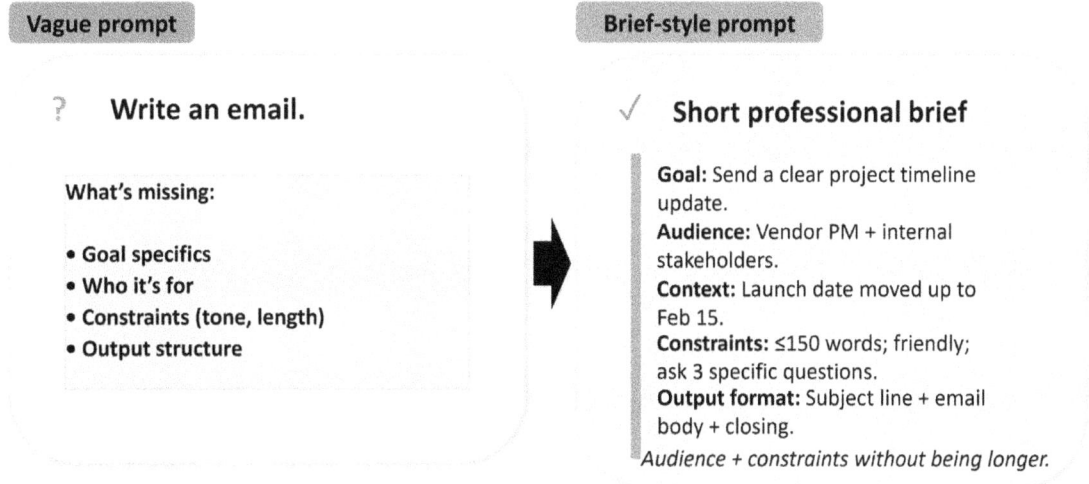

Vague prompt

? **Write an email.**

What's missing:

- Goal specifics
- Who it's for
- Constraints (tone, length)
- Output structure

Brief-style prompt

✓ **Short professional brief**

Goal: Send a clear project timeline update.
Audience: Vendor PM + internal stakeholders.
Context: Launch date moved up to Feb 15.
Constraints: ≤150 words; friendly; ask 3 specific questions.
Output format: Subject line + email body + closing.
Audience + constraints without being longer.

More context = less randomness.

Section 4.3: The Four Ingredients of a Business-Ready Prompt

We introduced the Goal–Context–Constraints triad in Chapter 2. In professional practice, it helps to add one more ingredient:

1. **Goal:** what you want and why
2. **Context:** what the assistant must know to do it correctly
3. **Constraints:** tone, length, format, boundaries
4. **Output format:** what the deliverable should look like

Figure 4.2 – Anatomy of a professional prompt

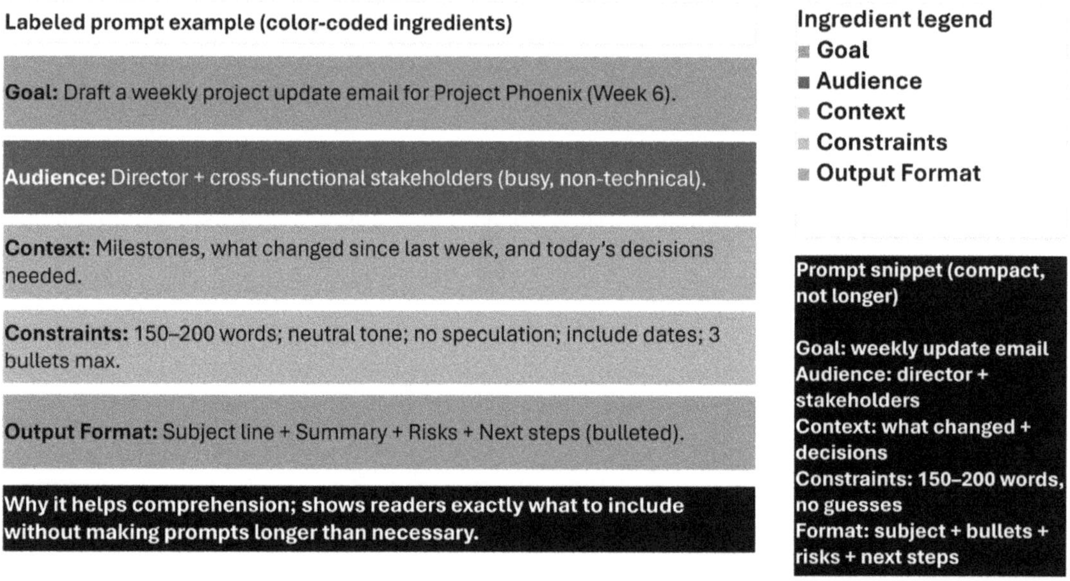

Labeled prompt example (color-coded ingredients)

Goal: Draft a weekly project update email for Project Phoenix (Week 6).

Audience: Director + cross-functional stakeholders (busy, non-technical).

Context: Milestones, what changed since last week, and today's decisions needed.

Constraints: 150–200 words; neutral tone; no speculation; include dates; 3 bullets max.

Output Format: Subject line + Summary + Risks + Next steps (bulleted).

Why it helps comprehension; shows readers exactly what to include without making prompts longer than necessary.

Ingredient legend
- Goal
- Audience
- Context
- Constraints
- Output Format

Prompt snippet (compact, not longer)

Goal: weekly update email
Audience: director + stakeholders
Context: what changed + decisions
Constraints: 150–200 words, no guesses
Format: subject + bullets + risks + next steps

That last item matters because "useful" is often a formatting question.

If you're writing for executives, you want a short, structured memo. If you're writing to a customer, you want clarity and warmth. If you're creating an SOP, you want numbered steps, roles, and exceptions.

A complete prompt can be as short as 6–10 lines. The goal is not length. The goal is completeness.

Here is a strong, general-purpose template:

Professional Prompt Template (Fundamental)

> *"Role: Act as a [role] supporting [type of work].*
> *Goal: I need [deliverable] so that [purpose].*
> *Audience: [who will read/use it].*
> *Context: [3-8 key facts, sanitized].*
> *Constraints: [tone], [length], [must include], [must avoid].*
> *Output format: [headings, bullets, table, steps, etc.].*
> *Uncertainty rule: If something is missing, label it "Missing" and ask questions instead of guessing.*
> *Verification: End with a short checklist of what I should verify before using this."*

That template turns prompting into a routine, not a guessing game.

Section 4.4: Role Instructions - The Fastest Way to Improve Output Quality

ChatGPT's default voice is "helpful generalist." In business, you often need a specific posture:

- Executive assistant (concise, action-oriented)
- Operations analyst (process, risk, dependencies)
- HR partner (neutral, policy-aware, careful wording)
- Customer support lead (empathetic, clear, accountable)
- Project manager (owners, dates, decisions, follow-ups)

You can set that posture in one line: "Act as a project manager writing for executives."

This does not make ChatGPT a real project manager. It simply guides tone and structure.

A useful professional rule: **Use roles to shape format and priorities, not to outsource authority.**

> *Avoid prompts like:*
> "Act as a lawyer and tell me what I'm legally required to do."
>
> *Prefer:*
> "Act as a professional editor. Rewrite this policy draft for clarity and neutrality. Do not make legal claims. Flag any areas that need legal review."

This keeps judgment and responsibility in the right place.

Section 4.5: Context That Helps vs. Context That Hurts

Not all context is equal.

Helpful context is the minimum information required to make the output accurate, aligned, and usable. It often includes:

- The decision or ask you need from the reader
- The current status (on track, at risk, blocked)
- Key constraints (budget, timeline, policy)
- Stakeholder sensitivities (what to emphasize or avoid)

- Definitions (what terms mean in your organization)

Unhelpful context is anything that increases risk without improving the output:

- Sensitive personal data
- Confidential customer details
- Internal financials that aren't necessary for the writing task
- Passwords, credentials, security procedures
- Legal strategies or privileged information

A calm approach is to sanitize. Sanitization does not mean stripping meaning. It means generalizing identifiers while keeping the structure.

> **Instead of:**
> "John Smith at Acme is angry because we missed the shipment and the contract penalty is $50,000."
>
> **Use:**
> "A key customer is dissatisfied due to a missed delivery. We need to acknowledge impact, explain next steps, and avoid making promises we can't guarantee."

You keep the business purpose and constraints while removing sensitive specifics.

Section 4.6: Output Format - Your Best Tool for Controlling Usefulness

Many "bad outputs" are not wrong, they're just unusable.

ChatGPT might give you a long narrative when you needed:

- A subject line + 8-sentence email
- A one-page memo with headings
- A checklist
- A table of options
- A script for a meeting
- A standard operating procedure format

Professionals reduce frustration by specifying format.

Examples:

> *Email format prompt line:*
> "Output: subject line + greeting + 10-sentence body + 3 bullet next steps."
>
> *Decision memo format prompt line:*
> "Output: 1-paragraph summary, then Options A/B/C with tradeoffs, then recommendation, then risks, then decision needed."
>
> *SOP format prompt line:*
> "Output: Purpose, Scope, Roles, Definitions, Procedure (numbered steps), Exceptions, Quality checks, Revision history."

When you specify format, you're doing what managers do: setting acceptance criteria.

Section 4.7: Tone Control without Awkwardness

Professionals often avoid using ChatGPT because they fear sounding unnatural. The irony is that tone is one of the easiest things to control. If you describe it like a business person, not like a poet.

Tone descriptors that work well:

- Neutral and direct
- Warm and collaborative
- Calm and confident
- Firm but respectful
- Executive concise
- Customer-friendly and accountable
- Policy-neutral and non-accusatory

Tone control becomes much easier when you also include:

- Relationship context (manager, peer, customer, vendor)
- Emotional context (frustrated stakeholder, sensitive situation, urgent timeline)
- Stakes (low-risk scheduling vs. high-stakes escalation)

Example tone instruction that prevents trouble: "Tone: calm and accountable. Do not blame. Do not over-apologize. Do not promise dates we can't guarantee."

That line alone prevents a common professional error: accidental commitments.

Section 4.8: The "Do Not" List - Boundaries That Prevent Expensive Mistakes

A "do not" list is one of the simplest ways to reduce anxiety.

In business writing, costly errors often come from what you accidentally include:

- A promise that becomes a commitment
- A statement that implies fault
- A detail that violates confidentiality
- A claim that sounds legal or definitive without support
- A tone that escalates conflict

So include boundaries.

Examples:

> "Do not include specific dollar figures."
>
> "Do not mention internal staffing constraints."
>
> "Do not assign blame."
>
> "Do not use legal language."
>
> "Do not reference private employee details."
>
> "Do not claim certainty, use cautious wording where appropriate."

This is not paranoia. It is professional risk management.

Section 4.9: The Clarifying-Questions Switch - How to Stop Guessing

One of the most powerful lines you can add to a prompt is: "Ask me questions before drafting if you need more information."

Even better is to limit it so it stays efficient: "Before drafting, ask me up to 7 clarifying questions. If you can draft without answers, draft and label gaps as 'Missing.'"

This creates a calm collaboration pattern:

- You provide a brief
- The assistant asks focused questions

- You answer quickly
- The assistant drafts with fewer assumptions

Figure 4.3 – The clarifying-questions switch

Prompt → Clarifying questions → Answers → Draft with fewer assumptions

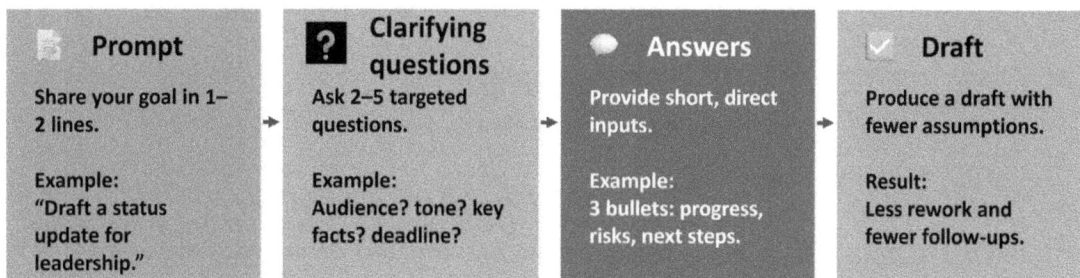

Prompt	Clarifying questions	Answers	Draft
Share your goal in 1–2 lines.	Ask 2–5 targeted questions.	Provide short, direct inputs.	Produce a draft with fewer assumptions.
Example: "Draft a status update for leadership."	Example: Audience? tone? key facts? deadline?	Example: 3 bullets: progress, risks, next steps.	Result: Less rework and fewer follow-ups.

Why this works

Clarifying questions turn a vague request into a brief.

That reduces hidden assumptions, improves accuracy, and lowers the chance of "confident formatting" masking uncertainty.

Quick checklist
- Audience
- Purpose
- Must-include facts
- Constraints
- Output format

In real workplaces, this is exactly how good assistants operate.

Section 4.10: Iteration - How Professionals "Steer" without Starting Over

A common beginner mistake is restarting from scratch each time.

Professional steering is incremental. You keep what works and adjust what doesn't.

Useful steering commands:

> "Keep the structure but shorten by 30%."
>
> "Keep the facts identical; adjust tone to be warmer."
>
> "Make the ask clearer and move it to the top."
>
> "Replace vague phrases with specific next steps."
>
> "Add a risk section and a mitigation plan."
>
> "Rewrite for an executive audience: fewer adjectives, more decisions."

You don't need to re-explain the entire prompt. You can direct edits like you would with a human editor.

This is where GPT-5's stronger instruction-following helps: it responds well to precise revision requests.

Figure 4.4 – Steering commands: revise without restarting

Steering commands (examples)

1 Move ask to top

2 Shorten ~30%

3 Make tone warmer

4 Add bullets for clarity

These edits *steer* the same draft—no need to start over.

Sample draft (v0)

Subject: Project Phoenix update

Hi team,
I wanted to share a quick update on Project Phoenix.
We are generally on track for the Jan 15 date, but there are a few blockers.
We still need approvals from Legal and Data before we can proceed.

Can you review the attached doc and reply by Friday?
Thanks,
Ava

After edits (v1) — same intent, clearer + shorter

Hi team — quick ask first: please review the attached 1-pager and reply by Fri EOD.

Status: On track for Jan 15 launch.
Blockers: awaiting Legal + Data approvals.
Next steps: approvals → finalize plan → rollout.

Thanks! — Ava

Section 4.11: Prompt Debugging - A Professional Diagnostic Checklist

When output is poor, don't argue with it. Diagnose it.

Use this checklist:

Prompt Debugging Checklist (Fundamental)

1. Was the goal clear? If not, rewrite the goal in one sentence.
2. Was the audience specified? If not, add who will read it and what they care about.
3. Was context provided (facts, status, constraints)? If not, add 5–10 key facts.
4. Were constraints stated (tone, length, boundaries)? If not, specify tone, length, and "do not" items.

5. Was the output format defined? If not, specify a format that matches the deliverable.
6. Did you allow uncertainty? If not, allow "Missing/Unverified" and clarifying questions.

This reduces anxiety because it turns "this is unpredictable" into "I know what to fix."

Figure 4.5 – Prompt debugging checklist (diagnostic card)

Troubleshoot misfires fast: answer these 6 questions before you re-prompt.

Output Contract — Prompt Debugging Checklist

1 Goal: What do you want the draft to accomplish (decision, action, outcome)?

2 Audience: Who will read it, and what do they care about or need to decide?

3 Context: What facts, background, examples, or source material should be used?

4 Constraints: Tone, length, must-include, must-avoid, policy/legal boundaries?

5 Format: What structure do you want (sections, bullets, table, email, memo)?

6 Uncertainty & verification: What is unknown, and how should it be labeled/checked?

Rule of thumb: More relevant context + clearer constraints = less randomness. End your prompt with a quick verification checklist.

Section 4.12: Few-Shot Examples - How to Teach the Style You Want

Sometimes the fastest way to get the right output is to show a small example.

You don't need technical terms. You can say: "Here is an example of the style I want. Match it."

For instance:

```
"Use this style example (tone and structure only):
Subject: Decision needed: Q1 onboarding timeline
Body:

Current status: …
```

```
Risk: …

Decision needed by Friday: …

Next steps: …"
```

Then provide your content separately.

This reduces the "translation" burden: you're not describing tone abstractly; you're demonstrating it.

Section 4.13: Prompt Libraries - Why You Should Stop Writing from Scratch

The most productive business users do not "prompt creatively" every time.

They build a small library of reusable prompt templates for common tasks:

- Weekly planning
- Meeting agendas and notes
- Status updates
- Decision memos
- SOP drafts
- Customer replies
- Performance feedback phrasing (careful and neutral)
- Marketing drafts (later chapters deepen this)

A prompt library reduces cognitive load because you don't have to invent structure under stress.

It also improves consistency, which is a professional advantage.

We will build a full prompt library later in the capstone, but you will start in this chapter with a few foundational templates.

Section 4.14: Worked Example 1 - A Project Update Email That Reduces Follow-Ups

Let's take a common situation: you need to update leadership on a project that is "mostly on track" but has an emerging risk.

```
Weak prompt:
"Write a project update email."
```

> *Professional prompt:*
> *"Act as a project manager writing for executives.*
> *Goal: Send a short update that maintains trust and gets one decision unblocked.*
> *Audience: VP + Directors (busy, wants clarity).*
> *Context (sanitized): Project is on track overall; one dependency from another team is late; timeline risk if not resolved by next week; we have a fallback option but it costs more time.*
> *Constraints: neutral tone, no blame, no promises we can't guarantee, keep under 150 words.*
> *Output format: subject line + 10-sentence email + 3 bullet next steps with owners.*
> *Uncertainty rule: If any detail is missing, label it 'Missing' and ask me a question instead of guessing.*
> *Verification: End with a 5-item pre-send checklist."*

Why this works:

- It defines success (trust + decision)
- It defines the audience and their preferences
- It provides real context without sensitive detail
- It prevents accidental blame or overpromising
- It enforces a usable format

Your edits afterward are faster because the draft starts close to "professional usable."

Section 4.15: Worked Example 2 - Turning Messy Notes into a Decision Memo

Scenario: You ran a meeting with conflicting opinions and need a decision memo that fairly captures options.

> *Professional prompt:*
> *"Act as an operations analyst.*
> *Goal: Create a decision memo that summarizes options and tradeoffs so a director can decide.*
> *Audience: Director (needs clarity, not drama).*
> *Source material (use as truth; do not add facts):*
> *[Paste sanitized meeting notes.]*
> *Constraints: neutral language, no names (use 'Team A/Team B'),*

> *highlight risks and assumptions, keep to one page.*
> *Output format:*
>
> *One-paragraph situation summary*
>
> *Options A/B/C (benefits, risks, cost/time implications as described in notes)*
>
> *Key assumptions (label as assumptions)*
>
> *Recommendation (based on stated priorities: speed, quality, cost)*
>
> *Decision needed + deadline*
> *Verification: List 5 questions to confirm before finalizing."*

This prompt uses a key professional tactic: source-first transformation. It tells ChatGPT not to invent facts and to work with your notes as truth.

Section 4.16: Worked Example 3 - SOP Drafting Without "Fantasy Processes"

Many people ask ChatGPT to "write an SOP," then get a generic process that doesn't match reality.

The fix is to ground it in your real workflow.

> *Professional prompt:*
> *"Act as a process improvement specialist.*
> *Goal: Draft an SOP that makes our current process consistent and trainable.*
> *Audience: new team members and cross-functional partners.*
> *Current process (sanitized):*
>
> *Step 1: …*
>
> *Step 2: …*
>
> *Common exceptions: …*
>
> *Pain points: …*
> *Constraints: must fit current staffing; no new tools; use plain language; avoid jargon.*
> *Output format: Purpose, Scope, Roles, Inputs, Procedure (numbered steps), Exceptions, Quality checks, Metrics, Revision notes.*
> *Uncertainty rule: If steps are unclear, ask up to 7 clarifying questions before finalizing.*

> Verification: Provide a 'walkthrough test' checklist to validate the SOP against real work."

This turns SOP drafting into a collaboration rather than a guessing exercise.

Practice Exercises

Exercise 1 — Convert a vague request into a professional brief

> *Prompt:*
> "Turn my vague request into a professional prompt using: Role, Goal, Audience, Context, Constraints, Output format, Uncertainty rule, Verification checklist.
> Vague request: [paste your vague request].
> My work context: [brief sanitized context]."

Exercise 2 — Build a one-line role instruction for your job

> *Prompt:*
> "Help me write 5 role instructions that match my work.
> My role: [your role].
> Common outputs: [emails, SOPs, plans, etc.].
> Each role instruction should be one sentence and should improve structure and tone without claiming authority."

Exercise 3 — Tone control drill (neutral vs warm vs executive)

> *Prompt:*
> "Rewrite the text below three ways:
> (A) Neutral and direct
> (B) Warm and collaborative
> (C) Executive concise
> Keep the facts identical. Do not add promises or new details.
> Text: [paste]."

Exercise 4 — Add a "do not" list to prevent accidental risk

> *Prompt:*
> "I need to write a message about: [topic].
> Create a 'do not include' list of 8 items tailored to this situation (confidentiality, unintended promises, blame, legal claims, sensitive details).
> Then draft the message in a safe, professional way.
> Audience: [who].

```
Tone: [tone].
Length: [limit]."
```

Exercise 5 — Activate the Clarifying-Questions Switch

Prompt:
"Before drafting, ask me up to 7 clarifying questions needed to produce a high-quality [email/memo/SOP]. After I answer, draft it.
Constraints: if anything remains unknown, label it 'Missing' instead of guessing.
Deliverable type: [type].
Audience: [who].
Goal: [purpose]."

Exercise 6 — Format control: request a deliverable you can actually use

Prompt:
"Create a deliverable in this exact format:

Subject line:

Opening sentence (purpose):

3 bullets (status/impact/ask):

2 sentences (risks and mitigation):

Closing sentence (next step):
Topic: [topic].
Audience: [who].
Tone: calm and professional.
Do not include: [boundaries]."

Exercise 7 — Prompt debugging on a bad output

Prompt:
"I received an output that wasn't useful. Here is my original prompt: [paste]. Here is the output: [paste].
Diagnose what was missing using this checklist: goal, audience, context, constraints, output format, uncertainty rule.
Then rewrite my prompt to fix the issue and explain the changes in plain English."

Exercise 8 — Few-shot style teaching (match a model example)

Prompt:
"Here is a short example of the style I want (tone and structure). Match it for my new content.
Style example: [paste 5-10 lines of a preferred email/memo style–sanitized].
New content facts: [paste facts].
Output format: same as the example.
Rules: do not add new facts; label unknowns as 'Missing.'"

Exercise 9 — Build your first three prompt-library entries

Prompt:
"Help me create three reusable prompt templates for my work:

Project update email

Decision memo

Meeting summary with actions
My role: [role].
Constraints: [privacy/policy/tone].
Each template should be copy-paste ready with placeholders in brackets."

Exercise 10 — Steering practice: revise without restarting

Prompt:
"Draft this deliverable: [describe].
Then I will give you revision commands. After each command, revise without changing the underlying facts unless I explicitly change them.
Initial constraints: [tone/length/format].
Topic/context: [paste sanitized context]."

Exercise 11 — Create an "output contract" you can paste anywhere

Prompt:
"Write a short 'output contract' (max 7 rules) that I can paste at the end of any prompt.
It must: prevent guessing, protect confidentiality, enforce professional formatting, and end with a verification checklist.
Then show a sample prompt using it for a customer reply email."

Skill Check

After completing this chapter, you should be able to:

- Write a business-ready prompt as a brief (not a vague question)
- Include the four ingredients: Goal, Context, Constraints, and Output Format
- Use role instructions to shape structure and tone reliably
- Control tone using professional descriptors and relationship context
- Add a "do not" list to reduce accidental commitments, blame, or sensitive details
- Trigger clarifying questions to prevent guessing and hallucinations
- Debug weak prompts using a calm diagnostic checklist
- Begin a reusable prompt library that reduces cognitive load and increases consistency

Chapter 5: Thinking, Planning, and Decision-Making with ChatGPT

Most professionals don't struggle because they can't work hard. They struggle because they must think in public while the clock is running.

You are asked to make decisions with incomplete information, explain those decisions clearly, and keep projects moving, often while juggling interruptions, changing priorities, and competing stakeholder expectations. This chapter is about using ChatGPT to support that "thinking work" in a calm, structured way.

The goal is not to let ChatGPT decide for you. The goal is to reduce cognitive load by externalizing the parts of thinking that are heavy but repeatable:

- Turning vague situations into clear problem statements
- Generating options and tradeoffs
- Surfacing assumptions and risks
- Planning next steps and sequencing work
- Creating decision records so you don't re-litigate the same issues

When used well, ChatGPT becomes a planning partner and a clarity engine. You still own judgment, final decisions, and accountability.

Section 5.1: Why Decisions Feel Heavier Than They Used To

In modern work, decisions feel heavier for three reasons.

First, more decisions are made "upstream."
Teams are expected to anticipate problems earlier. That's good, but it means you are often deciding before you have perfect data.

Second, decisions are more visible.
Even small choices are documented in chats, tickets, and emails. Decisions can be revisited months later by people who were not present.

Third, decisions have more stakeholders.
A choice that used to affect one team now affects customers, partner teams, compliance, leadership narratives, budgets, and timelines.

All of this increases mental strain because it expands what you must consider, defend, and communicate.

ChatGPT can help with the structure of decision-making: how you define the problem, how you compare options, how you articulate tradeoffs, and how you capture the decision clearly so the organization can move forward.

A key concept for this chapter is a calm reframe: You don't need AI to "think for you." You need a system that helps you think with less friction.

Section 5.2: What ChatGPT is Good for in "Thinking Work"

ChatGPT is strongest at tasks that involve language-based reasoning and structure, such as:

- Organizing messy inputs into coherent categories
- Generating questions you might not have considered
- Producing alternative framings of a situation
- Creating options and outlining pros and cons
- Drafting plans, checklists, and decision memos
- Simulating stakeholder perspectives (carefully)
- Turning your notes into a decision record

It is weaker at tasks that require ground truth it cannot verify: exact facts, real-time operational status, legal certainty, and proprietary knowledge you did not provide.

So the professional approach is: **Use ChatGPT to generate structure, options, and drafts. Use your expertise and real-world verification to decide and finalize.**

If you keep that boundary, the tool reduces anxiety because it supports your process without replacing your responsibility.

Section 5.3: A Simple Decision Model You Can Reuse - Frame → Options → Test → Decide → Record

Many decision mistakes happen because people skip steps when rushed. You can reduce risk by using a repeatable model.

Here is a practical model for business decisions:

1. Frame the decision (define the problem and success criteria)
2. Generate options (at least two real alternatives)
3. Test options (tradeoffs, risks, assumptions, constraints)
4. Decide (choose and align)

5. Record (capture the "why" and the "what")

This model is not academic. It's a tool for speed and clarity.

Figure 5.1 – Decision workflow

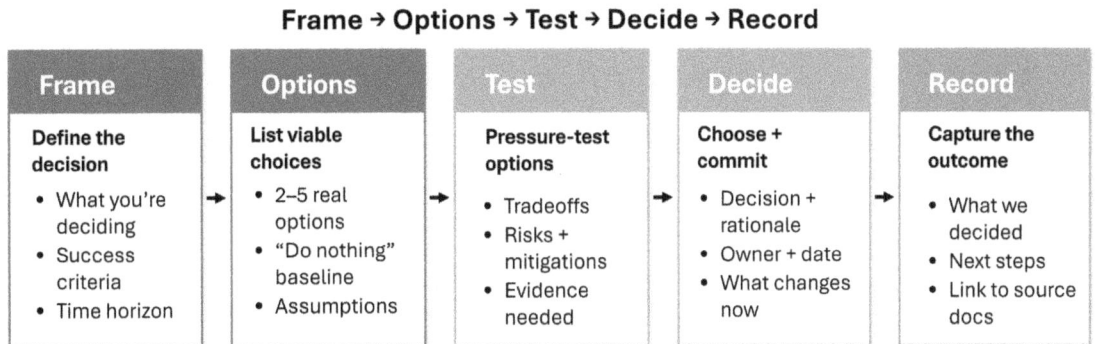

Frame → Options → Test → Decide → Record

Frame	Options	Test	Decide	Record
Define the decision	**List viable choices**	**Pressure-test options**	**Choose + commit**	**Capture the outcome**
• What you're deciding • Success criteria • Time horizon	• 2–5 real options • "Do nothing" baseline • Assumptions	• Tradeoffs • Risks + mitigations • Evidence needed	• Decision + rationale • Owner + date • What changes now	• What we decided • Next steps • Link to source docs

Tip: Treat this as a repeatable template — the "Record" step prevents re-litigating decisions later.

ChatGPT can help at every step:

1. **Framing:** turning vague discomfort into a precise question
2. **Options:** creating a short list of viable paths
3. **Testing:** surfacing risks, dependencies, and second-order effects
4. **Deciding:** drafting a recommendation memo in a neutral tone
5. **Recording:** writing a decision record for future clarity

We will build prompt patterns for each step.

Section 5.4: Framing: Turning "Mess" into a Decision You Can Act On

Framing means defining what decision you are actually making.

Professionals often believe they are stuck because "the problem is complicated." Often the real issue is that the decision is not framed clearly. The team is trying to solve multiple problems at once, or they are debating solutions without agreeing on what "success" means.

A good decision frame includes:

- The decision statement (what is being chosen)
- The objective (what you are optimizing for)
- Constraints (non-negotiables: budget, policy, timeline, ethics)
- Success criteria (what "good" looks like)

- Stakeholders (who is affected, who must agree)

In plain English: framing is deciding what matters and what doesn't.

Figure 5.2 – Problem framing vs. solution jumping

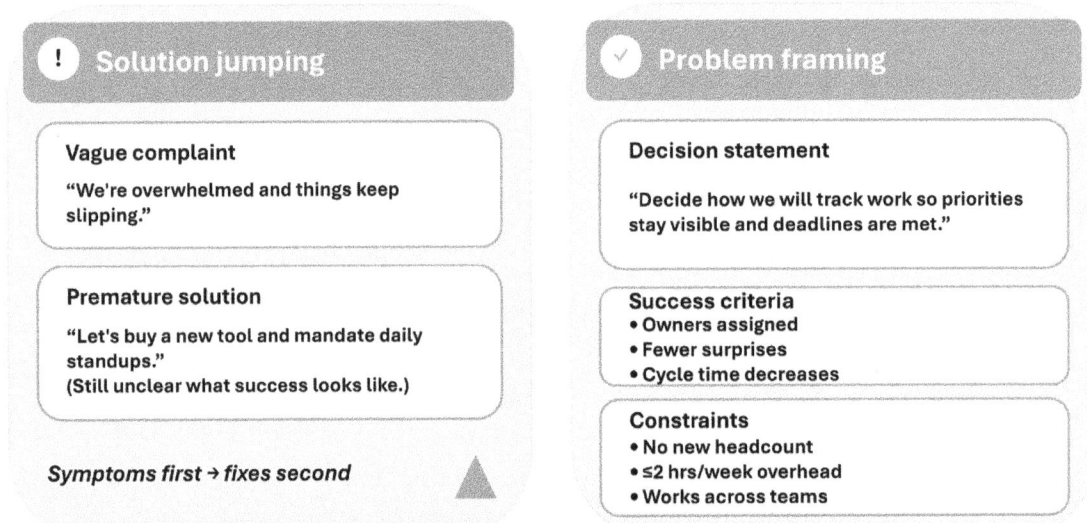

! Solution jumping

Vague complaint

"We're overwhelmed and things keep slipping."

Premature solution

"Let's buy a new tool and mandate daily standups."
(Still unclear what success looks like.)

Symptoms first → fixes second

✓ Problem framing

Decision statement

"Decide how we will track work so priorities stay visible and deadlines are met."

Success criteria
• Owners assigned
• Fewer surprises
• Cycle time decreases

Constraints
• No new headcount
• ≤2 hrs/week overhead
• Works across teams

Frame the decision first. Solutions get better—and faster—when success criteria and constraints are explicit.

```
Prompt: Decision framing assistant
"Help me frame the decision below.
Situation (sanitized): [describe].
Output:

A one-sentence decision statement (what we are choosing)

The objective (what we are optimizing for)

Constraints (non-negotiables)

Success criteria (how we will judge the outcome)

Stakeholders and what each cares about
Rules: Ask up to 7 clarifying questions if needed. Do not guess
facts."
```

Common framing errors (and how to fix them)

```
Error: Framing as a complaint
"We're overwhelmed and nothing works."
```

> *Fix: Convert to a choice*
> *"What process changes will reduce cycle time by 20% without adding headcount this quarter?"*
>
> *Error: Framing as a solution*
> *"We need a new tool."*
>
> *Fix: Frame as an outcome*
> *"How will we reduce handoff errors and improve visibility using current tools?"*
>
> *Error: Framing too broadly*
> *"How do we improve customer experience?"*
>
> *Fix: Narrow by scope and time*
> *"What two changes can we implement in 30 days to reduce customer confusion in onboarding emails?"*

ChatGPT can help you rewrite frames until the decision becomes actionable.

Section 5.5: Options - How to Get Real Alternatives (Not Just Variations of the Same Idea)

When teams are stressed, they generate one idea and debate it endlessly. That increases anxiety because there is no comparison. People feel trapped.

A professional trick is to require at least two viable alternatives plus "do nothing" as a baseline.

"Do nothing" is not laziness. It is a reference point. It helps you measure whether change is worth the cost and risk.

Define "options" in plain English: Options are different paths you could take. A real option changes something meaningful: scope, timing, ownership, process, or investment.

> *Prompt: Generate options with meaningful differences*
> *"Generate 4 options for this decision, and make them meaningfully different (not minor variations).*
> *Decision frame: [paste your framed decision].*
> *Constraints: [list].*
> *Output format:*
> *Option name, short description, what changes, benefits, risks, required effort, and who it impacts.*

> *Include 'Do nothing' as an option.*
> *Rules: If you lack information, ask questions instead of*
> *inventing details."*

If the options feel generic, that's a signal your frame lacks constraints or context. Add what matters most: time, budget, risk tolerance, and stakeholder priorities.

Section 5.6: Tradeoffs - How to Compare Options Like a Professional

Tradeoffs are the heart of business decisions.

A tradeoff in plain English is what you gain and what you give up. You can rarely maximize everything at once. You choose what to prioritize.

Common business tradeoffs:

- Speed vs. quality
- Cost vs. flexibility
- Consistency vs. customization
- Short-term relief vs. long-term sustainability
- Central control vs. team autonomy
- Simplicity vs. completeness

ChatGPT can help you articulate tradeoffs in a way that feels fair and decision-ready.

> *Prompt: Tradeoff comparison table*
> *"Create a tradeoff comparison for Options A/B/C/Do nothing.*
> *Decision frame: [paste].*
> *Options: [paste].*
> *Output: A table that compares options across: speed, cost,*
> *quality, risk, effort, stakeholder impact, and reversibility.*
> *Definitions:*
>
> *'Reversibility' means how hard it is to undo the choice later.*
> *Rules: Use plain English. Label assumptions explicitly."*

Reversibility is especially useful. Some choices are easy to change later; others create lock-in. If a decision is reversible, you can move faster with less anxiety.

Figure 5.3 – Tradeoff table example

Speed vs Quality vs Cost vs Risk vs Reversibility — plain-English ratings for each option.

Criterion	Option A (Quick fix)	Option B (Balanced)	Option C (Full rebuild)	Do nothing
Speed	Fast (same day)	Medium (1–2 weeks)	Slow (1–2 months)	Fast now / slower later
Quality	Good enough	High	Best-in-class	Unchanged / inconsistent
Cost	Low	Medium	High	Low now / hidden later
Risk	Medium (patch debt)	Low–Medium	Medium–High	High (drift & errors)
Reversibility	Easy to undo	Moderate	Hard to reverse	Easy, but costly later

Tip: Keep ratings short and consistent so tradeoffs are easy to compare at a glance.

Section 5.7: Assumptions - The Quiet Source of Most Decision Failures

An assumption is something you are treating as true without proof.

Assumptions are not bad. They are unavoidable. The problem is hidden assumptions; when teams argue about options but never name the beliefs underneath.

Examples of hidden assumptions:

- "Leadership will support this."
- "Customers won't mind the change."
- "The other team can deliver by that date."
- "This can be done without more workload."
- "This is a one-time effort, not ongoing maintenance."

A professional move is to surface assumptions and decide how to test them.

> *Prompt: Assumption audit*
> *"List the assumptions in this plan and classify them as:*
>
> *Confirmed (we have evidence)*
>
> *Unconfirmed (we think it's true)*
>
> *Risky (if wrong, the plan fails)*
> *Plan: [paste plan or option].*
> *Then propose fast tests for each risky assumption (low cost, ethical, within 1-2 weeks if possible).*
> *Rules: Keep it practical and business-appropriate. Ask questions if needed."*

This prompt reduces anxiety because it replaces vague fear with a concrete list of what needs confirmation.

Figure 5.4 – Assumption audit worksheet

Use this to surface uncertainties early, assign tests, and reduce downstream rework.

Assumption	Status (Confirmed / Unconfirmed / Risky)	How to test	Owner	Date

Tip: Start with the top 3 "risky" assumptions — assign an owner and a concrete test within 48 hours.

Section 5.8: Risks - Using a Pre-Mortem to Protect Trust

A pre-mortem is a structured risk exercise.

In a pre-mortem, you imagine that your plan failed and you ask: "What went wrong?" This is not pessimism. It is professional foresight.

Why it works: People are often reluctant to voice risks because it can sound negative. The pre-mortem makes risk discussion normal and productive.

```
Prompt: Pre-mortem
"Run a pre-mortem on this plan.
Assume it failed in 90 days.
Plan: [paste].
Output:

Top 10 reasons it failed

Early warning signs for each

Mitigations we can implement now

What we should monitor weekly
Rules: Label assumptions. Do not invent specific facts."
```

If the plan affects customers or leadership trust, add one more line: "Include reputational risks and communication risks."

That ensures you consider how the message lands, not only the mechanics.

Section 5.9: Prioritization - Getting Out of the "Everything Is Urgent" Trap

A common anxiety pattern in modern work is priority fog: everything feels important, so you bounce between tasks, and nothing gets finished cleanly.

ChatGPT can help you prioritize by converting a list into a structured decision.

But prioritization must be based on criteria, not mood.

Plain-English criteria that work well:

1. **Impact:** how much difference it makes
2. **Urgency:** time sensitivity

3. **Effort:** time/complexity required
4. **Risk:** consequences of delay or failure
5. **Dependencies:** what unlocks other work
6. **Strategic alignment:** supports key goals

> *Prompt: Prioritization matrix*
> *"Help me prioritize this list of tasks using clear criteria.*
> *Tasks: [paste list].*
> *Context: [goal of the week/month].*
> *Constraints: [deadlines, staffing, policy].*
> *Output:*
>
> *Ask me any missing questions needed to prioritize well*
>
> *Then rank tasks into: Do now, Schedule, Delegate, Defer*
>
> *Provide a short rationale for each*
>
> *Identify the top 3 dependencies that unblock the most progress*
> *Rules: Avoid hype. Be direct."*

This kind of structured prioritization reduces cognitive load because it turns a swarm of tasks into a plan.

Section 5.10: Planning - Turning a Goal into a Workable Sequence

Planning is different from dreaming.

A plan includes:

- Steps in a sensible order
- Owners (even if it's just "me")
- Time estimates (rough is fine)
- Dependencies
- Decision points
- A definition of "done"

ChatGPT can help you produce a first plan quickly, and then you can adjust it with real constraints.

> *Prompt: Practical planning draft*
> *"Create a practical plan to accomplish this goal.*
> *Goal: [goal].*
> *Timeframe: [deadline].*

```
Constraints: [budget, staffing, tools, policy].
Known risks: [if any].
Output format:

Step-by-step plan (numbered)

For each step: purpose, owner, time estimate range, dependency,
and deliverable

A 'definition of done' checklist
Rules: If information is missing, ask questions instead of
guessing."
```

A calm professional note: time estimates from ChatGPT are placeholders. Use them as a starting point, then adjust based on your reality. The value is the structure, not the precision.

Section 5.11: Stakeholder Thinking without Drama

Stakeholder issues can make decisions feel personal. They don't have to.

A stakeholder is anyone affected by the decision or who can influence it. Stakeholder management is not manipulation. It is clarity: understanding what different people need to feel comfortable moving forward.

ChatGPT can help you map stakeholder needs and prepare communication that reduces friction.

```
Prompt: Stakeholder map and messaging
"Help me map stakeholders for this decision and create a
communication plan.
Decision: [paste].
Stakeholders: [list or 'unknown'].
Output:

Stakeholder map: who, what they care about, likely concerns, what
evidence they need

Messaging plan: what to communicate, when, and through what
channel (email/meeting/1:1)

Draft a short executive update and a separate partner-team
message
Constraints: neutral tone, no blame, avoid sensitive details."
```

This reduces anxiety because you stop guessing what people will react to. You prepare thoughtfully.

Section 5.12: Bias And Blind Spots - How to Ask for a Challenge without Getting Lectured

All humans have blind spots. Under stress, blind spots get worse.

A practical way to use ChatGPT is to request "challenge mode" and make it specific. You don't want a motivational speech. You want a quality check.

```
Prompt: Bias and blind-spot check
"Challenge my plan like a professional reviewer.
Plan: [paste].
Context: [constraints].
Output:

7 potential blind spots or weak assumptions

5 risks that are easy to underestimate

3 counterarguments a skeptical stakeholder might raise

5 improvements that keep the plan realistic
Tone: direct, calm, no flattery."
```

This prompt is especially useful before you present to leadership or send a sensitive message.

Section 5.13: Decision Records - Stop Re-Litigating the Same Choice

One of the biggest hidden drains in organizations is decision recycling.

A decision gets made, but the reasoning isn't captured clearly. Weeks later, someone asks, "Why did we do it this way?" The team spends time reconstructing context, defending choices, and reopening debates.

A decision record prevents that.

A decision record is a short document that captures:

- The decision
- The date and owner

- The context
- The options considered
- The tradeoffs
- The reason for the choice
- The risks and mitigations
- The next review point (when you will reconsider)

This is not bureaucracy. It is memory. It reduces cognitive load for everyone.

```
Prompt: Decision record draft
"Create a one-page decision record from the information below.
Decision: [what we chose].
Context: [why].
Options considered: [A/B/C + do nothing].
Tradeoffs: [key tradeoffs].
Risks/mitigations: [if known].
Output format: Decision record with headings: Decision,
Date/Owner, Context, Options, Rationale, Risks, Next steps,
Review date.
Rules: If something is missing, label it 'Missing.' Keep it
neutral and factual."
```

If you adopt only one practice from this chapter, adopt decision records. They create calm by reducing future confusion.

Figure 5.5 – Decision record one-pager template

Decision

One-sentence decision statement (what are we doing / not doing?)

Owner: _____ Date: _____

Context

Why this decision matters now (background, drivers, constraints).

Key stakeholders: _____

Options

- Option A — _____
  Pros: _____ Cons: _____

- Option B — _____
  Pros: _____ Cons: _____

- Option C (if needed) — _____

Rationale

What tradeoffs did we accept? Why this option wins today?

Risks

- Risk 1 — _____ (mitigation: _____)
- Risk 2 — _____ (mitigation: _____)

Next Steps

- Task 1 — Owner / due date
- Task 2 — Owner / due date
- Task 3 — Owner / due date

Dependencies: _____

Review Date

Revisit on: _____ Success check: _____

Tip: Keep this to one page. Link to supporting docs in the context section.

Section 5.14: A Full Worked Example - From Messy Situation to Decision-Ready Output

Let's walk through a realistic scenario.

Situation (sanitized):
A process handoff between two teams is causing delays. Customers are confused. Team A believes Team B is the bottleneck. Team B believes Team A's inputs are inconsistent. Leadership wants improvement without new tools or headcount this quarter.

Step 1: Frame the decision
You prompt ChatGPT to produce a decision statement and success criteria.

Outcome (what you want to get to):
Decision statement: "What change to the handoff process will reduce delays and customer confusion within 30 days without new tools or headcount?"
Success criteria: fewer rework loops, clearer ownership, faster cycle time, fewer customer questions.

Step 2: Generate options
You request meaningful alternatives.

Possible options might include:

- Option A: Standardize Team A input checklist and define "ready" criteria
- Option B: Introduce a daily 10-minute handoff huddle with clear owners
- Option C: Assign a rotating "handoff coordinator" role (internal shift, no headcount increase)
- Do nothing: maintain the current approach and accept the delay cost

Step 3: Test options
You request tradeoffs, risks, and assumption audits.

You discover key assumptions:

- People will adopt the checklist
- The huddle won't become another meeting burden
- The coordinator role won't burn out staff

You propose fast tests:

- Run the checklist with a small pilot for one week

- Run the huddle twice weekly first
- Rotate the coordinator weekly and monitor workload

Step 4: Decide

You choose a combination or sequence and often the most realistic approach is incremental:

- Start with the checklist (low effort, high consistency)
- Add a brief huddle only if metrics don't improve
- Keep the coordinator role as a temporary escalation path

Step 5: Record

You generate a decision record and share it. Now the organization can move forward with clarity.

Notice what happened: ChatGPT did not "solve" the problem. It helped you structure the thinking. That structure created speed and reduced conflict.

Practice Exercises

Instructions: Use sanitized information. Treat outputs as drafts. For Level 2 and Level 3 decisions, verify facts and align with policy before sharing.

Exercise 1 — Frame a real decision you're currently avoiding

```
Prompt:
"I'm avoiding this decision because it feels messy: [describe].
Help me frame it. Output: decision statement, objective,
constraints, success criteria, stakeholders. Ask up to 7
clarifying questions if needed. Keep it calm and practical."
```

Exercise 2 — Generate meaningful options (not variations)

```
Prompt:
"Using this decision frame: [paste], generate 4 meaningfully
different options plus 'Do nothing.' For each: what changes,
benefits, risks, effort, who it impacts, and reversibility."
```

Exercise 3 — Tradeoff comparison table (copy-paste ready)

```
Prompt:
"Create a tradeoff comparison table for these options: [paste].
Criteria: speed, cost, quality, risk, effort, stakeholder impact,
reversibility.
Use plain English. Label assumptions explicitly."
```

Exercise 4 — Assumption audit + fast tests

Prompt:
"Run an assumption audit on Option A: [paste].
Classify assumptions as Confirmed/Unconfirmed/Risky and propose
fast, low-cost tests for risky assumptions. Include owners and a
2-week timeline."

Exercise 5 — Pre-mortem (90-day failure rehearsal)

Prompt:
"Run a pre-mortem on this plan: [paste].
Assume it failed in 90 days. List 10 failure reasons, early
warning signs, mitigations, and what to monitor weekly. Label
assumptions. Do not invent facts."

Exercise 6 — Prioritize a list using criteria that match your reality

Prompt:
"Here's my task list: [paste].
My goal this week: [goal].
Constraints: [deadlines/staffing].
Prioritize into Do now, Schedule, Delegate, Defer with rationale.
Identify the top 3 dependencies that unlock progress."

Exercise 7 — Build a 10-step plan with owners and a definition of done

Prompt:
"Create a practical plan for this goal: [goal].
Deadline: [date].
Constraints: [constraints].
Output: numbered steps with purpose, owner, time estimate range,
dependency, deliverable; then a definition-of-done checklist."

Exercise 8 — Stakeholder map and two messages (executive + partner team)

Prompt:
"Decision: [paste].
Map stakeholders (who, what they care about, likely concerns,
what evidence they need).
Then draft two messages:
(A) Executive update (concise, decision-ready)
(B) Partner team message (collaborative, clear asks)
Constraints: neutral tone, no blame, no sensitive details."

Exercise 9 — Challenge mode: stress-test your recommendation

Prompt:
"Here is my recommendation: [paste].
Challenge it like a professional reviewer: list 7 blind spots, 5
underestimated risks, 3 counterarguments, and 5 improvements.
Tone: direct, calm, no flattery."

Exercise 10 — Write a one-page decision record you can share

Prompt:
"Create a one-page decision record from the information below.
Decision: [paste].
Context: [paste].
Options considered: [paste].
Rationale: [paste].
Risks/mitigations: [paste].
Output format: Decision, Date/Owner, Context, Options, Rationale,
Risks, Next Steps, Review Date. Label unknowns as 'Missing.'"

Exercise 11 — Debug-the-thinking: when the team is stuck in a circular debate

Prompt:
"My team is stuck debating this issue: [describe].
Diagnose why we're stuck (frame unclear, success criteria
missing, hidden assumptions, stakeholder misalignment, lack of
options, etc.).
Then propose a 30-minute meeting plan to get unstuck, including:
agenda, questions to answer, and what decision we need by the
end."

Exercise 12 — Create your personal "decision support template" for future use

Prompt:
"Build me a reusable decision-support prompt template I can paste
for future decisions.
It must include: framing, options, tradeoffs, assumptions, risks,
stakeholder considerations, and a decision record output.
Keep it copy-paste ready with placeholders in [brackets].
Include an 'uncertainty rule' that prevents guessing."

Skill Check

After completing this chapter, you should be able to:

- Frame a messy situation into a clear decision statement with success criteria
- Generate meaningful options, including a "do nothing" baseline
- Compare options using explicit tradeoffs and the concept of reversibility
- Surface hidden assumptions and design fast tests to confirm or reduce risk
- Run a pre-mortem to identify failure modes and mitigations before committing
- Prioritize work using criteria instead of urgency fog
- Convert goals into practical step-by-step plans with dependencies and definitions of done
- Map stakeholders and prepare communication that reduces friction and preserves trust
- Create a one-page decision record that prevents future re-litigating and rework

Chapter 6: Writing At Work - Emails, Reports, Proposals

Most professionals do not "write" at work the way writers write. They write the way operators write: to move work forward, reduce confusion, and protect trust.

That kind of writing has a specific challenge: You are rarely writing because you feel inspired. You are writing because something needs to happen.

- An email must clarify the next steps.
- A report must make a decision possible.
- A proposal must earn confidence.
- A status update must prevent surprises.

This chapter teaches a calm, repeatable method for using ChatGPT to produce strong first drafts and better revisions across the most common workplace writing tasks without hype, without sounding robotic, and without increasing risk.

You will learn:

- A professional writing workflow that reduces blank-page stress
- How to control tone and avoid accidental commitments
- Email templates for common scenarios
- How to draft reports and proposals that are structured and decision-ready
- How to use "review loops" and verification checklists
- How to build a writing pipeline you can reuse daily

A note on boundaries: this chapter assumes you are using ChatGPT as a drafting and editing assistant. You remain responsible for maintaining confidentiality, ensuring factual accuracy, and obtaining final approval, particularly for external communications.

Section 6.1: Why Work Writing Feels Hard (Even for Smart People)

Work writing is cognitively expensive because it combines four things at once:

1. **Content:** what happened, what matters, what you need
2. **Audience:** who will read this and how they will interpret it
3. **Stakes:** what could go wrong if this is misunderstood
4. **Constraints:** tone, length, policy, politics, timing

When people say, "I'm not a good writer," they often mean: "I can't hold all of those factors in my head at once under time pressure." That is cognitive load.

ChatGPT helps because it externalizes the first draft. Once a draft exists, your job becomes easier: you edit, verify, and align it to your reality.

This chapter is built around a core principle: Use ChatGPT to draft structure and phrasing; use your judgment to ensure truth, fit, and professionalism.

Section 6.2: The Work Writing Method - Brief → Draft → Review → Revise → Send

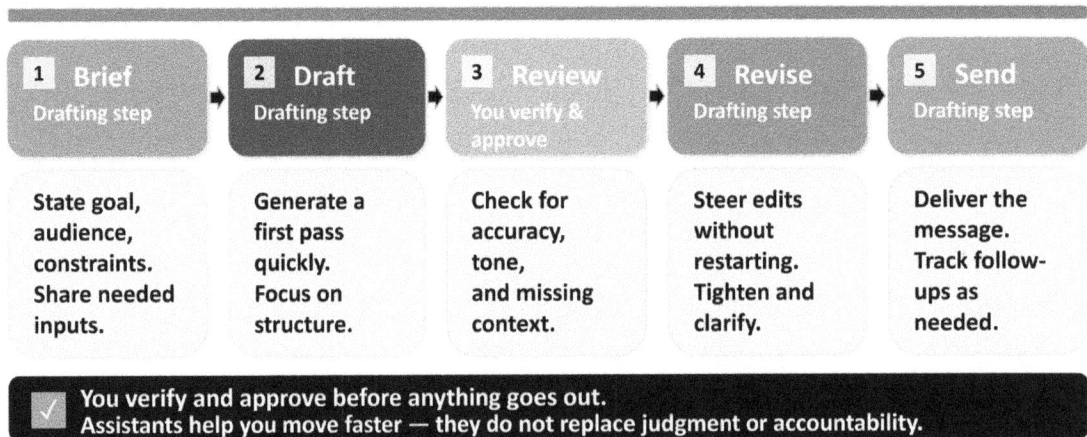

To write calmly and professionally with ChatGPT, use a five-step method:

1. **Brief:** provide goal, audience, context, constraints, and boundaries
2. **Draft:** generate a first version in a usable format
3. **Review:** check for accuracy, tone, unintended promises, and gaps
4. **Revise:** steer changes without restarting
5. **Send:** deliver with confidence, and capture reusable templates

This method turns "writing" into a predictable workflow.

Figure 6.1 – Work writing pipeline

Brief → Draft → Review → Revise → Send

1 Brief	2 Draft	3 Review	4 Revise	5 Send
Drafting step	Drafting step	You verify & approve	Drafting step	Drafting step
State goal, audience, constraints. Share needed inputs.	Generate a first pass quickly. Focus on structure.	Check for accuracy, tone, and missing context.	Steer edits without restarting. Tighten and clarify.	Deliver the message. Track follow-ups as needed.

☑ You verify and approve before anything goes out.
Assistants help you move faster — they do not replace judgment or accountability.

Many people skip the brief and jump straight to drafting, then wonder why the output feels generic. The brief is where professionalism happens.

A short brief can be enough:

- Purpose
- Audience
- Key facts
- Tone
- Constraints
- Ask/next step

If you supply that, you will spend less time rewriting later.

Section 6.3: The Most Important Email Skill - Put the Ask Up Front

In business writing, clarity beats elegance.

A common reason emails generate follow-ups is that the ask is buried. The reader finishes the email thinking, "So what do you want from me?"

A practical rule: **If you need a decision, a response, or an action, put it in the first two sentences. This is not rude. It is respectful of attention.**

Figure 6.2 – Email structure: Ask-first format

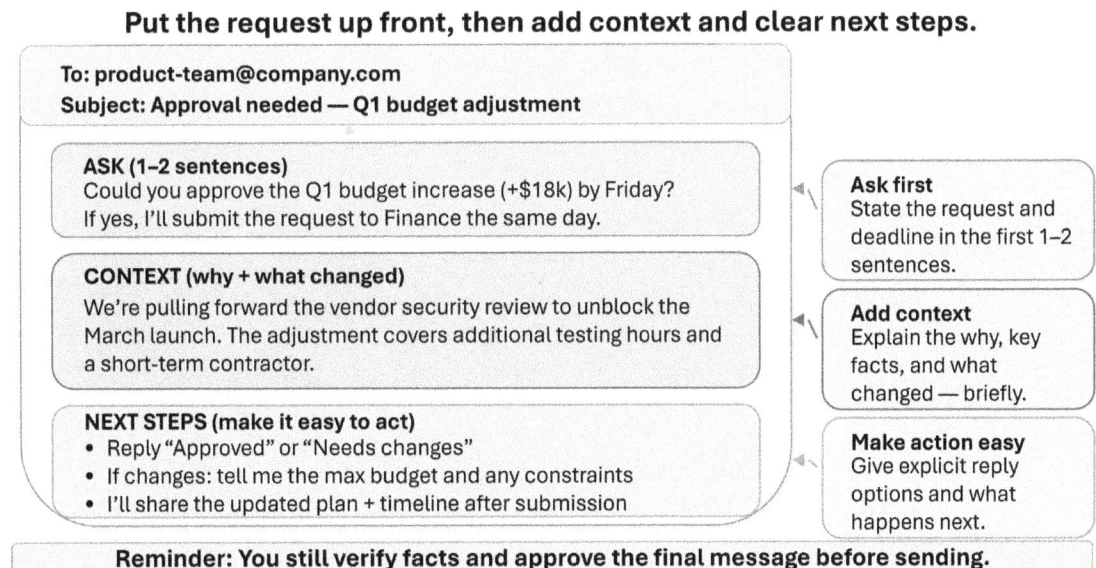

Put the request up front, then add context and clear next steps.

To: product-team@company.com
Subject: Approval needed — Q1 budget adjustment

ASK (1–2 sentences)
Could you approve the Q1 budget increase (+$18k) by Friday?
If yes, I'll submit the request to Finance the same day.

Ask first
State the request and deadline in the first 1–2 sentences.

CONTEXT (why + what changed)
We're pulling forward the vendor security review to unblock the March launch. The adjustment covers additional testing hours and a short-term contractor.

Add context
Explain the why, key facts, and what changed — briefly.

NEXT STEPS (make it easy to act)
- Reply "Approved" or "Needs changes"
- If changes: tell me the max budget and any constraints
- I'll share the updated plan + timeline after submission

Make action easy
Give explicit reply options and what happens next.

Reminder: You still verify facts and approve the final message before sending.

You can ask ChatGPT to enforce this:

> **Prompt: Ask-first email drafting**
> "Draft an email where the ask is in the first two sentences.
> Goal: [what you need from the reader].
> Audience: [who].
> Context: [key facts].
> Tone: [neutral/warm/firm but respectful].
> Constraints: [length, boundaries].
> Output: subject line + email body + 3 bullet next steps with owners.
> Do not: overpromise, assign blame, include sensitive details.
> End with: a 6-item pre-send checklist."

Section 6.4: Email Types - A Professional Playbook

Most workplace emails fall into repeatable categories. If you build templates for these, you reduce cognitive load permanently.

We will cover nine high-frequency types:

1. Request (asking for information or action)
2. Update (status and next steps)
3. Follow-up (closing loops politely)
4. Clarification (reducing ambiguity)
5. Escalation (raising risk without drama)
6. Apology + correction (fixing an error professionally)
7. Boundary-setting (saying no or renegotiating scope)
8. Stakeholder alignment (getting buy-in)
9. Customer-facing response (accountable and clear)

For each type, you will see a structure and a prompt pattern.

Figure 6.3 – Prompt comparison: vague vs. structured (email example)

| GOAL | AUDIENCE | CONSTRAINTS | OUTPUT | *Highlights show what makes a prompt "decision-ready."* |

Vague prompt

Write an email to the team about the new onboarding process.

What's missing:

| Goal? | Audience? |
| Constraints? | Output? |

Structured prompt

GOAL	Announce updated onboarding and ask managers to share with new hires.
AUDIENCE	Engineering team (ICs + managers). Tone: upbeat & practical.
CONSTRAINTS	≤150 words, ask-first, include [LINK], collect questions by Fri.
OUTPUT	Return: subject + 3 short paragraphs + "What changed" bullets.

Sample output (vague)

Subject: Onboarding update

Hi team,

We've made improvements to our onboarding process and will roll them out soon.
Please take a look and share feedback when you have a moment.

Thanks,

Sample output (structured)

Subject: Please share the updated onboarding checklist (Jan 15)

Quick ask: managers—please share this with any new hires starting next week.

Doc: [LINK]

What changed:
• Day 1 setup steps clarified
• Access requests updated
• First-week checklist added

Email Type 1: Request

Structure:

- Purpose + ask (first two sentences)
- Context (what they need to know)
- Deadline (if applicable)
- Why it matters (optional, short)
- Next step / thanks

```
Prompt:
"Write a request email.
Ask: [what you need].
Audience: [role/relationship].
Context: [2-5 facts].
Deadline: [date/time].
Tone: warm, direct, respectful.
Constraints: under [word count].
Output: subject line + email.
Do not: guilt, vague urgency, or unnecessary details."
```

Email Type 2: Update

Structure:

- Status headline (on track / at risk / blocked)
- Key progress since last update
- Risks + mitigations
- Decisions needed / asks
- Next steps + owners

> **Prompt:**
> "Draft a short project update for executives.
> Status: [on track/at risk/blocked].
> Progress: [bullets].
> Risks: [bullets].
> Asks/decisions needed: [bullets].
> Tone: neutral, confident, no blame.
> Output: subject line + 10-sentence email + 3 bullet next steps with owners.
> Rule: If something is missing, label it 'Missing' and ask me."

Email Type 3: Follow-Up

Structure:

- Reminder of the prior thread
- What you need
- A clear deadline or "by end of day" suggestion
- Offer help / alternative
- Thank you

> **Prompt:**
> "Write a polite follow-up email.
> What I'm following up on: [topic].
> What I need: [ask].
> When I need it: [deadline].
> Tone: friendly, brief, not passive-aggressive.
> Output: subject line + 6-8 sentence email."

Email Type 4: Clarification

Structure:

- State what you heard/understood
- Identify ambiguity
- Ask specific questions

- Propose a default assumption (optional)
- Confirm next steps

> **Prompt:**
> "Write a clarification email that reduces ambiguity.
> What I understand so far: [summary].
> What's unclear: [points].
> Questions: [list].
> Tone: collaborative, not accusatory.
> Output: subject line + short email."

Email Type 5: Escalation

Structure:

- Calm headline of risk
- Evidence (facts, not opinions)
- Impact if unchanged
- Options or recommendation
- Decision needed + deadline

> **Prompt:**
> "Draft an escalation email that is calm and factual.
> Risk: [risk].
> Facts/evidence: [facts].
> Impact: [impact].
> Options: [option A/B].
> Decision needed: [decision].
> Deadline: [date].
> Tone: neutral, no blame, executive-ready.
> Output: subject + email + 5-item verification checklist."

Email Type 6: Apology + Correction

Structure:

- Acknowledge
- Correct
- Impact and mitigation
- Next steps
- Prevent recurrence (optional)

> **Prompt:**
> "Write an apology-and-correction email.
> Mistake: [what happened].

```
Correction: [what is true now].
Impact: [impact].
Next steps: [actions].
Tone: accountable, calm, not over-apologetic.
Do not: assign blame or include unnecessary detail."
```

Email Type 7: Boundary-Setting (Saying No or Renegotiating Scope)

Structure:

- Acknowledge request
- State constraint
- Offer alternatives
- Confirm next step

Prompt:
```
"Help me say no professionally while maintaining trust.
Request: [request].
Constraint: [time/budget/policy].
Alternatives I can offer: [options].
Tone: respectful, calm, collaborative.
Output: email + short call script version."
```

Email Type 8: Stakeholder Alignment

Structure:

- Shared goal
- Current situation
- Proposal
- Tradeoffs
- Ask for agreement/feedback
- Next steps

Prompt:
```
"Draft a stakeholder alignment email.
Shared goal: [goal].
Proposal: [proposal].
Tradeoffs: [tradeoffs].
What I need from them: [agreement/feedback].
Tone: collaborative, confident, clear.
Output: email + 3 likely objections + suggested responses."
```

Email Type 9: Customer-Facing Response

Structure:

- Acknowledge and empathize (brief)
- Confirm understanding
- Provide solution or next steps
- Set expectations (timelines carefully)
- Close with support

> **Prompt:**
> "Draft a customer response email.
> Customer issue: [issue].
> What we can do: [solution].
> Constraints: [what we can't promise].
> Tone: empathetic, accountable, clear, not defensive.
> Output: subject + email + a short internal note summarizing commitments made."

That last internal note is a professional safeguard. It prevents accidental commitments from being forgotten.

Section 6.5: The Unintended Promise Problem (And How to Prevent It)

One of the biggest risks in business writing is promising something unintentionally.

It happens when:

- You use absolute language ("will," "guarantee," "always")
- You propose a date without confirming feasibility
- You over-apologize and imply fault or liability
- You write with confidence when you should write with caution

To prevent this, adopt two practices:

> **Practice 1: Add a boundary instruction**
> "Do not make promises about dates unless I provide them."
>
> **Practice 2: Add a verification checklist item**
> "Confirm all commitments and timelines before sending."

You can also ask ChatGPT to highlight commitments explicitly:

> ***Prompt: Commitment highlighter***
> *"After drafting, list every commitment this email makes (dates, actions, promises, expectations).*
> *If any commitment is implied but not stated, flag it.*
> *Then suggest safer wording that preserves accountability without overpromising."*

This is a high-value prompt for customer communications and leadership updates.

Figure 6.4 – "Unintended promise" checklist

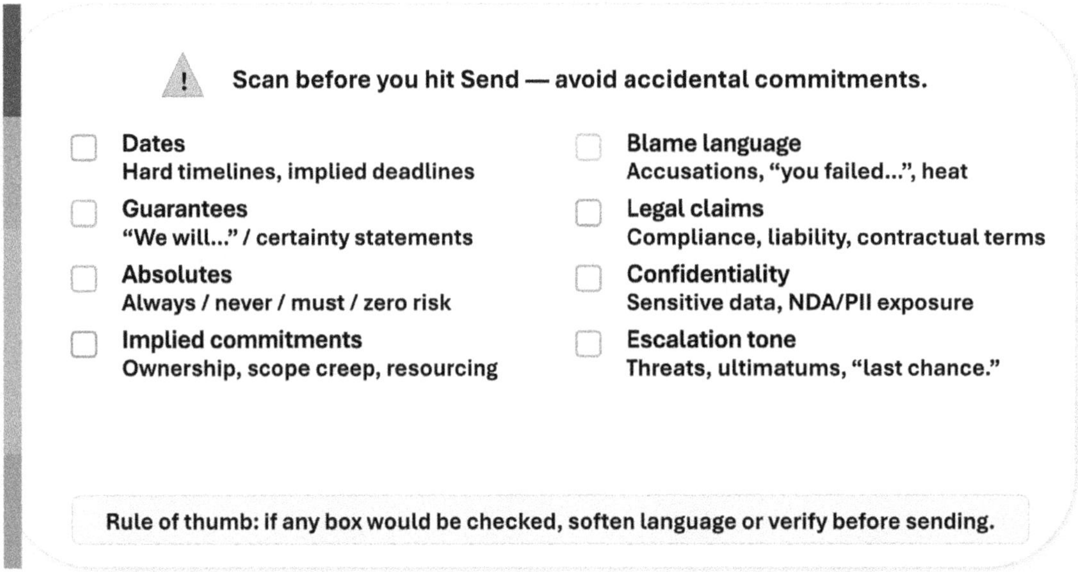

Scan before you hit Send — avoid accidental commitments.
Dates
Hard timelines, implied deadlines
Guarantees
"We will..." / certainty statements
Absolutes
Always / never / must / zero risk
Implied commitments
Ownership, scope creep, resourcing
Blame language
Accusations, "you failed...", heat
Legal claims
Compliance, liability, contractual terms
Confidentiality
Sensitive data, NDA/PII exposure
Escalation tone
Threats, ultimatums, "last chance."
Rule of thumb: if any box would be checked, soften language or verify before sending.

Section 6.6: Report Writing - Think "Decision-Ready," not "Information-Dense"

A report is not a data dump. It is a tool for decision-making.

Figure 6.5 – Decision-ready report structure (one page)

Use these headings to keep a report scannable, verifiable, and action-oriented.

Summary
- What happened (1–3 sentences)
- What decision is needed (or what you recommend)
- What success looks like

Findings
- Key facts + evidence (link/appendix if needed)
- What changed since last update
- Any notable metrics or customer signals

Implications
- Why the findings matter
- Who/what is impacted (users, timeline, cost, risk)
- What happens if we do nothing

Options
- Option A: tradeoffs (speed / cost / quality)
- Option B: tradeoffs
- Option C (if applicable)

Recommendation
- Choose one option and explain why
- Call out assumptions and what to verify

Risks
- Top risks + mitigations
- Decision reversibility/blast radius

Next Steps
- Tasks, owners, and dates
- What you will report back, and when

A decision-ready report includes:

- Executive summary (what matters and why)
- Key findings (the evidence)
- Implications (so what?)
- Options (what can be done)
- Recommendation (if appropriate)
- Risks (what could go wrong)
- Next steps (what happens now)

ChatGPT can help you structure and draft reports using your source material.

```
Prompt: Report drafting from source material
"Act as a business analyst.
Goal: Draft a decision-ready report for [audience].
Source material (use as truth; do not add facts): [paste].
Constraints: plain English, neutral tone, keep it to [length].
Output format:

Executive summary (5 bullets max)

Findings (with evidence from source material)

Implications

Options (2-3)
```

> *Recommendation (state assumptions)*
>
> *Risks*
>
> *Next steps*
> *Rule: If information is missing, label it 'Missing' and ask questions."*

To keep reports grounded, include the "do not add facts" rule. That prevents invention.

Section 6.7: Proposals - The Real Job is Building Trust

A proposal is not just a description of what you'll do. It is an argument for why you can be trusted to do it.

Professional proposals typically succeed because they:

- Show understanding of the problem
- Define scope clearly
- Demonstrate a sensible plan
- Address risks and dependencies
- Clarify what success looks like
- Make responsibilities explicit
- Communicate credibility without arrogance

ChatGPT helps by drafting structure and phrasing, but you must supply the real specifics.

A proposal should reduce uncertainty for the reader.

Proposal structure (general, reusable):

1. Summary (what you will deliver and why it matters)
2. Background / problem statement
3. Goals and success criteria
4. Scope (in scope / out of scope)
5. Approach / methodology (how work will be done)
6. Timeline and milestones
7. Roles and responsibilities
8. Risks and mitigations
9. Assumptions and dependencies
10. Pricing or resourcing (if relevant)
11. Next steps

> *Prompt: Proposal draft generator*
> *"Act as a proposal writer for business audiences.*
> *Goal: Draft a proposal for [client/stakeholder] to [deliverable].*
> *Audience: [who].*
> *Context (sanitized): [problem, constraints, goals].*
> *Success criteria: [list].*
> *Scope: in-scope [list], out-of-scope [list].*
> *Constraints: plain English, confident but not salesy, no hype,*
> *avoid absolute promises.*
> *Output format: use the 11-section structure above with headings.*
> *Uncertainty rule: If details are missing, label them 'Missing'*
> *and ask me questions.*
> *Verification: End with a checklist of items I must confirm*
> *(dates, resourcing, scope)."*

Then do a second pass: "Now rewrite for clarity and concision. Remove redundancy. Ensure tone is professional and calm."

This two-pass approach prevents proposals from becoming bloated.

Figure 6.6 – Proposal structure map (trust-building elements)

A proposal reduces uncertainty by making expectations explicit across scope, time, ownership, and risk.

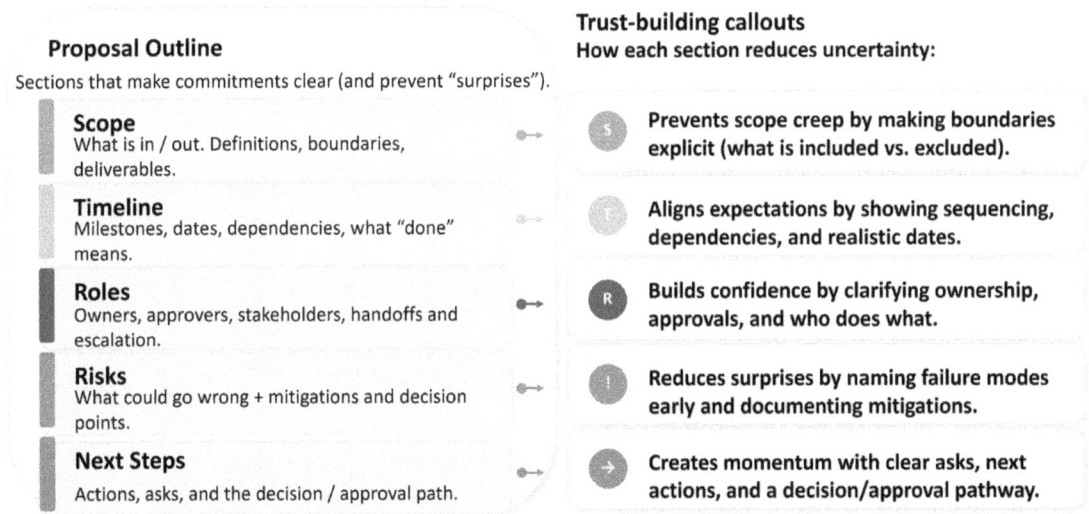

Proposal Outline
Sections that make commitments clear (and prevent "surprises").

Trust-building callouts
How each section reduces uncertainty:

Scope
What is in / out. Definitions, boundaries, deliverables.

(S) Prevents scope creep by making boundaries explicit (what is included vs. excluded).

Timeline
Milestones, dates, dependencies, what "done" means.

(T) Aligns expectations by showing sequencing, dependencies, and realistic dates.

Roles
Owners, approvers, stakeholders, handoffs and escalation.

(R) Builds confidence by clarifying ownership, approvals, and who does what.

Risks
What could go wrong + mitigations and decision points.

(!) Reduces surprises by naming failure modes early and documenting mitigations.

Next Steps
Actions, asks, and the decision / approval path.

(→) Creates momentum with clear asks, next actions, and a decision/approval pathway.

Tip: If reviewers ask follow-up questions, add a section (or tighten one) — the goal is fewer surprises later.

Section 6.8: Executive Writing - The "So What / Now What" Rule

Executives rarely lack intelligence. They lack time.

Executive writing succeeds when it answers two questions quickly:

So what?
Now what?

So what:

- What changed?
- Why should I care?
- What is the impact?

Now what:

- What decision do you need?
- What action do you want?
- What is the timeline?

ChatGPT can produce executive summaries if you give it a strict format.

> **Prompt: Executive summary converter**
> "Convert the information below into an executive summary that answers: So what? Now what?
> Information: [paste].
> Output:
>
> 1 sentence: So what
>
> 1 sentence: Now what
>
> 3 bullets: key facts
>
> 2 bullets: risks
>
> 1 bullet: decision needed (if any)
> Tone: concise, neutral."

This is a high-impact daily tool for leaders and managers.

Section 6.9: Writing Pipelines - How to Use ChatGPT without Feeling Like You're "Cheating"

Some professionals feel uneasy using AI for writing because it can feel like outsourcing competence.

A calmer perspective is this: Using a drafting assistant is not cheating. It is using a tool to reduce friction, like using spellcheck, templates, or a standard report format.

The ethical line is not "did AI help draft this?" The ethical line is "is this accurate, honest, and appropriately authored and reviewed?"

In most workplaces, the expectation is not that you craft every sentence from scratch. The expectation is that your work is correct, clear, and professional.

A writing pipeline helps you maintain that standard:

Pipeline Step 1: Draft quickly (ChatGPT)
Pipeline Step 2: Verify facts and commitments (you)
Pipeline Step 3: Align tone and stakeholder sensitivity (you + ChatGPT revisions)
Pipeline Step 4: Final read-out loud (you)
Pipeline Step 5: Send and record template improvements (you)

The "read-out loud" step is underrated. It catches awkward phrasing and unintended tone.

Section 6.10: Editing with ChatGPT - Make it Your "Second Set of Eyes"

ChatGPT is often more valuable as an editor than as a writer.

Editing tasks it supports well:

- Tightening and shortening
- Making language more neutral or more warm
- Removing ambiguity
- Improving structure and headings
- Identifying missing information
- Spotting implied commitments
- Highlighting jargon and rewriting in plain English

> *Prompt: Professional edit pass*
> *"Edit the text below for clarity, professionalism, and concision.*
> *Goals: reduce ambiguity, avoid unintended promises, keep tone calm.*
> *Constraints: do not change factual meaning; do not add new facts; keep under [word count].*
> *After editing, list:*
>
> *Any implied commitments*
>
> *Any ambiguous phrases*
>
> *3 questions that would improve accuracy*
> *Text: [paste]."*

This is a powerful "review loop" prompt you can reuse across emails, memos, and proposals.

Section 6.11: Common Writing Failures (And the Fix Prompts)

Failure: Too long

> *Fix prompt:*
> *"Shorten this by 30% while keeping meaning. Remove redundancy. Keep the ask and next steps clear."*

Failure: Too vague

> *Fix prompt:*
> *"Replace vague phrases with specific actions, owners, and deadlines where possible. If unknown, label as 'Missing.'"*

Failure: Too harsh

> *Fix prompt:*
> *"Rewrite to be firm but respectful. Remove blame. Keep accountability and clarity."*

Failure: Too soft / unclear ask

> *Fix prompt:*
> *"Make the ask explicit and move it to the top. Add a clear deadline and next step."*

Failure: Sounds robotic

> *Fix prompt:*
> *"Make this sound more natural while staying professional. Keep sentences varied. Avoid clichés."*

Failure: Risky commitments

> *Fix prompt:*
> *"Highlight every promise or timeline. Suggest safer wording that maintains accountability without guaranteeing."*

When you treat writing problems as fixable patterns, anxiety decreases. You stop feeling like you "failed." You simply run the appropriate revision.

Section 6.12: Worked Example - A Customer Email That Stays Accountable without Overpromising

Scenario (sanitized): A customer is unhappy about a delay. You need to respond quickly and preserve trust. You can offer a solution, but the exact ship date is not confirmed.

Brief to ChatGPT:

- Goal: acknowledge, explain next steps, avoid promising a date
- Audience: customer
- Tone: empathetic, accountable, calm
- Constraints: no blame, no internal details, no guarantees

> *Prompt:*
> *"Draft a customer response email.*
> *Customer issue: delay in delivery.*
> *What we know: order is in progress; we are confirming timeline; we will update within 24 hours.*
> *What we can do: offer expedited shipping once ready, or offer a refund if they prefer.*
> *Constraints: do not promise a ship date; do not blame; avoid internal operational details.*
> *Tone: empathetic, accountable, calm.*
> *Output: subject + email + internal note listing commitments made."*

The internal note might say:

- Commitment: provide update within 24 hours
- Offer: expedited shipping once ready OR refund option
- No ship date promised

That internal note protects you and your team. It turns customer communication into a controlled promise set.

Section 6.13: Building Your "Writing Prompt Library" for Daily Use

At the end of this chapter, you should have at least five reusable prompts:

1. Ask-first email template
2. Executive update template
3. Customer response template (with commitment tracking)
4. Decision-ready report template
5. Proposal structure template

You do not need 50 prompts. You need a few that match your work.

Later in the capstone, you will build a full personal prompt library, but you can start now with these foundational tools.

Practice Exercises

Exercise 1 — Ask-first email for a real request

```
Prompt:
"Draft an ask-first email.
Ask: [what you need].
Audience: [who].
Context: [facts].
Deadline: [deadline].
Tone: [tone].
Constraints: under [word count], no blame, no overpromises.
Output: subject + email + 3 bullet next steps."
```

Exercise 2 — Executive update in 150 words

> **Prompt:**
> "Write a 150-word executive update.
> Status: [on track/at risk/blocked].
> Progress: [bullets].
> Risks: [bullets].
> Decision needed: [decision].
> Tone: concise, neutral, no blame.
> Output: subject + email + 3 bullets (next steps with owners)."

Exercise 3 — Follow-up that doesn't sound passive-aggressive

> **Prompt:**
> "Write a polite follow-up on this thread: [summary].
> What I need: [ask].
> Deadline: [deadline].
> Tone: friendly, brief, respectful.
> Output: subject + 6–8 sentence email."

Exercise 4 — Escalation email that stays factual

> **Prompt:**
> "Draft an escalation email.
> Risk: [risk].
> Evidence: [facts].
> Impact: [impact].
> Options: [A/B].
> Decision needed: [decision].
> Deadline: [deadline].
> Tone: neutral, calm, no blame.
> Output: email + 5-item verification checklist."

Exercise 5 — Customer response with commitment tracking

> **Prompt:**
> "Draft a customer response email.
> Issue: [issue].
> What we know: [facts].
> What we can do: [solutions].
> Constraints: [what we can't promise].
> Tone: empathetic and accountable.
> Output: subject + email + internal note listing commitments made."

Exercise 6 — Rewrite a message three ways (tone control)

> *Prompt:*
> *"Rewrite this message three ways:*
> *(A) Neutral and direct*
> *(B) Warm and collaborative*
> *(C) Firm but respectful*
> *Keep facts identical. Do not add commitments.*
> *Message: [paste]."*

Exercise 7 — Convert messy notes into a decision-ready report

> *Prompt:*
> *"Use the source material below (do not add facts) to draft a decision-ready report for [audience].*
> *Source material: [paste].*
> *Output format: summary, findings, implications, options, recommendation (state assumptions), risks, next steps.*
> *Label unknowns as 'Missing.'"*

Exercise 8 — Proposal draft using the 11-section structure

> *Prompt:*
> *"Draft a proposal using this structure: Summary, Background, Goals, Scope, Approach, Timeline, Roles, Risks, Assumptions, Resourcing, Next steps.*
> *Context: [paste].*
> *Audience: [who].*
> *Constraints: plain English, calm, confident, not salesy.*
> *Do not: promise unconfirmed dates or include sensitive details."*

Exercise 9 — Editing pass: shorten by 30% and remove ambiguity

> *Prompt:*
> *"Edit the text below: shorten by 30%, remove ambiguity, keep tone calm and professional.*
> *Do not change factual meaning or add new facts.*
> *After editing, list implied commitments and ambiguous phrases.*
> *Text: [paste]."*

Exercise 10 — Commitment audit on an email before sending

> *Prompt:*
> *"Analyze this email for commitments.*
> *List every explicit and implied promise (dates, actions, expectations).*

> *Then suggest safer wording for any risky commitments while*
> *keeping accountability.*
> *Email: [paste]."*

Exercise 11 — Build your top 5 reusable writing prompts

> **Prompt:**
> *"Based on my role and typical writing tasks, create 5 reusable*
> *prompt templates I can save.*
> *My role: [role].*
> *My common writing: [emails, reports, proposals, updates].*
> *Constraints: [privacy/tone/policy].*
> *Each template should be copy-paste ready with placeholders."*

Skill Check

After completing this chapter, you should be able to:

- Use a repeatable writing workflow: Brief → Draft → Review → Revise → Send
- Draft ask-first emails that reduce follow-up confusion
- Produce executive updates that answer "so what / now what" quickly
- Write follow-ups and escalations that stay calm, factual, and professional
- Create customer responses that are empathetic and accountable without overpromising
- Draft decision-ready reports from your source material without inventing facts
- Build proposal drafts that clarify scope, timeline, roles, risks, and assumptions
- Run editing and commitment-audit review loops to prevent costly writing mistakes
- Start a reusable writing prompt library tailored to your daily work

Chapter 7: Productivity Systems Powered by AI

Productivity is not a personality trait. It is not "discipline" in the moral sense. It is a set of agreements you make with yourself about how work will move from incoming to done.

Most professionals do not fail because they lack effort. They fail because their system is informal, overloaded, and constantly interrupted. The result is familiar:

- You capture tasks in too many places
- You hold "open loops" in your head
- You respond to urgency instead of priority
- You rewrite the same messages because context is scattered
- You complete lots of activity but don't feel control

This chapter is about building a productivity system that reduces cognitive load by making work visible, structured, and repeatable, and then using ChatGPT as a drafting and thinking assistant inside that system.

We will avoid complicated frameworks. You do not need a perfect app stack. You need a few dependable workflows:

- A capture workflow (nothing important lives only in your head)
- A daily planning workflow (today has a plan you can actually execute)
- A weekly review workflow (your system gets cleaned and reset)
- A writing pipeline (your communication becomes faster and more consistent)
- Guardrails (privacy, accuracy, and commitment control)

By the end of this chapter, you will have a practical, business-ready productivity system that you can run with simple tools, a calendar, email, task list, and ChatGPT, without turning your life into a management project.

Section 7.1: What a "System" Is (Plain English)

A productivity system is a repeatable way of answering five questions:

1. What is coming in?
2. What do I need to do about it?
3. When will I do it?
4. What does "done" look like?
5. How do I keep the system clean?

If you do not have clear answers, your brain becomes the system. That is the hidden tax of modern work: you carry the whole operation in your head.

A system is not restrictive. A system is what creates flexibility. When you trust your system, you can relax, because you know nothing important is being forgotten.

ChatGPT's role here is not to "manage your life." Its role is to reduce friction inside the system:

- Drafting your daily plan
- Turning messy notes into clear tasks
- Creating checklists and definitions of done
- Writing and rewriting communication
- Helping you run reviews and reflect on what's working

Think of ChatGPT as the assistant that helps you operate the system, not as the system itself.

Section 7.2: The Four Leaks That Drain Productivity (And How AI Helps Plug Them)

Most productivity problems come from four leaks. If you fix these, you will feel the difference quickly.

Leak 1: Open loops in your head

An open loop is anything you're tracking mentally: "I need to email them," "I should follow up," "I have to remember that meeting," "I owe someone a draft."

Open loops increase cognitive load because your brain keeps pinging you to avoid forgetting.

How AI helps: Convert vague mental loops into clear tasks and next steps.

Leak 2: Unclear next actions

Many "tasks" are not actions. They are projects disguised as tasks: "Prepare budget," "Fix onboarding," "Improve process." That ambiguity creates avoidance.

How AI helps: Turn ambiguous work into next actions, checklists, and definitions of done.

Leak 3: Context fragmentation

Information is scattered across email threads, chats, docs, and meetings. You spend time searching instead of doing.

How AI helps: Summarize, structure, and create "context packets" you can reuse.

Leak 4: Rework in writing and decisions

Unclear emails create follow-up questions. Unrecorded decisions get revisited. Drafts take too long to start.

How AI helps: Draft faster, enforce structure, and generate decision records.

Figure 7.1 – The four leaks

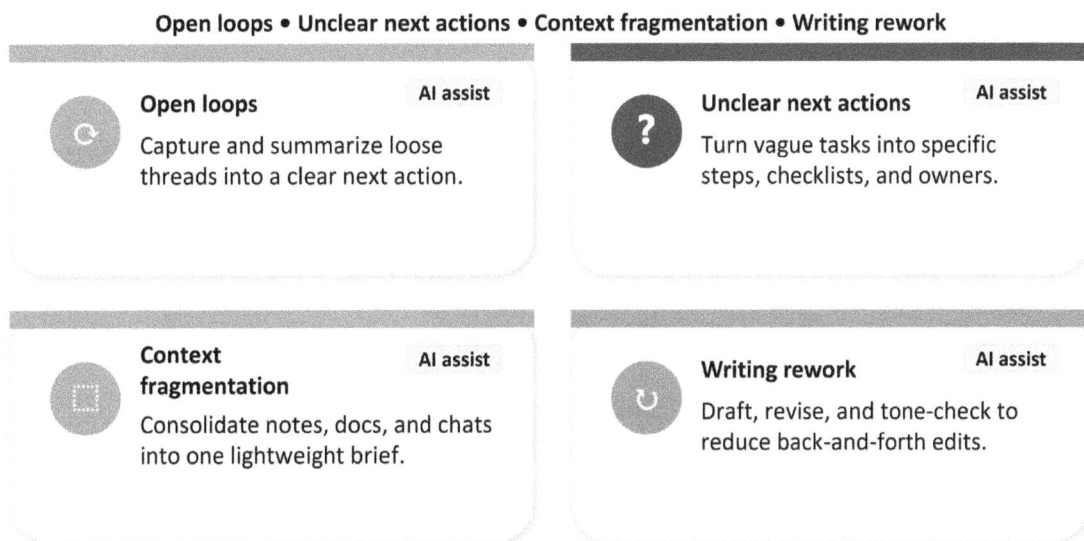

Open loops • Unclear next actions • Context fragmentation • Writing rework

Open loops — AI assist Capture and summarize loose threads into a clear next action.	**Unclear next actions** — AI assist Turn vague tasks into specific steps, checklists, and owners.
Context fragmentation — AI assist Consolidate notes, docs, and chats into one lightweight brief.	**Writing rework** — AI assist Draft, revise, and tone-check to reduce back-and-forth edits.

Tip: Fixing the leaks often starts by externalizing the next action.

A calm reminder: plugging leaks is not about being "busy." It's about reducing friction so your effort turns into usable output.

Section 7.3: The Foundation - Capture, Clarify, Organize, Execute, Review

This chapter uses a simple system backbone. It's not a brand-name method. It's a practical sequence:

1. **Capture**: Collect inputs into a trusted place
2. **Clarify**: Decide what each input means and what to do next
3. **Organize**: Put tasks where they belong (calendar, task list, reference)
4. **Execute**: Work your plan with realistic expectations
5. **Review**: Reset weekly so the system stays clean

Figure 7.2 – The productivity system loop: Capture → Clarify → Organize → Execute → Review

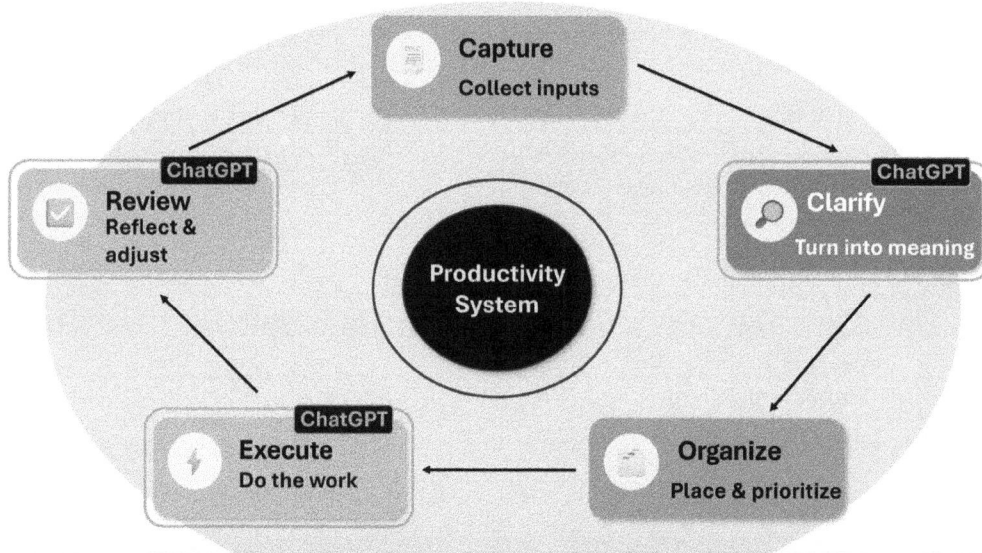

ChatGPT is most useful in steps 2–5. Capture is mostly about your habits and tools. Clarify and plan are where language and structure matter and where AI shines.

Section 7.4: Capture - How to Stop Trusting Your Brain to Remember

Capture is the first non-negotiable. If you skip it, everything else becomes fragile.

A professional capture system has three channels:

1. **Calendar**: time-specific commitments (meetings, deadlines, appointments)
2. **Task list**: actions you must take (work you control)
3. **Notes/reference**: information you may need later (work you don't want to rewrite)

The mistake many professionals make is using email as a task list and their head as a notes system.

A calmer approach:

- Email is a communication tool, not a memory system.
- Your brain is for thinking, not for storing open loops.

A capture rule that changes everything: **If it takes more than two minutes or depends on the future, capture it.**

Capture does not mean "organize perfectly." Capture means "get it out of your head."

How ChatGPT supports capture (without seeing sensitive info)

You don't need to paste confidential content. You can paste sanitized summaries.

```
Prompt: Capture-to-task converter
"Turn the items below into clear tasks with next actions.
Rules: If a task is unclear, propose a clarifying question.
Output: a checklist grouped into (A) quick actions under 10
minutes, (B) tasks 10-60 minutes, (C) projects that need multiple
steps.
Items: [paste your list or quick notes—sanitized]."
```

This prompt is a pressure-release valve. It takes mental clutter and turns it into visible, structured work.

Section 7.5: Clarify - Turn Inboxes and Notes into Next Actions

Clarify is where most professionals get stuck. They capture, but they don't decide what anything means, so the pile grows.

Clarify has four decisions:

1. Is this actionable?
2. If yes, what is the next action?

3. What is "done"?

4. Where does it belong (calendar, task list, delegate, defer, reference)?

ChatGPT can help you clarify quickly by forcing specificity.

> **Prompt: Next action + definition of done**
> "Help me clarify the items below. For each item:
>
> Is it actionable?
>
> Next action (verb-first)
>
> Definition of done (1-3 bullet checks)
>
> Suggested category: calendar / task list / delegate / defer / reference
> Items: [paste items—sanitized].
> Tone: direct and practical."

Why "verb-first" matters

A next action should begin with a verb:

- Email ...
- Draft ...
- Review ...
- Call ...
- Decide ...
- Schedule ...

If your task does not start with a verb, it is likely not clear enough to execute. This is a simple but powerful diagnostic.

Section 7.6: Organize - Where Work Goes so it Doesn't Haunt You

Once clarified, each item should have a home:

Calendar (time-specific)

Use the calendar for:

- Meetings
- Appointments
- Hard deadlines
- Time blocks for focused work (optional but powerful)

Do not put vague tasks on the calendar unless you are time-blocking deliberately.

Task list (action-specific)

Use a task list for:

- Actions you can do without a fixed time
- Projects broken into next actions
- Follow-ups

A task list must be short enough to review daily. If it becomes a warehouse, it stops functioning.

Reference (information)

Reference is not a graveyard. It's where you store:

- SOPs
- meeting notes
- decision records
- templates
- context packets

ChatGPT can help you convert references into reusable formats, especially SOPs and decision records (Chapters 5 and 8 deepen this).

Section 7.7: The Daily Plan - A Calm Routine You Can Actually Follow

A daily plan is not a wish list. It is a realistic agreement with time.

A calm daily planning routine takes 10–15 minutes and includes:

1. Review calendar (time is already spoken for)
2. Choose 1–3 priority outcomes (not 15 tasks)
3. Identify "must do today" tasks (true deadlines or commitments)
4. Plan around energy (deep work vs shallow work)
5. Add buffer for reality (interruptions happen)

The "Three Outcomes" rule

Instead of listing everything, choose three outcomes:

- **Outcome 1:** a meaningful deliverable
- **Outcome 2:** a key communication
- **Outcome 3:** an operational step that prevents future pain

You can do more than three tasks. But outcomes keep you aligned with what matters.

```
Prompt: Daily plan generator (professional, calm)
"Help me draft a realistic daily plan.
Context:

Meetings/time blocks today: [paste schedule summary]

Must-do tasks (deadlines/commitments): [list]

Optional tasks: [list]

Energy notes: [morning is best for deep work / afternoons are
admin, etc.]
Output:

Top 3 outcomes for today

A time-aware plan that fits around meetings

A short 'if interrupted' fallback plan

A 6-item end-of-day shutdown checklist
Rules: be realistic; build buffer; do not overload."
```

This prompt gives you structure while preserving your judgment. If it suggests too much, you revise: "Reduce scope by 20%."

Figure 7.3 – Daily plan template

Calendar-first • Three outcomes • Buffer • Shutdown

📅 Calendar-first (time blocks)

Drag blocks onto your calendar first; protect focus time.

9:00

10:00   Deep work

11:00

12:00   Meetings / calls

1:00   Buffer / catch-up

◎ Top 3 outcomes (must ship today)

1️⃣ Outcome text...

2️⃣ Outcome text...

3️⃣ Outcome text...

💬 Shutdown checklist (10 minutes)

☐ Capture open loops (unanswered emails, TODOs) into tomorrow's list.

☐ Confirm your next day's Top 3 outcomes and first time block.

☐ Send any blocking messages (asks, updates) while context is fresh.

☐ Close tabs, file drafts, and park "later" items in a trusted place.

☐ End the day: quick review → clear next action → log off.

◐ Buffer (protect it)

Reserve: 30–90 min for interruptions + small tasks.

If a meeting slips, it lands here.

If nothing breaks: advance tomorrow's work.

The shutdown checklist (why it matters)

A shutdown checklist is a short routine that prevents overnight cognitive load. It typically includes:

- Capture loose ends
- Update task list
- Confirm tomorrow's first action
- Close open documents
- Note one win (optional but stabilizing)
- End

You can ask ChatGPT to customize your shutdown checklist to your role.

Section 7.8: Weekly Review - How to Keep the System Clean and Trustworthy

The weekly review is what turns a productivity method into a productivity system.

Without review, your task list becomes stale, your calendar becomes reactive, and your brain starts carrying open loops again.

A weekly review typically includes:

1. Clear inboxes (email, tasks, notes)
2. Update project lists
3. Review commitments and deadlines
4. Decide next week's priorities
5. Identify risks and constraints
6. Prepare Monday with a clean start

A calm weekly review script you can reuse

You can run your weekly review with ChatGPT as a guide. You don't have to share sensitive info; use categories and summaries.

> *Prompt: Weekly review coach*
> "Act as my weekly review coach. Ask me questions one at a time.
> Goal: clean up open loops and prepare next week.
> You must cover: inbox cleanup, project review, deadlines, key
> stakeholders, risks, and next-week priorities.
> When finished, produce:
>
> A prioritized list of next-week outcomes
>
> A short 'risk watchlist'
>
> A Monday startup plan
> Tone: calm, direct."

This creates a structured conversation that prevents you from skipping important maintenance steps.

Why does weekly review reduce anxiety? Because anxiety is often "unmade decisions." The weekly review forces decisions into the open when you have time to think rather than when you're ambushed mid-week.

Figure 7.4 – Weekly review checklist

Printable card • 10–15 minutes • Reset your week

☐ ● **Clear inboxes**
Email, chat, notes, downloads

☐ ● **Review projects**
Scan active work and stalled threads

☐ ● **Confirm deadlines**
Update dates and dependencies

☐ ● **Choose next-week outcomes**
Pick 1–3 outcomes that matter

☐ ● **Risk watchlist**
Flag blockers, unknowns, and surprises

☐ ● **Monday plan**
First steps + calendar-first blocks

If anything feels fuzzy: capture it → clarify the next action → schedule it. (You verify and approve.)

Section 7.9: The Meeting System - Before, During, After (With AI Support)

Meetings are a major productivity lever, not because meetings are evil, but because poorly structured meetings create rework.

A strong meeting system has three stages.

Before: Set purpose and outputs

A meeting should produce something:

- a decision
- a plan
- alignment
- an owner and next steps

```
Prompt: Agenda builder
"Create a 30-minute meeting agenda for [purpose].
Audience: [roles].
Desired outputs: [decision/plan/alignment].
Constraints: include timeboxes, a decision point, and clear next
```

```
steps.
Tone: practical."
```

During: Capture decisions and actions

You don't need perfect notes. You need decisions, owners, and deadlines.

```
Prompt: Notes-to-actions converter
"Turn these meeting notes into:

Decisions made

Action items (owner, deadline, next step)

Open questions

Risks/concerns raised
Rules: do not invent details; label unknowns as 'Missing.'
Notes: [paste sanitized notes]."
```

After: Send a recap that prevents rework

```
Prompt: Meeting recap email
"Draft a meeting recap email with:

Purpose (1 sentence)

Decisions

Action items with owners and deadlines

Next meeting or follow-up plan
Tone: neutral and clear.
Do not: blame or add new facts."
```

If you adopt only one change to meetings: always send a recap for meetings that involve decisions or cross-team commitments. It reduces downstream confusion dramatically.

Figure 7.5 – Meeting system: Before / During / After

A simple loop that turns conversation into decisions, actions, and durable records.

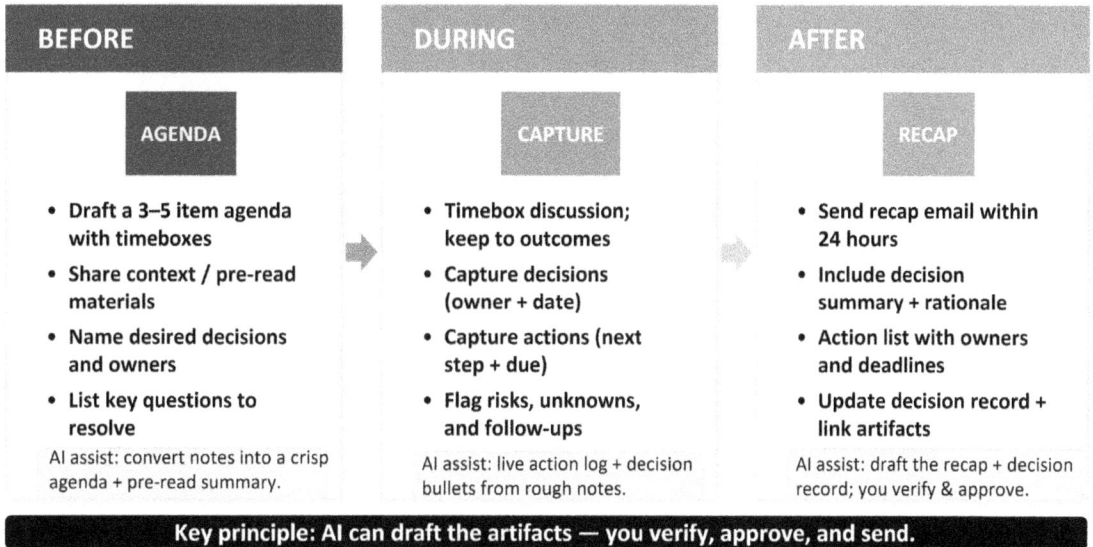

BEFORE	DURING	AFTER
AGENDA	**CAPTURE**	**RECAP**
• Draft a 3–5 item agenda with timeboxes • Share context / pre-read materials • Name desired decisions and owners • List key questions to resolve	• Timebox discussion; keep to outcomes • Capture decisions (owner + date) • Capture actions (next step + due) • Flag risks, unknowns, and follow-ups	• Send recap email within 24 hours • Include decision summary + rationale • Action list with owners and deadlines • Update decision record + link artifacts
AI assist: convert notes into a crisp agenda + pre-read summary.	AI assist: live action log + decision bullets from rough notes.	AI assist: draft the recap + decision record; you verify & approve.

Key principle: AI can draft the artifacts — you verify, approve, and send.

Section 7.10: The Writing Pipeline as a Productivity System (Not a One-Off)

Chapter 6 taught writing tactics. Now we integrate writing into your productivity system.

A writing pipeline reduces friction by standardizing:

- Inputs (brief)
- Drafting (first pass)
- Review loops (accuracy, tone, commitments)
- Reuse (templates)

The standard brief (copy-paste)

> "Brief:
>
> Deliverable type:
>
> Audience:
>
> Goal:
>
> Key facts (sanitized):

```
Tone:

Constraints (length, do-not list):

Ask/next step:

Risk level (1/2/3):"
```

When you maintain this brief format, you stop starting from scratch.

The review loop (copy-paste)

```
"Review loop:

List all commitments and deadlines in the draft

Flag ambiguous phrases

Identify missing information

Suggest safer wording for any risky claims

Provide a verification checklist before sending"
```

This turns writing into a controlled process.

Section 7.11: The "Context Packet" Practice - Stop Re-Explaining Your Work

A context packet is a short, sanitized reference you maintain for an ongoing project. It answers:

- What is this project and why does it matter?
- Who is involved?
- What are constraints?
- What decisions have been made?
- What's the current status?
- What's next?

You can store context packets in a notes app or document. The value is that you can paste the packet into ChatGPT to get consistent drafts without re-explaining.

```
Prompt: Context packet creator
"Create a context packet for this project based on the notes
below.
Rules: keep it under 250 words; replace names with roles; remove
sensitive details; include purpose, stakeholders, constraints,
```

```
current status, next steps, and open risks.
Notes: [paste sanitized notes]."
```

A context packet is a professional productivity tool because it reduces startup time. It also makes delegation easier because you can share a packet with a colleague.

Figure 7.6 – Context packet template

Project header card (fill in before prompting)

Purpose
What are we trying to accomplish? (1–2 sentences)
Example: Decide whether to launch X in Q2 and what "done" looks like.

Stakeholders (roles)
Who cares / who approves?
• Sponsor:
• Reviewer:
• Implementer:

Status
Where things stand right now.
Example: In discovery; options drafted; awaiting data.

Constraints
Hard boundaries.
Example: Budget ≤ $50k; must ship by May 30; legal review required.

Decisions
What decisions are needed?
Example: Choose vendor; pick rollout scope; confirm success metrics.

Next steps
Concrete actions + owners.
Example: Draft memo (A); pull numbers (B); review Friday (C).

Risks
What could go wrong / block progress?
Example: Data quality; stakeholder misalignment; timeline slip.

Section 7.12: Automation without Coding - "Templates + Routines" First

Many people hear "AI productivity" and imagine complex automations. Most business value comes earlier, from simpler things:

- Templates you reuse
- Routines you repeat
- Checklists that reduce errors
- Drafts that start faster
- Reviews that prevent rework

Before you automate anything, standardize it.

A simple rule: **If you can't do it consistently by hand, you can't automate it reliably.**

ChatGPT helps you standardize by creating templates and checklists tailored to your work. Once standardized, you can choose to automate later (Chapter 12 will cover automation without coding in more depth).

Section 7.13: Measuring The Value - Time Saved is Not the Only Metric

If you want to know whether your AI-powered system is working, don't measure "how often I use ChatGPT." Measure outcomes:

- Fewer follow-up questions after emails
- Faster time from vague task to clear plan
- Less time staring at blank pages
- More consistent meeting outputs (actions/owners)
- Reduced rework on deliverables
- Lower cognitive load (subjective but real)

A simple weekly measurement:

- One example of time saved
- One example of rework avoided
- One system improvement you will make

```
Prompt: Weekly system improvement
"Help me review my AI-supported productivity system this week.
Ask me for:

one win

one friction point

one recurring rework problem
Then propose 3 small system tweaks I can implement next week.
Tone: calm and practical."
```

Systems improve through small iterations, not dramatic overhauls.

Section 7.14: Common Failures in AI-Powered Productivity (And How to Fix Them)

Failure 1: You use ChatGPT randomly, not as part of a system

Fix: Choose one workflow (daily plan, meeting recap, email drafting) and standardize it.

Failure 2: You over-share context to get better results

Fix: Sanitize. Use roles and summaries. Build context packets without sensitive details.

Failure 3: You treat outputs as final

Fix: Use review loops and verification checklists, especially for Level 2 work.

Failure 4: Your task list becomes a warehouse

Fix: Weekly review + limit daily outcomes.

Failure 5: You create too many templates and don't use them

Fix: Maintain a small prompt library of your top 5 workflows. Expand only when stable.

A calm rule for sustainability: **Consistency beats sophistication.**

Practice Exercises

Instructions: Use sanitized information. Treat outputs as drafts. Build small, reusable templates. If you work in a regulated environment, follow your organization's AI policy.

Exercise 1 — Build your capture list (one place per category)

```
Prompt:
"Help me design a capture system.
My tools: [calendar app], [task list], [notes app].
List the best 'home' for: meeting commitments, deadlines, follow-
ups, ideas, reference material, and waiting-for items.
Then give me a 7-day habit plan to make capture automatic."
```

Exercise 2 — Convert mental clutter into next actions

> *Prompt:*
> *"Turn this brain-dump into clear next actions.*
> *Rules: verb-first tasks, group by quick tasks / medium tasks /*
> *projects, and ask clarifying questions for anything ambiguous.*
> *Brain-dump: [paste sanitized list]."*

Exercise 3 — Create definitions of done for your top 5 recurring tasks

> *Prompt:*
> *"Here are 5 recurring tasks I do: [list].*
> *For each, create a definition of done checklist (5 items max)*
> *that prevents rework and improves quality.*
> *Keep it plain English and role-appropriate."*

Exercise 4 — Draft tomorrow's daily plan using the Three Outcomes rule

> *Prompt:*
> *"Help me draft a daily plan for tomorrow.*
> *Schedule summary: [meetings/time blocks].*
> *Must-do: [list].*
> *Optional: [list].*
> *Energy: [notes].*
> *Output: top 3 outcomes, time-aware plan with buffer, fallback*
> *plan if interrupted, shutdown checklist."*

Exercise 5 — Create your shutdown checklist (personalized)

> *Prompt:*
> *"Design a 7-step end-of-day shutdown checklist for my work.*
> *It must: capture open loops, prepare tomorrow's first action, and*
> *reduce cognitive load.*
> *Keep it under 2 minutes to execute."*

Exercise 6 — Run a weekly review with ChatGPT as a coach

> *Prompt:*
> *"Be my weekly review coach. Ask questions one at a time.*
> *Cover inbox cleanup, project review, deadlines, risks, and next-*
> *week priorities.*
> *End with: next-week outcomes, risk watchlist, Monday plan."*

Exercise 7 — Turn a meeting into outputs (agenda + recap)

> *Prompt (agenda):*
> *"Create a 30-minute meeting agenda for [purpose] with timeboxes and a decision point."*
>
> *Prompt (recap):*
> *"Turn these notes into decisions, action items (owner/deadline), open questions, and a recap email. Do not invent facts. Notes: [paste]."*

Exercise 8 — Build a context packet for an active project

> *Prompt:*
> *"Create a context packet under 250 words for this project.*
> *Include purpose, stakeholders (roles), constraints, current status, decisions, next steps, risks.*
> *Replace names with roles and remove sensitive details.*
> *Notes: [paste]."*

Exercise 9 — Build your top 5 prompt-library entries (system-focused)

> *Prompt:*
> *"Create 5 reusable prompt templates for my productivity system:*
>
> *Daily plan*
>
> *Weekly review*
>
> *Meeting notes → actions*
>
> *Ask-first email*
>
> *Decision record*
> *My role/context: [brief].*
> *Constraints: privacy, calm tone, verification checklists.*
> *Make them copy-paste ready with placeholders."*

Exercise 10 — Debug-the-system: find your biggest leak

> *Prompt:*
> *"My system feels messy. Diagnose where the biggest leak is: open loops, unclear next actions, fragmentation, or writing rework.*
> *Ask me 10 diagnostic questions.*
> *Then propose 3 targeted changes I can implement this week and how to measure improvement."*

Exercise 11 — Create a "waiting for" tracker workflow (follow-ups)

> *Prompt:*
> *"Help me design a 'Waiting For' workflow for follow-ups.*
> *I need a simple method to track delegated items and pending responses.*
> *Output: a weekly routine, how to write follow-up messages, and a template I can reuse."*

Exercise 12 — Build your personal productivity scorecard (simple metrics)

> *Prompt:*
> *"Help me build a simple weekly scorecard for productivity that measures outcomes, not busyness.*
> *Include 6 metrics max (examples: rework avoided, fewer follow-ups, decisions captured, time saved, cognitive load rating).*
> *Make it easy to fill out in 5 minutes."*

Skill Check

After completing this chapter, you should be able to:

- Explain what a productivity system is and why it reduces cognitive load
- Implement a capture workflow so open loops stop living in your head
- Clarify inputs into verb-first next actions and definitions of done
- Build a realistic daily plan anchored to the calendar and three outcomes
- Run a weekly review that resets priorities, deadlines, and risks
- Use ChatGPT to convert notes into tasks, agendas, recaps, and decision records without inventing facts
- Create and use context packets to reduce re-explaining and improve consistency
- Build a small prompt library for your top workflows
- Diagnose your system's biggest leak and improve it through small weekly iterations

Chapter 8: ChatGPT for Business Operations & SOPs

Operations is where good intentions either become reliable results or become recurring problems.

If you've ever heard any of the following, you've seen an operations gap:

- "It depends who's working that day."
- "We do it differently on each team."
- "I know how to do it, but I couldn't explain it quickly."
- "We keep fixing the same issue."
- "Training takes forever."
- "We don't have time to document."

Those are not character flaws. They are system signals.

This chapter shows how to use ChatGPT to strengthen business operations by building clear processes, Standard Operating Procedures (SOPs), checklists, and role-ready training materials, without turning your workplace into paperwork.

You will learn how to:

- Identify which processes should be documented first
- Map a process in plain English
- Create an SOP that people actually follow
- Build checklists that prevent errors without slowing work
- Capture exceptions and decision points (the "real world" part)
- Create training materials and job aids from your SOPs
- Use ChatGPT to improve processes without inventing "fantasy workflows"
- Maintain SOPs over time with lightweight governance

The core principle stays the same: ChatGPT can draft structure, language, and templates quickly.

You provide real-world truth, constraints, and final approval.

Section 8.1: What Operations Means in Modern Work

"Operations" can sound like a department. In practice, operations is the part of work that must be repeatable.

Operations is:

- How requests move from intake to delivery
- How decisions are made and recorded
- How handoffs happen between people and teams
- How quality is checked
- How exceptions are handled
- How training and onboarding happen
- How work is measured and improved

If knowledge work is clarity, operations is consistency. And consistency is what reduces rework.

When processes are unclear:

- New hires learn through rumor
- Experienced staff become single points of failure
- Quality varies
- Customers receive inconsistent experiences
- Leaders get surprises instead of predictable outcomes

A practical goal for operations is not perfection. It is reliability.

SOPs are one of the simplest ways to build reliability if they are written in a usable way.

Section 8.2: Why SOPs Fail (And How to Write Ones That Work)

Most SOPs fail for predictable reasons:

1. They are too long and too vague at the same time
   They include lots of words but few executable steps.

2. They describe the "ideal" process, not the real one
   People don't follow them because they don't match reality.

3. They ignore exceptions
   Real work has edge cases. If the SOP doesn't cover them, the SOP becomes irrelevant.

4. They are written for compliance, not for the worker
   The tone is legalistic. The steps are unclear. The document is not a tool.

5. They are not maintained
   They drift out of date and people stop trusting them.

To write SOPs that work, use this definition: A good SOP is a job aid that helps a competent person perform a task consistently, safely, and efficiently, especially under time pressure.

That definition implies five qualities:

1. Clear steps (not just descriptions)
2. Role clarity (who does what)
3. Inputs and outputs (what starts the process; what "done" looks like)
4. Exceptions (what changes when conditions change)
5. Quality checks (how you prevent mistakes)

ChatGPT can help you draft SOPs that include these qualities as long as you provide truth and constraints.

Section 8.3: The First Rule of AI in Operations - Don't Ask it to Invent Your Process

A common mistake is asking ChatGPT: "Write an SOP for onboarding."

If you do that without providing your real workflow, you will likely receive a generic process that sounds fine but doesn't match your organization. That creates distrust.

A better approach is:

- You provide the current process (even if messy)
- You provide pain points and constraints
- ChatGPT turns it into a clean, structured draft
- You verify and adjust
- Then you test it in real work

This is the "source-first" habit from Chapter 2 applied to operations.

This prevents fantasy workflows.

Section 8.4: Which Processes to Document First - The High-Leverage List

You cannot document everything at once. Start where documentation reduces the most pain.

High-leverage processes usually have one or more of these traits:

- **High frequency:** done often
- **High risk:** errors are costly
- **High variability:** different people do it differently
- **High training burden:** new hires struggle
- **Cross-team handoffs:** coordination causes delays
- **Customer impact:** affects experience and trust
- **Recurring rework:** the same problems keep returning

A practical prioritization method: Choose one process that is frequent and annoying, and one process that is risky and important.

That pairing builds momentum (quick win + meaningful impact).

> **Prompt: SOP prioritization helper**
> "Help me choose which processes to document first.
> List of processes: [paste list].
> For each, score 1–5 on: frequency, risk, variability, training burden, customer impact, and rework.
> Then recommend the top 3 processes to document first and explain why.
> Keep it practical."

Section 8.5: Process Mapping in Plain English - See the Work Before You Write It

An SOP should be based on a process map. Not a fancy diagram, just a clear sequence.

A plain-English process map includes:

- **Trigger:** what starts the process
- **Inputs:** what you need to begin
- **Steps:** what happens (with ownership)
- **Decision points:** where the path changes
- **Outputs:** what "done" produces
- **Handoffs:** where responsibility changes
- **Quality checks:** where errors are caught

Figure 8.1 – Process map in plain English: Trigger → Steps → Decision points → Outputs

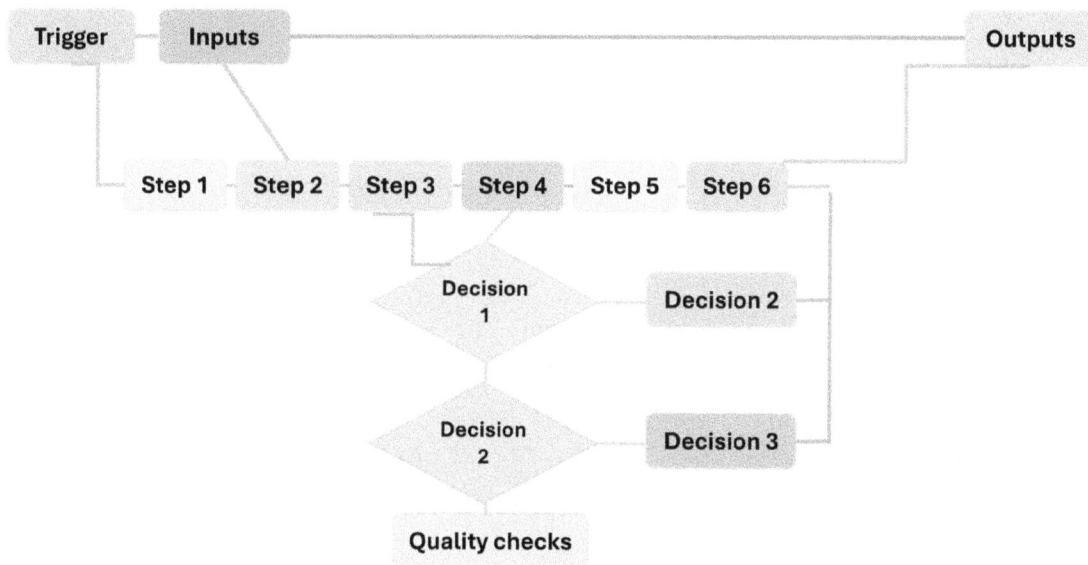

You can map a process in 10 minutes with simple bullets.

Example (generic structure):

Trigger: Customer request received
Inputs: Request details, customer account info (sanitized), required forms
Steps:

1. Intake specialist logs request
2. Specialist checks completeness
3. If incomplete → request missing info
4. If complete → assign to owner
5. Owner executes work
6. Quality check
7. Communicate outcome to customer
   Output: Request resolved and recorded
   Quality checks: completeness check; final review; customer confirmation

ChatGPT can help you convert messy descriptions into a clean map.

> **Prompt: Process map builder**
> "Turn the process description below into a plain-English process map.
> Include: trigger, inputs, steps with owners, decision points, outputs, handoffs, quality checks, and common exceptions.
> Rules: Do not invent tools or policies. If information is missing, label it 'Missing' and ask questions.
> Process description: [paste sanitized description]."

Once the process map exists, SOP writing becomes easier.

Section 8.6: The SOP Template That Works in Real Life

Many SOP templates are either too thin or too heavy. Here is a balanced template designed for working professionals.

SOP Template (Practical)

1. Title and ID
2. Purpose (why this exists)
3. Scope (where it applies; where it doesn't)
4. Roles and responsibilities
5. Definitions (terms that matter)
6. Inputs (what you need to start)

7. Tools/systems used (only what's actually used)
8. Procedure (numbered steps)
9. Decision points and exceptions
10. Quality checks (how to prevent errors)
11. Outputs and records (what is created/saved)
12. Metrics (optional: how you know it's working)
13. Revision history (date, change summary, owner)

Figure 8.2 – SOP template (one-page layout)

Purpose

Scope

Roles

Procedure
1.
2.
3.
4.
5.

Inputs

Exceptions

Quality checks
1.
2.

Revision history

Date   Author   Change

Outputs

This template works because it matches real operational needs:

- It clarifies responsibility
- It makes steps executable
- It captures exceptions
- It defines quality and "done"
- It supports training and audits without becoming legal language

Prompt: SOP draft generator (source-first)
"Draft an SOP using the template below.
Rules: Use only the process details I provide. Do not invent

> tools, approvals, or policy requirements. If something is missing, label it 'Missing' and ask me questions.
> Template: Title/ID, Purpose, Scope, Roles, Definitions, Inputs, Tools, Procedure, Decision points/exceptions, Quality checks, Outputs/records, Metrics, Revision history.
> Process map/notes: [paste sanitized process map or notes].
> Audience: new team member.
> Tone: plain English, calm, practical."

Section 8.7: Making SOP Steps Executable - The "Step Standard"

People ignore SOPs when steps are vague.

An executable step includes:

- Action (verb-first)
- Owner (role)
- Input (what they need)
- Output (what it produces)
- Quality check (how to avoid mistakes)
- Time expectation (optional, rough)

> **Vague step:**
> "Ensure the request is complete."
>
> **Executable step:**
> "Intake Specialist: Confirm the request includes (A) customer name or ID, (B) request type, (C) required document attached. If any item is missing, send the 'Missing Info' email template within 2 business hours."

Figure 8.3 – Step standard: Vague vs. executable SOP step

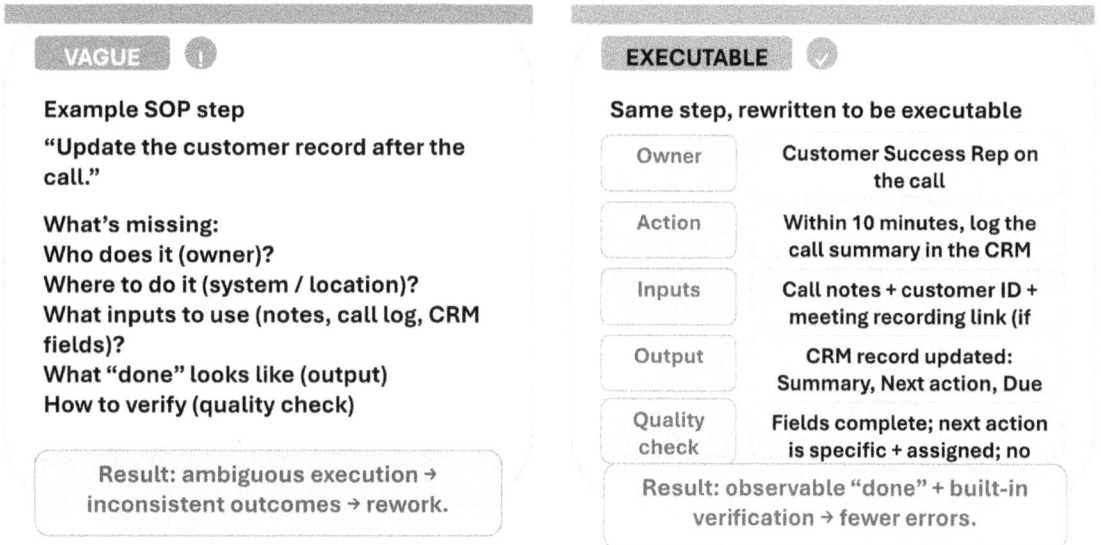

VAGUE ⓘ	EXECUTABLE ✓
Example SOP step	**Same step, rewritten to be executable**
"Update the customer record after the call."	**Owner**: Customer Success Rep on the call
	Action: Within 10 minutes, log the call summary in the CRM
What's missing:	**Inputs**: Call notes + customer ID + meeting recording link (if
Who does it (owner)?	
Where to do it (system / location)?	**Output**: CRM record updated: Summary, Next action, Due
What inputs to use (notes, call log, CRM fields)?	
What "done" looks like (output)	**Quality check**: Fields complete; next action is specific + assigned; no
How to verify (quality check)	
Result: ambiguous execution → inconsistent outcomes → rework.	Result: observable "done" + built-in verification → fewer errors.

ChatGPT can help you rewrite vague steps into executable steps, especially if you provide quality criteria.

> *Prompt: Step sharpening*
> "Rewrite the SOP steps below to be executable.
> For each step, include: owner (role), verb-first action, required inputs, expected output, and a quality check.
> Do not add new tools or approvals. If you need information, ask questions.
> Steps: [paste steps]."

Section 8.8: Exceptions and Decision Points - The Part of SOPs That Makes Them Trustworthy

Most real processes are not straight lines. They are branching paths.

Decision points are where the process changes based on conditions:

- If request is incomplete → gather missing info
- If customer is priority tier → expedite
- If risk level is high → escalate for review
- If deadline is missed → notify stakeholder and update plan

Exceptions are situations that require a different path. If you ignore exceptions, people will treat the SOP as "not for real work."

A practical way to capture exceptions is to include:

- Common exceptions (the ones that happen often)
- High-impact exceptions (rare but risky)
- Escalation triggers (when to involve leadership or another function)

> **Prompt: Exception capture**
> "Review this SOP draft and identify:
>
> Likely decision points
>
> Common exceptions
>
> High-impact exceptions
>
> Escalation triggers
> Then propose short exception-handling steps in plain English.
> Rules: Do not invent policy requirements; ask questions where
> necessary.
> SOP draft: [paste]."

Section 8.9: Checklists - The Most Underrated Operations Tool

Checklists are not bureaucracy. They are memory aids for high-value consistency.

A good checklist is:

- Short enough to use
- Specific enough to prevent errors
- Written in the language of the worker
- Positioned at the point of use (not buried in a doc)

There are three common checklist types:

1. Intake checklist (prevent incomplete starts)
2. Quality checklist (prevent defects before delivery)
3. Handoff checklist (prevent dropped work)

Figure 8.4 – Checklist types: Intake vs. quality vs. handoff

INTAKE	QUALITY	HANDOFF
☐ Goal stated in one sentence	☐ Facts verified / sources noted	☐ Summary at top (3–5 lines)
☐ Stakeholders listed (roles)	☐ Numbers & dates double-checked	☐ Decision / recommendation stated
☐ Success criteria defined	☐ Assumptions labeled clearly	☐ Artifacts linked (docs, files)
☐ Deadline & time zone confirmed	☐ Tone matches audience	☐ Tasks captured with owners
☐ Inputs/links collected	☐ Structure matches requested format	☐ Due dates added to tracker
☐ Constraints noted (length, tone)	☐ Jargon minimized / defined	☐ Open questions listed
☐ Risks/unknowns flagged	☐ Edge cases considered	☐ Risks + mitigations noted
☐ Next action identified	☐ Spelling/grammar pass complete	☐ Next meeting / checkpoint scheduled
☐ Owner assigned	☐ Call-to-action is explicit	☐ Status updated for stakeholders
Printable card • adapt to your team	*Printable card • adapt to your team*	*Printable card • adapt to your team*

Use Intake to prevent missing info • Quality to reduce errors • Handoff to make work transferable

ChatGPT can convert SOP steps into checklists.

```
Prompt: Checklist extraction
"From this SOP, create three checklists:
A) Intake checklist
B) Quality checklist
C) Handoff checklist
Constraints: each checklist must be 8-12 items max, plain
English, verb-first, and usable under time pressure.
SOP: [paste]."
```

Checklists are also excellent for reducing anxiety because they reduce "Did I forget something?" That is cognitive load relief in operational form.

Section 8.10: SOPs as Training - Turn One Document into Multiple Job Aids

A single SOP can generate several practical training assets:

- A one-page quick reference ("cheat sheet")
- A step-by-step onboarding guide
- A role-specific version (what *you* do vs what the system does)
- A scenario-based training quiz
- A "common mistakes and fixes" guide

ChatGPT is very good at transforming a single source into different formats; again, as long as you supply the source and prevent invention.

> **Prompt: SOP-to-training pack**
> "Create a training pack from this SOP.
> Rules: Do not add new steps or policies. Use the SOP as truth.
> Output:
>
> One-page quick reference (bullet format)
>
> A new-hire walkthrough (step-by-step with tips)
>
> 10-question knowledge check quiz (with answers)
>
> Common mistakes + how to avoid them
> SOP: [paste]."

This is a powerful operational multiplier: one SOP becomes a training system.

Figure 8.5 – SOP-to-training pack: One SOP → four training assets

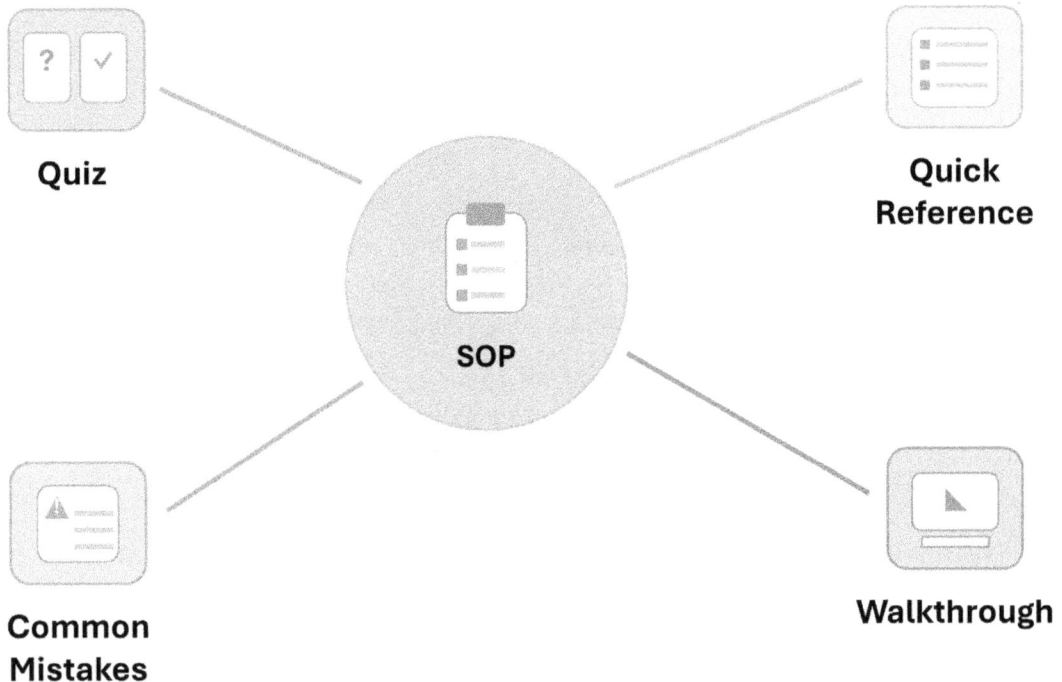

Quiz

Quick Reference

SOP

Common Mistakes

Walkthrough

Section 8.11: Quality And Metrics - Measure What Matters without Over measuring

Operations improves when feedback exists. But measurement can become its own burden if you measure everything.

A practical approach is to choose 2–4 metrics per process:

- Cycle time (how long it takes)
- First-pass quality (how often it works without rework)
- On-time completion (reliability)
- Customer clarity (reduced questions/complaints)
- Handoff defects (dropped steps, missing info)

ChatGPT can help you choose metrics and define how to measure them.

```
Prompt: Metrics selection
"For this process, recommend 3-4 metrics that reflect speed,
quality, and reliability without adding heavy overhead.
Process: [describe].
Constraints: measurement must be simple and use existing tools.
Output: metric name, definition, how to measure, frequency, and
what 'good' looks like."
```

The phrase "what good looks like" matters. Without it, metrics are numbers without meaning.

Section 8.12: Process Improvement with ChatGPT - Fix the System, Not the Person

When a process fails, organizations often blame people: "They didn't follow the steps."

Sometimes that's true. But often the process is unclear, too slow, too complex, or misaligned with incentives.

A calm operations mindset is: Assume people are trying. Improve the system.

ChatGPT can support process improvement by helping you:

- Identify bottlenecks
- Surface root causes

- Generate improvement options
- Design pilots
- Create before/after SOP revisions
- Build communication for change adoption

However, process improvement can also go wrong if the assistant invents causes. Keep it grounded.

> **Prompt: Root cause analysis (grounded)**
> "Help me analyze this recurring problem using a root-cause approach.
> Problem: [describe].
> Evidence we have (facts only): [list].
> Constraints: [tools, staffing, policy].
> Output:
>
> 5 possible root causes (label as hypotheses)
>
> What evidence would confirm or deny each
>
> 3 low-cost interventions to test
>
> How to measure improvement
> Rules: Do not claim certainty. Label assumptions and hypotheses."

This prompt enforces professional humility: hypotheses, not declarations.

Section 8.13: Change Adoption - How to Get People to Use the SOP

A perfect SOP that no one uses is wasted effort.

Adoption usually fails for one of these reasons:

- The SOP is hard to find
- The SOP is too long to use
- The SOP doesn't match real work
- The SOP adds friction without clear benefit
- People weren't involved in shaping it
- There is no reinforcement or ownership

A practical adoption plan includes:

- Put the SOP where people work (linked in tools, pinned, in onboarding)
- Provide a one-page quick reference

- Train using scenarios, not lectures
- Run a pilot and incorporate feedback
- Assign an owner for updates
- Review the SOP after 30–60 days

ChatGPT can help you draft an adoption plan and communication.

> **Prompt: SOP rollout plan**
> "Create a simple SOP rollout plan for a team of [size].
> Constraints: minimal meetings, practical training, no hype.
> Output:
>
> Rollout steps over 2-4 weeks
>
> A short announcement message
>
> A 15-minute training outline using scenarios
>
> A feedback method (lightweight)
>
> Ownership and revision plan
> SOP topic: [topic]."

Section 8.14: Governance - Keep SOPs Current without a Bureaucracy

SOP governance does not need a committee. It needs clarity.

A lightweight governance model:

- Every SOP has an owner (role)
- Every SOP has a review cadence (quarterly or semiannual)
- Changes are logged (revision history)
- Feedback is captured (simple form or channel)
- Major changes are communicated briefly

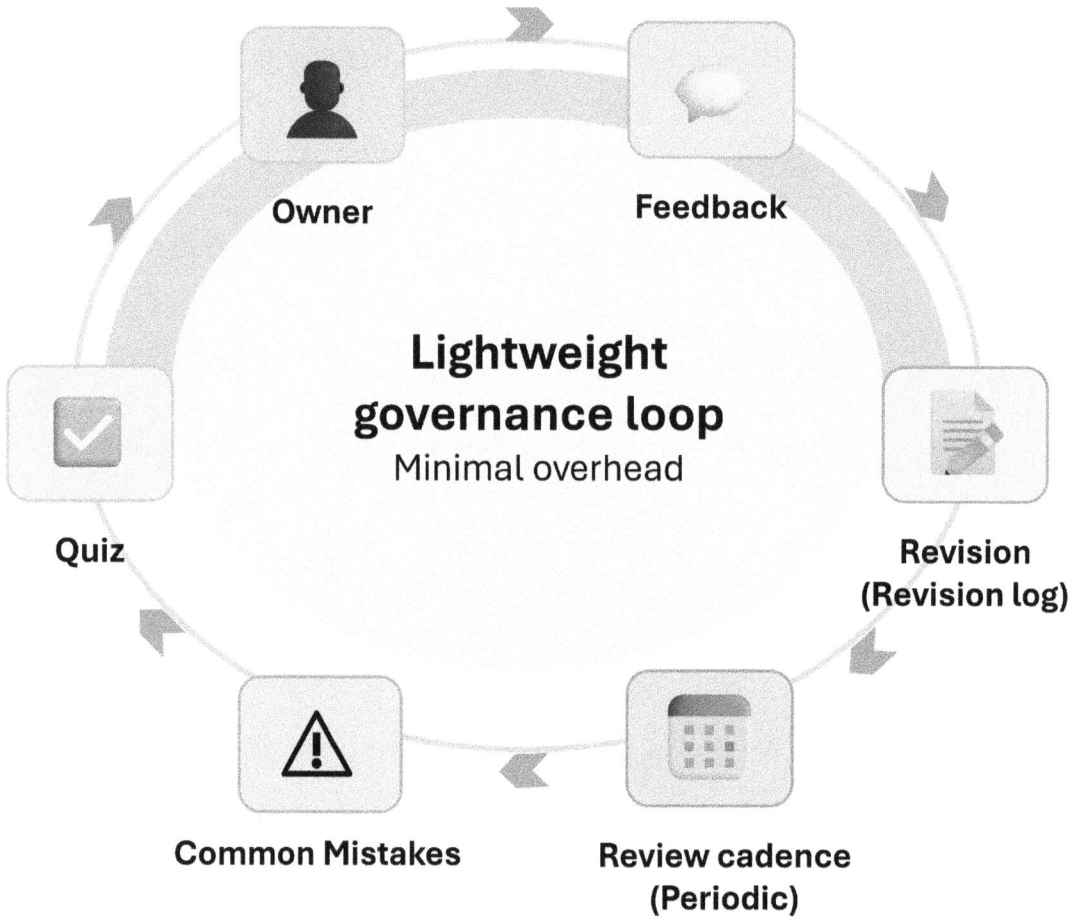

Lightweight
governance loop
Minimal overhead

Owner

Feedback

Revision
(Revision log)

Review cadence
(Periodic)

Common Mistakes

Quiz

ChatGPT can help you set a governance standard across SOPs.

> **Prompt: SOP governance standard**
> *"Help me create a lightweight SOP governance standard for our team.*
> *We need: ownership, review cadence, change control rules, revision history format, and how to collect feedback.*
> *Constraints: minimal overhead, plain English, suitable for a small team.*
> *Output: a one-page policy we can adopt."*

When SOPs are maintained, people trust them. Trust reduces cognitive load.

Section 8.15: A Full Worked Example - From Messy Work to a Usable SOP

Let's walk through an end-to-end example in a generic form you can copy.

Scenario (sanitized):

A team receives internal requests by email and chat. Requests are often missing information, leading to back-and-forth. Work gets delayed, and stakeholders complain about "no visibility."

Step 1: Capture the current process (even messy)

You list what actually happens:

- Requests arrive via email and chat
- Someone picks it up based on availability
- If info is missing, the team asks for it
- Work is done, sometimes without logging
- Stakeholders ask for status; the team responds ad hoc

Step 2: Build a process map

You use the process map builder prompt. You discover missing pieces:

- What counts as "complete request"?
- Who owns intake?
- Where is work tracked?
- What are service expectations?

Step 3: Draft the SOP using the template

You draft:

- Purpose: improve clarity and cycle time
- Scope: internal requests only
- Roles: requestor, intake owner, executor, reviewer
- Procedure: intake checklist, assignment, execution, update, closeout
- Exceptions: urgent requests, incomplete requests, escalations
- Quality checks: completeness check, closeout note

Step 4: Extract checklists

You create:

- Intake checklist
- Handoff checklist
- Closeout checklist

Step 5: Create training pack

You generate:

- One-page quick reference
- New hire walkthrough
- Quiz
- Common mistakes

Step 6: Pilot and revise

You run it for a week, collect feedback, and adjust:

- Clarify request completeness
- Set a response standard ("acknowledge within X hours")
- Add a status update rule

None of this requires fancy tools. It requires clarity, structure, and iteration. ChatGPT accelerates the drafting and formatting so you can spend your time on truth and adoption.

Practice Exercises

Instructions: Use sanitized descriptions. Treat outputs as drafts. Do not paste sensitive customer data, confidential internal numbers, or regulated information.

Exercise 1 — Choose your first SOP using a leverage score

```
Prompt:
"Help me choose my first SOP to document.
Here are 8-12 processes we run: [list].
Score each 1-5 on frequency, risk, variability, training burden,
customer impact, and rework.
Recommend the top 3 to document first and why."
```

Exercise 2 — Build a plain-English process map

```
Prompt:
"Turn this process description into a plain-English process map
with: trigger, inputs, steps with owners, decision points,
outputs, handoffs, quality checks, and exceptions.
Rules: do not invent tools or approvals; label unknowns as
'Missing' and ask questions.
Process: [paste sanitized description]."
```

Exercise 3 — Draft an SOP using the practical template

Prompt:
"Draft an SOP using this template: Title/ID, Purpose, Scope, Roles, Definitions, Inputs, Tools, Procedure, Decision points/exceptions, Quality checks, Outputs/records, Metrics, Revision history.
Rules: use only what I provide; do not invent policies/tools; ask questions if needed.
Process map/notes: [paste].
Audience: new hire.
Tone: plain English."

Exercise 4 — Sharpen steps into executable form

Prompt:
"Rewrite these SOP steps to be executable. For each: owner, verb-first action, required inputs, expected output, and a quality check.
Do not add tools or approvals. Ask questions where needed.
Steps: [paste]."

Exercise 5 — Extract three checklists (intake, quality, handoff)

Prompt:
"From this SOP, create three checklists: intake, quality, and handoff.
Each must be 8–12 items max, plain English, verb-first, usable under time pressure.
SOP: [paste]."

Exercise 6 — Capture exceptions and escalation triggers

Prompt:
"Review this SOP and identify decision points, common exceptions, high-impact exceptions, and escalation triggers.
Then add short exception-handling steps.
Rules: do not invent policies; ask questions where needed.
SOP: [paste]."

Exercise 7 — Convert an SOP into a training pack

Prompt:
"Create a training pack from this SOP.
Output: one-page quick reference, new-hire walkthrough, 10-

question quiz (with answers), common mistakes and prevention
tips.
Rules: do not add steps not in the SOP.
SOP: [paste]."

Exercise 8 — Root cause analysis without false certainty

Prompt:
"Help me analyze this recurring operational problem using
hypotheses, not certainty.
Problem: [describe].
Evidence (facts only): [list].
Constraints: [tools/staffing/policy].
Output: 5 root-cause hypotheses, evidence needed for each, 3 low-
cost tests, and how to measure improvement.
Label assumptions clearly."

Exercise 9 — Create a 2-week pilot plan for a process change

Prompt:
"Design a 2-week pilot plan for this process improvement:
[describe].
Constraints: no new tools, minimal meetings, protect service
levels.
Output: pilot scope, steps, owners, success metrics, risks, and a
feedback method.
End with a decision point: keep/adjust/stop."

Exercise 10 — Write a rollout message and a 15-minute training outline

Prompt:
"Write:

A short rollout announcement message for this SOP (calm,
practical)

A 15-minute training outline using 3 scenarios

A lightweight feedback request
SOP topic: [topic].
Audience: [team]."

Exercise 11 — Build a lightweight SOP governance standard

Prompt:
"Create a one-page SOP governance standard for a small team.
Must include: SOP owner role, review cadence, change control
rules, revision history format, and how feedback is collected.
Constraints: minimal overhead, plain English."

Exercise 12 — Create an SOP "audit checklist" for self-checking

Prompt:
"Create an SOP audit checklist to evaluate whether an SOP is
usable and trustworthy.
Include: clarity of steps, roles, inputs/outputs, exceptions,
quality checks, findability, and maintenance.
Keep it to 15 items max and written in plain English."

Skill Check

After completing this chapter, you should be able to:

- Identify which processes to document first based on leverage (frequency, risk, variability, training burden, customer impact, rework)
- Create a plain-English process map with triggers, steps, decision points, handoffs, outputs, and quality checks
- Draft an SOP using a practical template that matches real work and avoids invented steps
- Rewrite SOP steps into executable actions with owners, inputs, outputs, and quality checks
- Capture exceptions and escalation triggers so the SOP is trustworthy under real conditions
- Extract short, usable checklists (intake, quality, handoff) that reduce errors and cognitive load
- Convert an SOP into training assets (quick reference, walkthrough, quiz, common mistakes guide)
- Use ChatGPT to support grounded process improvement through hypothesis-driven analysis and small pilots
- Establish lightweight SOP governance so documents stay current and trusted

Chapter 9: Ethical Use, Accuracy, and Trust in AI Outputs

Ethics is not a separate topic from productivity. In modern work, ethics is how you protect trust while moving fast.

When professionals hesitate to use ChatGPT, they're often reacting to a reasonable fear:

"What if I rely on this and it's wrong?"
"What if I share something I shouldn't?"
"What if I accidentally mislead someone?"
"What if this crosses a line legally, professionally, or personally?"

This chapter answers those concerns calmly and practically.

You will learn how to:

- Use ChatGPT ethically without becoming rigid or paranoid
- Match verification effort to the stakes of the work
- Recognize common failure modes (especially confident errors)
- Build guardrails that prevent costly mistakes
- Create a "trust workflow" you can use every day
- Communicate responsibly when AI has assisted your work

The goal is not to make you afraid of AI. The goal is to make you confident in your judgment.

Ethical, accurate use is a system. Once you build that system, anxiety drops because you are no longer relying on luck.

Section 9.1: A Working Definition Of "Trust" at Work

In professional life, trust is not a feeling. Trust is a pattern:

- People believe your outputs are accurate enough
- Your commitments are reliable
- Your communication is honest and clear
- You correct mistakes responsibly
- You protect confidential information
- You make decisions with appropriate care

When you use ChatGPT, you are not borrowing "trust" from the tool. You are extending your trust pattern into a new workflow.

So the right question is not: "Can I trust ChatGPT?"

The right question is: "What trust standards apply to this task, and how do I meet them while using a drafting assistant?"

This reframing reduces anxiety. It puts you back in control.

Section 9.2: The Ethical Center - Human Judgment Remains Responsible

A common mistake in AI conversations is treating ethics as a debate about whether machines are "good" or "bad." That's not helpful for business users.

Ethical use in modern work is simpler:

- You choose what information to provide
- You choose what claims to make
- You choose what to verify
- You choose what to send
- You accept accountability

ChatGPT can accelerate drafting. It cannot assume responsibility. It cannot be accountable. It cannot know your organization's standards unless you provide them.

So your ethical stance is not "never use AI." Your ethical stance is:

Use AI as an assistant, never as an authority.

That single line will protect you in almost any professional scenario.

Section 9.3: The Three Risk Levels Revisited - Ethics as "Match the Care to the Stakes"

Ethics becomes practical when you connect it to risk.

Recall the risk levels from earlier chapters:

Level 1: Low-risk work

Examples:

- Rewriting an email for clarity (internal, low stakes)
- Turning your notes into an outline
- Brainstorming options
- Drafting a checklist for your own use

Ethical posture:

- Basic privacy hygiene
- Quick self-review before use

Level 2: Medium-risk work

Examples:

- Customer communication
- Proposals and statements that shape commitments
- SOPs that others will follow
- Internal documents that become reusable references
- Marketing claims that could be interpreted as factual

Ethical posture:

- Stronger verification
- Commitment check
- Tone and stakeholder sensitivity review
- "Do not invent facts" prompting
- Version control (save what you sent)

Level 3: High-risk work

Examples:

- Legal, HR, compliance, regulated content
- Financial advice or statements with material consequences
- Safety-related instructions
- Medical or health-related guidance
- Security procedures

Ethical posture:

- Use AI mainly for structure and plain-English rewriting
- Require authoritative sources and/or expert review
- Avoid definitive claims unless verified
- Follow your organization's policy and consult qualified professionals

This is not fear. It is professionalism.

The same tool can be used at all three levels. What changes is how you verify and what you allow the draft to claim.

Section 9.4: The Accuracy Trap - Why Confident Text Feels True

ChatGPT's most dangerous failure mode is not nonsense. It is plausible, polished wrongness.

The danger comes from a human bias: we tend to trust confident, structured communication. In business, structure often signals competence.

ChatGPT can produce:

- Clean headings
- Crisp bullet points
- Professional tone
- Well-formed explanations
- "Just-so" confidence

That presentation can cause you to accept claims too quickly, especially when you are tired, rushed, or overloaded.

So the ethical move is not "distrust everything." The ethical move is treat AI output as a draft that must earn trust through checks.

This chapter gives you those checks.

Section 9.5: The "3C" Method - Claims, Confidence, Checks

Here is a simple reliability method you can apply to any AI output in under two minutes.

Step 1: Identify Claims

A claim is any statement that asserts something about the world:

- "The policy requires..."
- "Customers prefer..."
- "This will reduce cycle time by..."
- "The deadline is..."
- "The law says..."
- "The standard practice is..."

Some outputs are mostly framing and wording (low claim density). Others are packed with claims (high claim density).

Step 2: Assign Confidence (yours, not the AI's)

Ask yourself:

- Do I already know this is true?
- Did I provide the source material?
- Is this a guess dressed up as an answer?

Label claims in your head as:

- Known true (I have evidence)
- Plausible but unverified
- Unknown or risky

Step 3: Perform Checks proportional to risk

Checks can be simple:

- Compare to your notes
- Confirm dates and numbers
- Ask a colleague
- Look up the authoritative policy
- Validate with a source document

The key is that you are making verification a routine, not an emotional event.

Figure 9.1 – The 3C method: Claims → Confidence → Checks

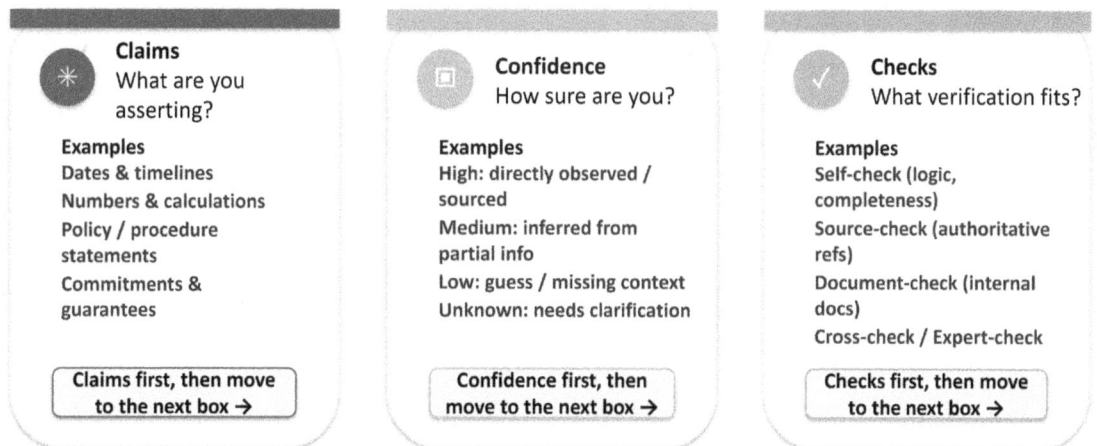

Claims — What are you asserting?	Confidence — How sure are you?	Checks — What verification fits?
Examples	**Examples**	**Examples**
Dates & timelines	High: directly observed / sourced	Self-check (logic, completeness)
Numbers & calculations	Medium: inferred from partial info	Source-check (authoritative refs)
Policy / procedure statements	Low: guess / missing context	Document-check (internal docs)
Commitments & guarantees	Unknown: needs clarification	Cross-check / Expert-check
Claims first, then move to the next box →	Confidence first, then move to the next box →	Checks first, then move to the next box →

Shortcut: Identify the claim type → state confidence → choose the lightest check that makes it safe.

> *Prompt: Build "3C" into your workflow*
> *"After your draft, list:*
>
> *The top 10 factual claims you made*
>
> *Which ones require verification*
>
> *A quick checklist to verify them*
> *Rules: do not add new facts; highlight any areas you are*
> *uncertain about."*

This prompt is powerful because it makes the assistant expose the claim structure rather than hiding behind polish.

Section 9.6: The Verification Ladder - A Simple Standard for "How Sure Do I Need to Be?"

Different tasks require different certainty.

Use this verification ladder:

1. **Self-check:** read it, confirm it aligns with what you know
2. **Source-check:** compare against your own notes or provided materials
3. **Document-check:** confirm against an authoritative internal document (policy, contract, SPEC)
4. **Cross-check:** confirm against a second independent source (another document, another person)
5. **Expert-check:** consult qualified professionals (legal, compliance, finance, security) when required

Figure 9.2 – Risk level and verification ladder

Risk level	Self-check	Source-check	Document-check	Cross-check	Expert-check
Level 1 **Low risk** Basic accuracy check (spelling, logic, completeness)	✓				
Level 2 **Medium risk** Confirm key facts & align with docs	✓	✓	✓		
Level 3 **High risk** Use authoritative sources + peer/pro review	✓	✓	✓	✓	✓

As risk rises, verification effort climbs the ladder (add checks—don't just "try harder").

Most Level 1 tasks stop at steps 1–2.

Most Level 2 tasks should include steps 1–3, often 4 for key claims.

Most Level 3 tasks should include steps 3–5 and careful scoping of what AI is allowed to draft.

This ladder reduces anxiety because it replaces guesswork with a consistent standard.

Section 9.7: Privacy And Confidentiality - What Not to Put in the Prompt

Confidentiality is not abstract. It is a habit: what you paste and what you avoid.

A calm baseline rule: **If you would not feel comfortable reading it out loud in a meeting with your leadership team, do not paste it into a general AI chat.**

Common categories to avoid sharing in prompts (unless your organization explicitly approves and you are using an approved environment):

- Customer personal data and account details
- Employee performance details and sensitive HR matters

- Legal strategies, privileged communications, or litigation context
- Non-public financial results, pricing, or deal terms
- Security procedures, credentials, access details
- Proprietary product roadmaps, source code, confidential IP
- Medical or highly sensitive personal information

This chapter cannot define your exact policy; organizations differ. The professional approach is: Use sanitization and abstraction.

Practical sanitization techniques (easy and effective)

1. Replace names with roles
   "Customer A," "Manager," "Vendor," "Team Lead"

2. Remove identifying numbers
   No account numbers, full addresses, IDs

3. Summarize sensitive sections
   Instead of pasting a full HR incident report, summarize the issue in neutral terms: "a performance concern" or "a policy question," then ask for phrasing guidance.

4. Focus on structure and tone
   Often you need language, not the details.

Figure 9.3 – Confidentiality Sanitization Examples

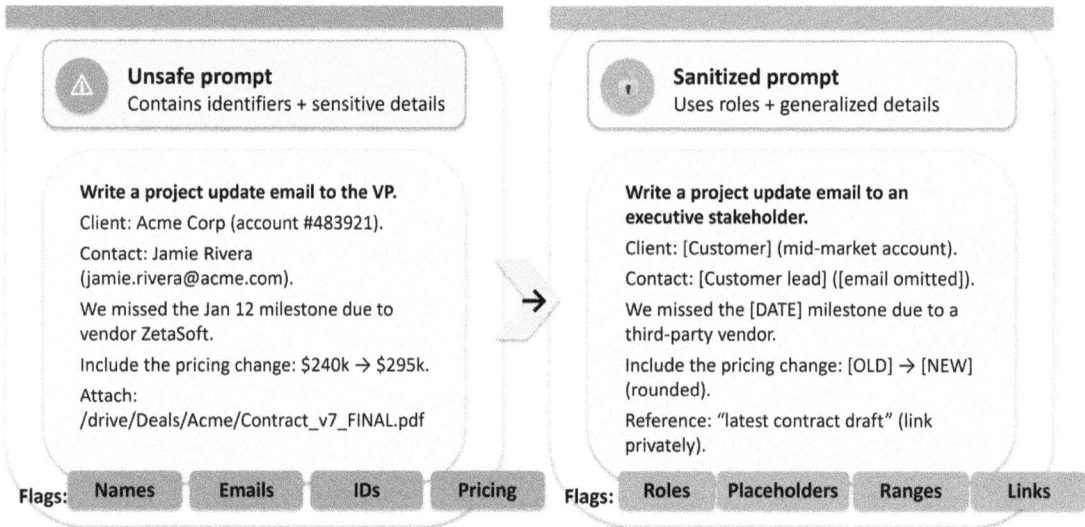

⚠ **Unsafe prompt** Contains identifiers + sensitive details		**Sanitized prompt** Uses roles + generalized details
Write a project update email to the VP. Client: Acme Corp (account #483921). Contact: Jamie Rivera (jamie.rivera@acme.com). We missed the Jan 12 milestone due to vendor ZetaSoft. Include the pricing change: $240k → $295k. Attach: /drive/Deals/Acme/Contract_v7_FINAL.pdf	→	Write a project update email to an executive stakeholder. Client: [Customer] (mid-market account). Contact: [Customer lead] ([email omitted]). We missed the [DATE] milestone due to a third-party vendor. Include the pricing change: [OLD] → [NEW] (rounded). Reference: "latest contract draft" (link privately).
Flags: Names Emails IDs Pricing		Flags: Roles Placeholders Ranges Links

> *Prompt: Confidentiality-first drafting*
> "Draft this without including any identifying details.
> Use role labels instead of names.

> *Do not include private numbers, addresses, or internal*
> *confidential terms.*
> *If you need details, ask questions in a way that preserves*
> *confidentiality."*

This keeps you safe while still giving you useful drafts.

Section 9.8: Intellectual Property and Plagiarism - Ethical Writing with AI

Many professionals worry about AI and plagiarism. The calm truth is: Ethical writing is about honest authorship and respectful use of sources.

In business work, you are often writing from common knowledge, internal experience, and original work. AI assistance is usually being used to draft phrasing, structure, and clarity.

But you must be careful when:

- You are rewriting someone else's copyrighted content
- You are producing academic material with citation requirements
- You are using AI to imitate a specific person's style in a misleading way
- You are generating marketing claims that sound like research

Practical ethics guidelines:

1. Don't ask for "rewrite this article verbatim."
   Instead, ask for a summary in your own words, using your own points, or ask for a new structure based on your original ideas.

2. If you use sources, keep track of them.
   In reports and proposals, cite where facts come from (internal documents, customer feedback summary, policy reference).

3. Avoid falsely implying research.
   If you haven't run a study, don't write like you did. Use cautious language: "Based on our observations," "Based on available feedback."

4. Don't use AI to impersonate a real person.
   In business, this can harm trust quickly.

A strong ethical move is to treat ChatGPT like an editor and drafting assistant, not like a source.

Section 9.9: Bias and Fairness - What Professionals Should Know without Getting Lost

Bias is not only a social issue. In business, bias is a quality issue.

Bias shows up when:

- A draft uses stereotypes or unfair assumptions
- A decision memo emphasizes one stakeholder unfairly
- A performance message uses loaded language
- A hiring or HR document contains subtle discrimination
- A customer response treats different customers inconsistently

ChatGPT is trained on large amounts of human text, and human text contains bias. So bias can appear in AI outputs.

The practical approach is not to panic. It is to review the output for:

- Loaded adjectives ("difficult," "emotional," "unprofessional")
- Inconsistent standards ("He was assertive" vs "She was aggressive")
- Unnecessary personal descriptors
- Assumptions about intent
- Overgeneralizations

> **Prompt: Bias and neutrality check**
> "Review this text for biased or loaded language and rewrite it to be neutral and professional.
> Rules: do not change factual meaning; remove assumptions about intent; avoid stereotypes; keep it respectful.
> Text: [paste]."

This is especially useful for HR-adjacent communication and conflict situations.

Section 9.10: Hallucinations and How to Prevent Them - "Abstain" is a Feature

The easiest way to reduce hallucinations is to allow the assistant to admit uncertainty.

Many users accidentally force hallucinations by writing prompts like: "Give me the exact policy requirements and cite sources," without providing the policy text and without enabling a reliable source workflow.

If the model can't verify, it may guess.

Your fix is simple:

- Provide the relevant source text (if appropriate)
- Or instruct the model to ask questions and label unknowns
- Or require an "Unverified" label for uncertain claims

Use this universal anti-hallucination clause: "Do not guess. If you are unsure, label it Unverified and ask me what information you need."

Then make it operational by adding: "List all claims that require verification before use."

This turns hallucination risk into a controlled workflow.

Section 9.11: Trusted Outputs Require "Guardrails" - The Professional Guardrails Set

Guardrails are not restrictions. Guardrails are what allow speed without accidents.

Here is a guardrails set you can paste into many prompts:

> *Guardrails Set (Copy-Paste)*
>
> *"Use plain English and a calm tone*
>
> *Do not invent facts, names, dates, or numbers*
>
> *If information is missing, write "Missing" and ask a question*
>
> *Do not include confidential or identifying details*
>
> *Avoid legal or medical claims; flag areas needing expert review*
>
> *End with: (1) commitments made, (2) claims to verify, (3) a short verification checklist"*

Figure 9.4 – Prompt guardrails set (printable prompt footer)

PROMPT FOOTER — Guardrails
Paste this at the end of a prompt to reduce guessing and increase safety.

No guessing	Confidentiality	Verification required
• Do not invent facts, numbers, or names. • If information is missing, ask up to 3 clarifying questions. • Label unknowns explicitly (Unknown / Needs confirmation). • Separate what's known vs assumed.	• Avoid sensitive or identifying details unless provided. • If examples are needed, use anonymized placeholders. • Do not reproduce secrets, credentials, or private data. • Flag anything that should be sanitized.	• End with a verification checklist. • Cite or name sources to verify critical claims. • Highlight high-risk statements (legal, finance, commitments). • Recommend expert review when appropriate.

End every draft with: "Known facts • Assumptions • Unknowns • Verification checklist."

This guardrail set works because it anticipates the most common business risks: invented details, accidental commitments, and confidentiality leaks.

Section 9.12: Disclosure - Do You Need to Say, "AI Helped"?

This is a common question, and the answer depends on your organization, your industry, and the nature of the work.

Here is a calm, practical approach:

1. Follow your organizational policy first.
    Some organizations require disclosure for certain documents or external communications. Others do not. If you're unsure, ask.

2. Focus on what matters: responsibility and accuracy.
    In most business settings, what people care about is whether the content is correct and whether you stand behind it.

3. Consider disclosure when:

    •   The audience expects original authorship (certain academic contexts, published thought leadership)

- The output could be misleading if readers assume human research occurred
- The work is regulated or contractually constrained

A safe professional practice is to be able to describe your process honestly if asked:

"I used AI to draft and edit for clarity. I reviewed and verified the content before sending."

That statement preserves trust without turning your workflow into a confession.

Section 9.13: Ethical Workflows by Scenario - What to Do in Real Business Cases

Let's make this concrete.

Scenario A: Customer email after a service issue (Level 2)

Risks:

- Overpromising timelines
- Admitting fault inappropriately
- Revealing internal details

Workflow:

- Provide sanitized facts and allowed remedies
- Use commitment audit
- Verify dates and policies
- Save what you sent

```
Prompt:
"Draft a customer response email.
Facts: [sanitized].
Allowed remedies: [list].
Constraints: do not promise timelines unless I provide them;
do not blame; do not reveal internal operations; keep it under
160 words.
End with a commitment list and verification checklist."
```

Scenario B: Internal SOP that people will follow (Level 2)

Risks:

- Invented steps or tools
- Missing exceptions
- Poor usability

Workflow:

- Source-first: provide current process map
- Draft SOP with "Missing" labels
- Test with real workers
- Revise and version-control

> *Prompt:*
> *"Create an SOP using only my process map as truth.*
> *Label missing info. Ask questions.*
> *End with an 8-item usability checklist and 5 questions to confirm before rollout."*

Scenario C: HR message about performance concerns (Level 3-ish)

Risks:

- Loaded language
- Legal exposure
- Inconsistent standards

Workflow:

- Use AI for neutral phrasing and structure only
- Avoid definitive claims
- Consider HR/legal review as required

> *Prompt:*
> *"Rewrite this message to be neutral, factual, and policy-aligned.*
> *Do not add new claims. Remove assumptions about intent.*
> *Flag any phrasing that could be interpreted as discriminatory or as a legal conclusion.*
> *Text: [paste sanitized text]."*

Scenario D: Proposal with pricing and timeline (Level 2, sometimes 3)

Risks:

- Unverified claims about capability
- Unintended commitments
- Misaligned scope

Workflow:

- Use AI to draft structure and clarify scope
- Commitment audit
- Cross-check dates and resourcing
- Save version and approvals

> *Prompt:*
> *"Draft a proposal with clear scope and assumptions.*
> *Do not promise unconfirmed dates.*
> *End with: a list of commitments, assumptions, and items requiring*
> *approval."*

This is ethical practice: use the tool where it helps and keep control where it matters.

Section 9.14: Building Your Personal "Trust Workflow" (A Daily 2-Minute Routine)

Here is a routine you can use daily.

Daily Trust Workflow

1. Identify the risk level (1/2/3)
2. Run the "commitment scan" (what am I promising?)
3. Run the "claims scan" (what must be true?)
4. Verify the top-risk claims (ladder step appropriate)
5. Save the final (especially for Level 2/3)

Figure 9.5 – Daily trust workflow (2-minute routine)

2-minute routine before you hit send
A quick pass to reduce errors, unintended promises, and trust leaks.

① **Risk level**
Low / Medium / High

② **Commitment scan**
Look for implied promises

③ **Claims scan**
Dates • numbers • policies

④ **Verify**
Do the right check

⑤ **Save**
Store the decision / record

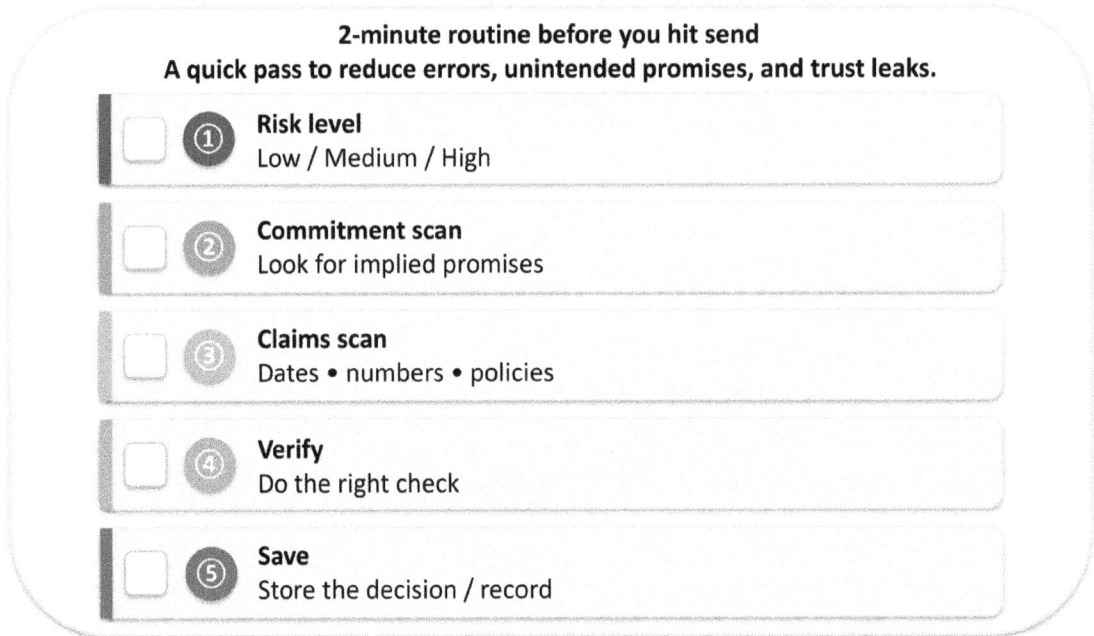

You can ask ChatGPT to support steps 2 and 3:

> *Prompt: Commitment + claims scan*
> *"Before I send this, perform two scans:*
>
> *Commitment scan: list every promise (explicit or implied)*
>
> *Claims scan: list factual claims that must be verified*
> *Then propose safer wording for risky commitments and give a*
> *verification checklist.*
> *Text: [paste].*
> *Rules: Do not add facts. Keep it concise."*

This prompt turns ethical diligence into a repeatable habit.

Figure 9.6 – Commitment audit examples: implied vs. explicit promises

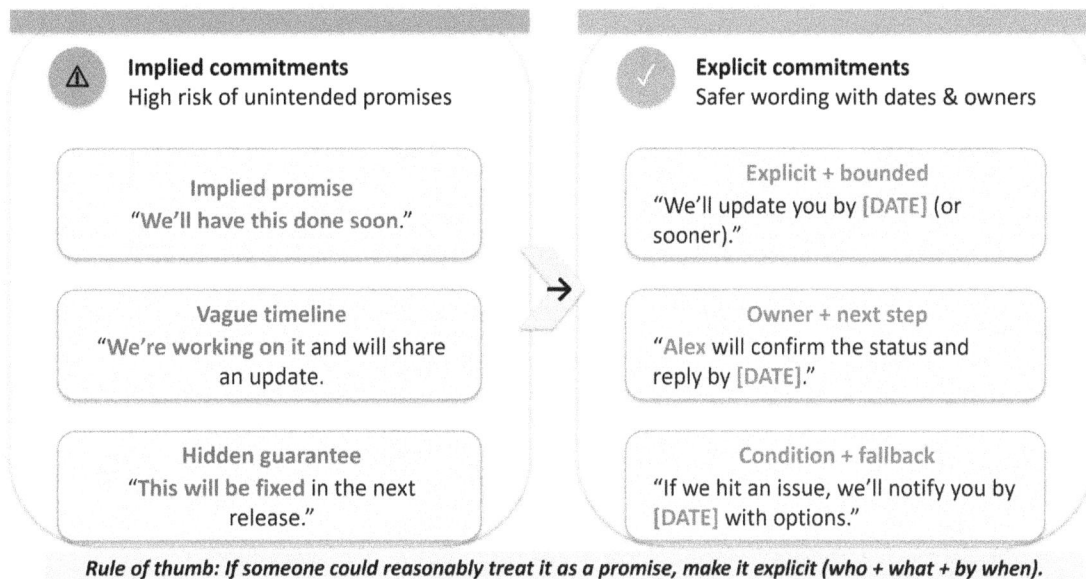

⚠ **Implied commitments**
High risk of unintended promises

Implied promise
"We'll have this done soon."

Vague timeline
"We're working on it and will share an update.

Hidden guarantee
"This will be fixed in the next release."

→

✓ **Explicit commitments**
Safer wording with dates & owners

Explicit + bounded
"We'll update you by [DATE] (or sooner)."

Owner + next step
"Alex will confirm the status and reply by [DATE]."

Condition + fallback
"If we hit an issue, we'll notify you by [DATE] with options."

Rule of thumb: If someone could reasonably treat it as a promise, make it explicit (who + what + by when).

Section 9.15: When Not to Use ChatGPT (And What to do Instead)

Ethical use includes knowing when not to use a tool.

Avoid using ChatGPT (or use only in highly constrained ways) when:

- You must handle regulated data and do not have an approved environment
- You are drafting security procedures or instructions that could create vulnerability
- You are producing legal advice or medical guidance (use professionals)
- You are asked to make authoritative claims without sources
- You are working with sensitive HR matters and lack policy clarity

What to do instead:

- Use ChatGPT for structure and plain-English rewriting of *approved content*
- Ask it to generate questions for your expert or counsel
- Ask it to create checklists for review, not answers
- Use internal approved tools for sensitive tasks

Prompt: "Questions for counsel / expert"
"Help me prepare for a conversation with
[legal/HR/compliance/security].

```
Context (sanitized): [summary].
Generate:

10 questions I should ask

5 risks to flag

3 decisions I need clarified
Tone: calm and practical.”
```

This is a high-value way to use AI ethically in high-stakes environments.

Practice Exercises

Use sanitized information. Treat outputs as drafts. For medium- and high-risk work, follow your organization's policy and required approvals.

Exercise 1 — Classify your work by risk level

```
Prompt:
“Here is a list of tasks I do regularly: [paste list].
Classify each into Risk Level 1/2/3 for AI assistance.
Explain why, and recommend the appropriate verification ladder
steps for each.”
```

Exercise 2 — Run the 3C method on a draft

```
Prompt:
“Apply the 3C method to this text.
Text: [paste].
Output:

List the top 10 claims

Mark each as Known/Unverified/Risky

Provide a verification checklist appropriate to Risk Level
[1/2/3]
Rules: do not add new facts.”
```

Exercise 3 — Build your guardrails footer

> *Prompt:*
> *"Create a 7-line guardrails footer I can paste into any prompt.
> It must prevent guessing, protect confidentiality, and require a
> commitment + claims scan at the end.
> Keep it plain English and business-ready."*

Exercise 4 — Commitment audit practice

> *Prompt:*
> *"Analyze this email for commitments.
> List every explicit and implied promise (dates, actions,
> expectations).
> Then rewrite the email to reduce risky commitments while
> preserving accountability.
> Email: [paste]."*

Exercise 5 — Confidentiality sanitization drill

> *Prompt:*
> *"Rewrite my prompt to remove confidential details while keeping
> enough context for a useful answer.
> Original prompt: [paste].
> Rules: replace names with roles, remove identifying numbers,
> generalize sensitive details, and add a boundary line ('Do not
> include identifying details').
> Then produce the sanitized prompt I should use."*

Exercise 6 — Bias and neutrality check

> *Prompt:*
> *"Review this text for biased or loaded language and rewrite it to
> be neutral, respectful, and professional.
> Do not change factual meaning. Remove assumptions about intent.
> Text: [paste]."*

Exercise 7 — High-stakes boundary setting (Level 3)

> *Prompt:*
> *"I need help with a high-stakes message (HR/legal/compliance
> adjacent).
> Rewrite for clarity and neutrality only. Do not add claims or
> advice.*

Flag phrases that require expert review.
Text: [paste sanitized text]."

Exercise 8 — Build a "verification plan" for a proposal or report

Prompt:
"I'm preparing a [proposal/report] that includes key claims.
Here is the draft: [paste].
Create a verification plan:

Claims that must be verified

Where to verify each (document/person/source)

What evidence to save

Who should review (if applicable)
Risk level: [2/3].
Rules: do not add new facts."

Exercise 9 — Create an "AI usage note" for your own documentation

Prompt:
"Draft a short internal note I can attach to my deliverables
explaining how AI was used responsibly.
It must include: what AI did (draft/edit), what I did
(review/verify), and what sources were used.
Tone: calm and professional. Keep it to 5–7 sentences."

Exercise 10 — Build a "safe prompt template" for customer communications

Prompt:
"Create a reusable prompt template for customer emails that
enforces:

empathy + accountability

no overpromising

confidentiality

commitment scan + verification checklist
Make it copy-paste ready with placeholders in [brackets]."

Exercise 11 — Design a team guardrails standard (one page)

> **Prompt:**
> "Create a one-page team standard for responsible AI use in knowledge work.
> Include:
>
> what's allowed
>
> what's not allowed
>
> how to sanitize
>
> risk levels and verification ladder
>
> commitment scan requirement for external messages
> Tone: calm, practical, non-punitive."

Exercise 12 — Practice "abstention": preventing forced answers

> **Prompt:**
> "Answer the question below, but you must abstain from guessing.
> If you lack information, label it 'Unverified' and ask me for what you need.
> Question: [paste].
> Afterward, list what would be required to answer responsibly at Risk Level [2/3]."

Skill Check

After completing this chapter, you should be able to:

- Classify tasks into risk levels and match verification effort to stakes
- Use the 3C method (Claims, Confidence, Checks) to evaluate AI outputs quickly
- Apply a verification ladder to reduce errors without slowing down low-risk work
- Protect confidentiality through sanitization and boundary instructions
- Identify and reduce unintended promises in emails and proposals
- Detect and rewrite biased or loaded language into neutral, professional phrasing
- Use AI ethically in high-stakes contexts by limiting it to structure and clarity, not authority

- Implement a daily trust workflow that includes commitment scans, claim scans, and saving final versions
- Create team-ready guardrails and documentation practices that preserve trust while enabling productivity

Chapter 10: Research, Learning, and Skill Development

Professionals don't stop learning after school. They just stop calling it learning.

They call it:

- "Figuring it out"
- "Getting up to speed"
- "Preparing for a meeting"
- "Learning the new process"
- "Understanding the market"
- "Training the team"
- "Becoming competent faster than the timeline allows"

In modern work, learning is constant. The pressure comes from two realities:

1. You are expected to learn quickly.
2. You are expected to perform while learning.

This chapter shows how to use ChatGPT as a learning partner that helps you:

- Understand new topics in plain English
- Build working knowledge efficiently
- Practice skills through structured exercises
- Learn from your own documents and experiences (safely)
- Create study plans and job-ready reference materials
- Avoid misinformation and overconfidence
- Turn learning into competence, not just information

A calm warning up front: **ChatGPT can explain and structure, but it can also be confidently wrong.** For anything where factual accuracy matters, you must use the verification habits from Chapter 9. Learning is safer than many tasks, but it still benefits from good standards.

Section 10.1: What "Learning" Looks Like in Business

Business learning is different from academic learning.

In academic settings, you often learn broad foundations before applying them.

In business, you often learn just enough to:

- Make a decision
- Hold a conversation

- Avoid a mistake
- Meet a deadline
- Deliver a project

That's not shallow. It's contextual.

So the goal is not "know everything." The goal is: Build usable knowledge, which is the ability to explain, apply, and execute.

ChatGPT supports usable knowledge by providing:

- Explanations that you can ask to be simpler or deeper
- Analogies and examples tailored to your domain
- Practice questions and scenarios
- Step-by-step guides
- Summaries and checklists
- "Teach it back" exercises to confirm understanding

This chapter will give you learning workflows that produce competence, not just notes.

Section 10.2: The Learning Loop - Explain → Apply → Practice → Feedback → Repeat

Learning becomes reliable when it is a loop.

Here is a practical loop you can use for almost anything:

1. **Explain**: get a plain-English explanation
2. **Apply**: connect it to your role and real tasks
3. **Practice**: do exercises that simulate real work
4. **Feedback**: identify mistakes and correct them
5. **Repeat**: revisit until it becomes automatic

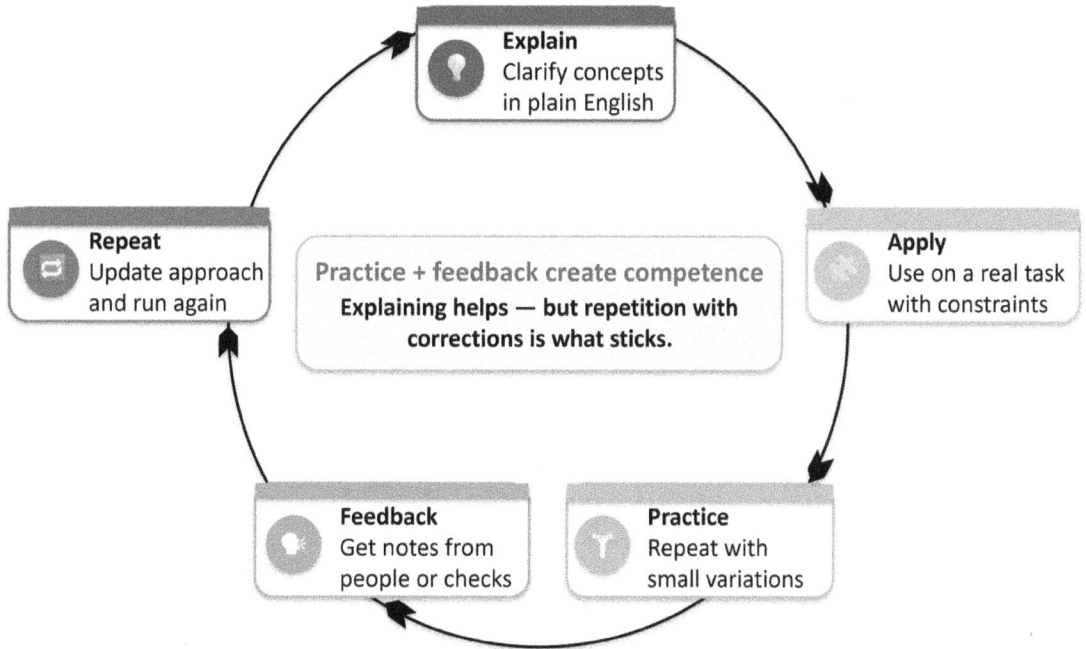

Explain
Clarify concepts in plain English

Apply
Use on a real task with constraints

Practice
Repeat with small variations

Feedback
Get notes from people or checks

Repeat
Update approach and run again

Practice + feedback create competence
Explaining helps — but repetition with corrections is what sticks.

Use the loop weekly: capture feedback, adjust your approach, and run the next iteration.

ChatGPT can help with every step, especially practice and feedback.

The most important shift for anxious learners: Don't use ChatGPT only to read. Use it to practice.

Reading creates familiarity. Practice creates skill.

Section 10.3: How to Ask for Explanations That Actually Help

Many people ask: "Explain X."

They receive:

- A generic definition
- A paragraph that sounds good
- And then they still feel unsure

The fix is to specify:

- Your current level
- Your goal
- Your context

- The format that helps you learn

Here are explanation formats that work well:

Format A: "Explain like I'm busy"

> **Prompt:**
> "Explain [topic] for a busy professional.
> Constraints: plain English, no jargon without definitions, 10 sentences max.
> Then give:
>
> 5 key terms with simple definitions
>
> 3 common mistakes people make
>
> 3 practical examples in a business setting."

Format B: "Layered explanation"

> **Prompt:**
> "Explain [topic] in three layers:
>
> 1-sentence explanation
>
> 1-paragraph explanation
>
> A deeper explanation with a simple example
> Rules: define any jargon; keep it practical."

Format C: "Explain with an analogy"

> **Prompt:**
> "Explain [topic] using an analogy from [your domain].
> Then explain the limits of the analogy so I don't misunderstand."

That last line is important. Analogies are helpful, but they can mislead if taken too literally.

Section 10.4: Learning New Subjects Fast - The "90-Minute Get-Up-To-Speed" Plan

Professionals often need to learn enough to participate intelligently in a meeting. Here is a structured approach you can run in under 90 minutes.

Step 1: Define your goal (5 minutes)

> What do I need to be able to do or say?
> Examples: "Ask good questions," "Explain the concept," "Make a recommendation," "Understand risks."

Step 2: Request a plain-English briefing (10 minutes)

```
Prompt:
"Create a briefing on [topic] for my role as [role].
Audience: me.
Goal: be able to [goal].
Output:

10 key points

5 terms defined

5 questions I should ask in a meeting

3 risks/pitfalls
Tone: calm and practical."
```

Step 3: Build a one-page cheat sheet (10 minutes)

```
Prompt:
"Turn the briefing into a one-page cheat sheet with headings and
bullets, designed for quick review before a meeting."
```

Step 4: Practice with scenarios (30 minutes)

```
Prompt:
"Give me 6 realistic scenarios related to [topic] I might face at
work.
For each scenario, ask me what I would do.
After I answer, give feedback and a better approach if needed."
```

Step 5: Create meeting questions and talking points (15 minutes)

> *Prompt:*
> *"Based on what we covered, generate:*
>
> *8 meeting questions (organized by priority)*
>
> *5 concise talking points I can use*
>
> *3 'watch-outs' I should mention*
> *Keep it plain English."*

Step 6: Review and verify key claims (20 minutes)

Use Chapter 9's 3C method and verify any factual claims you will repeat publicly.

Figure 10.2 – 90-minute get-up-to-speed plan (timeline)

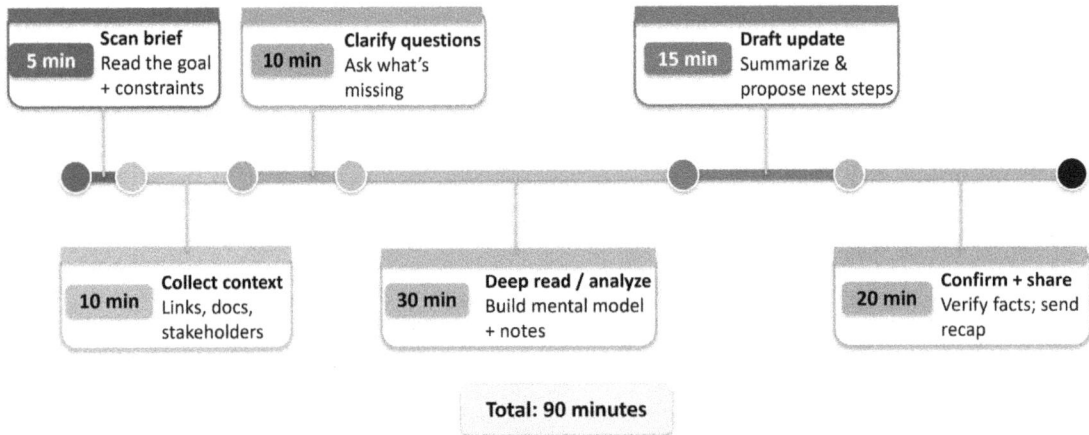

5 min	**Scan brief** Read the goal + constraints
10 min	**Clarify questions** Ask what's missing
15 min	**Draft update** Summarize & propose next steps
10 min	**Collect context** Links, docs, stakeholders
30 min	**Deep read / analyze** Build mental model + notes
20 min	**Confirm + share** Verify facts; send recap

Total: 90 minutes

Use this when joining a new project or taking over an ongoing thread.

This plan reduces anxiety because it replaces vague "I should learn this" with a concrete workflow and deliverables.

Section 10.5: Learning From Your Own Materials - Turn Experience into Training

One of the most valuable learning uses of ChatGPT is turning your own work into reusable knowledge.

Examples:

- Turning meeting notes into a training guide
- Turning an SOP into onboarding materials
- Turning a project postmortem into lessons learned
- Turning customer feedback into communication improvements
- Turning your own drafts into writing patterns you can reuse

This approach is safer and more accurate because the source material is yours.

The ethical practice is to sanitize and protect confidentiality.

> *Prompt: Lessons learned generator (source-first)*
> *"Turn the information below into a 'lessons learned' document.*
> *Source material (use as truth; do not add facts): [paste sanitized notes].*
> *Output:*
>
> *What happened (neutral summary)*
>
> *What worked*
>
> *What didn't*
>
> *Root causes (as hypotheses)*
>
> *Changes we should make*
>
> *A short checklist to prevent recurrence*
> *Rules: do not invent details; label assumptions."*

This transforms experience into organizational learning.

Section 10.6: Practice as the Path - Using ChatGPT as a Safe Simulator

Practice is the difference between knowing and doing.

ChatGPT can simulate:

- A skeptical stakeholder in a meeting
- A customer with concerns
- A manager asking for clarity
- A colleague needing a handoff
- A performance conversation (carefully and ethically)
- A negotiation or boundary-setting conversation

You are not using it to "replace humans." You are using it to rehearse.

```
Prompt: Role-play rehearsal (professional)
"Role-play with me.
You are [stakeholder role].
Scenario: [scenario].
My goal: [goal].
Rules: keep it realistic and professional; challenge me politely;
after each of my replies, give feedback: what worked, what could
be clearer, and a better version I could say."
```

This rehearsal reduces anxiety because it gives you a practice space without social risk.

Figure 10.3 – Role-play rehearsal framework

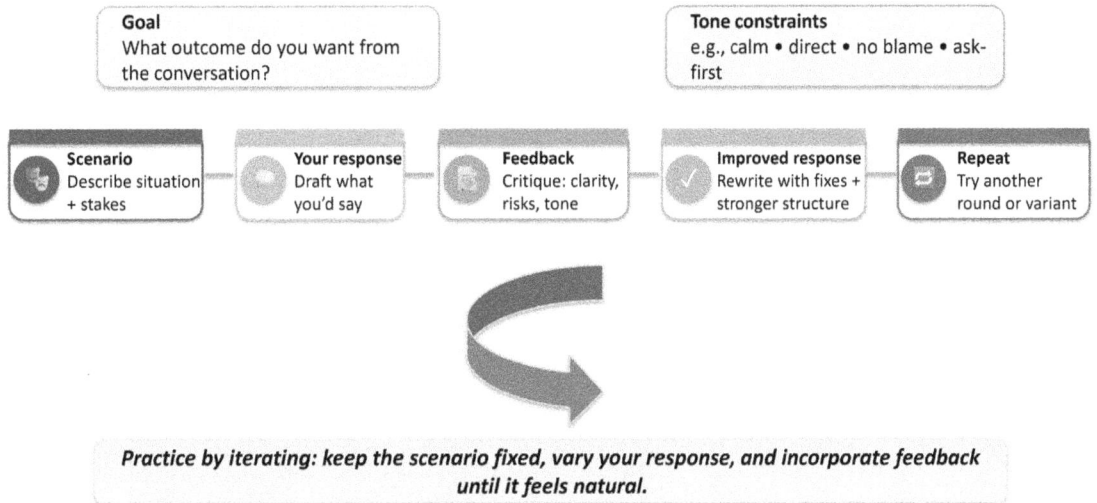

Goal		Tone constraints
What outcome do you want from the conversation?		e.g., calm • direct • no blame • ask-first

Scenario	Your response	Feedback	Improved response	Repeat
Describe situation + stakes	Draft what you'd say	Critique: clarity, risks, tone	Rewrite with fixes + stronger structure	Try another round or variant

Practice by iterating: keep the scenario fixed, vary your response, and incorporate feedback until it feels natural.

Section 10.7: Skill Development - Turning a Weakness into a Program

Most professionals have a skill they avoid:

- Presentations
- Difficult conversations
- Writing
- Prioritization
- Data interpretation
- Project planning
- Delegation
- Negotiation

Avoidance creates anxiety. Skill reduces anxiety.

ChatGPT can help you turn a skill gap into a structured program:

- Define the skill
- Identify sub-skills
- Create a practice plan
- Create exercises
- Provide feedback
- Track progress

Prompt: Skill development program
"Help me build a 4-week skill development program for [skill].
My role: [role].
Where I struggle: [describe].
Constraints: [time available per week].
Output:

Weekly focus

3 practice exercises per week

A checklist of what 'good' looks like

A way to measure improvement
Tone: calm, practical, supportive."

This is how you move from "I should be better at this" to "I am practicing it."

Figure 10.4 – Skill development plan (4-week grid)

Week	Weekly focus	Exercises	Measurement
WEEK 1	Inputs & clarity	Write briefs using Goal/Context/Constraints Ask 3 clarifying questions per task Do 1 two-pass draft per day	Track: # clarifying Qs Time-to-first-draft
WEEK 2	Reliability & verification	Use 3C method (Claims/Confidence/Checks) Verify dates/numbers in every draft Add a verification checklist footer	Track: # corrections needed Errors caught before send
WEEK 3	Writing for decisions	Create 2 decision memos Run assumption audits Practice ask-first emails + recaps	Track: stakeholder clarity Fewer follow-up questions
WEEK 4	Automation & consistency	Build reusable templates Create SOP/checklists for repeat work Run weekly review + improvements	Track: reuse rate Saved time/week

Keep it lightweight: pick one measurable behavior per week, then review + adjust.

Section 10.8: The Most Important Learning Practice - "Teach It Back"

A simple way to know whether you understand something is whether you can explain it clearly.

Teach-back means:

- You explain it in your own words
- You give an example
- You identify limits and risks
- You connect it to your work

ChatGPT can act as a coach.

> *Prompt: Teach-back coach*
> "I'm going to teach back what I think I learned about [topic].
> Your job:
>
> Tell me what I got right
>
> Correct misunderstandings
>
> Ask 5 probing questions
>
> Suggest a simpler explanation I can use with colleagues
> Ready? Here is my explanation: [paste]."

Teach-back converts passive learning into active competence.

Figure 10.5 – Teach-back worksheet

Use after you learn something new (a process, policy, or tool).
Goal: convert understanding into a clear explanation you can reuse.

Explain in 5 sentences
Write the core idea without jargon.
Keep each sentence short.

Give an example
Show a concrete case: inputs → steps → output.

Where does it break down?
List edge cases, risks, and failure modes.

What would you tell a colleague?
Your best advice: what to do first, what to avoid, what to verify.

Tip: If you can't teach it back clearly, you don't fully own it yet—repeat the loop.

Section 10.9: Reading and Summarizing Safely - How to Avoid "False Summaries"

Summarization is useful, but it has risks.

If you paste a document and ask for a summary, ChatGPT can summarize well—but it can also:

- Miss nuance
- Overgeneralize
- Misinterpret an ambiguous sentence
- Present uncertain interpretations as facts

To reduce risk, specify the kind of summary you need:

- Executive summary (what matters)
- Action summary (what to do)
- Risk summary (what could go wrong)
- Decision summary (what choices exist)

And require "quotes or references" within the document where possible (if allowed), so the summary stays grounded.

Prompt: Grounded summary
"Summarize this text in a way that stays grounded.
Output:

Executive summary (5 bullets)

Key details (10 bullets)

Decisions required (if any)

Risks/unknowns
Rules: Do not add facts. If you infer something, label it as an inference.
Text: [paste]."

This prompt teaches the assistant to separate facts from interpretation.

Figure 10.6 – Grounded summary template: facts vs. inferences

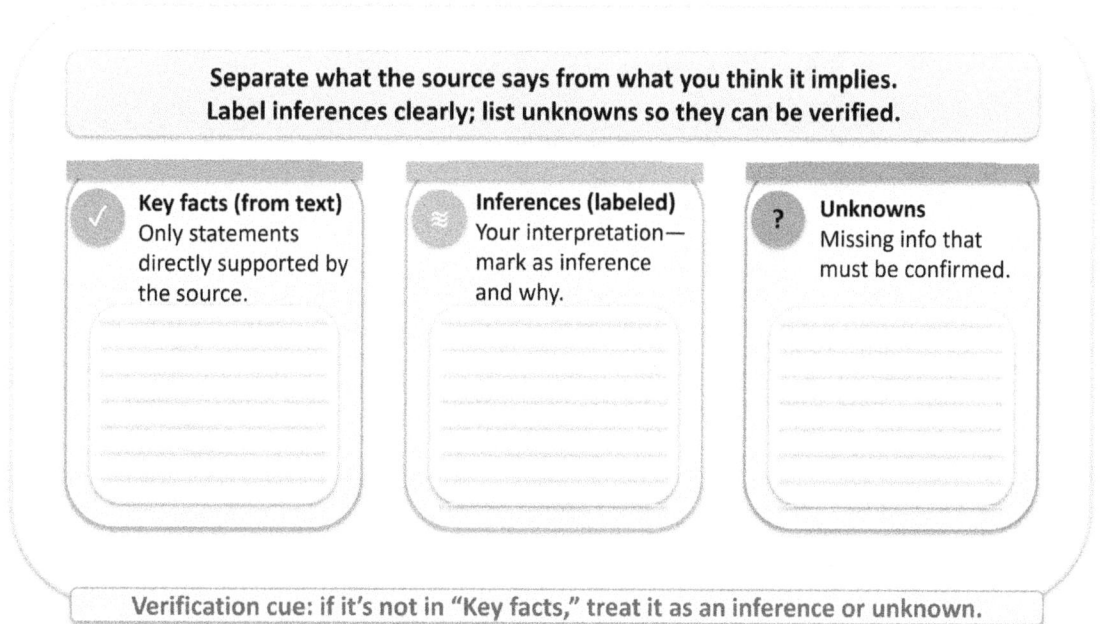

Separate what the source says from what you think it implies.
Label inferences clearly; list unknowns so they can be verified.

Key facts (from text)
Only statements directly supported by the source.

Inferences (labeled)
Your interpretation— mark as inference and why.

Unknowns
Missing info that must be confirmed.

Verification cue: if it's not in "Key facts," treat it as an inference or unknown.

Section 10.10: Learning to Write Better with Feedback Loops

Many professionals want to write better but don't know how to practice.

ChatGPT can provide feedback if you specify criteria.

Criteria examples:

- Clarity
- Brevity
- Professional tone
- Strong asks
- Logical structure
- Fewer assumptions
- Neutral language
- Reduced jargon

> **Prompt: Writing feedback coach**
> "Evaluate this writing using these criteria: clarity, concision, tone, structure, and actionability.
> Then:
>
> Give me a score (1-10) for each
>
> Explain what lowered the score (plain English)
>
> Rewrite it once
>
> Give me 3 micro-lessons I can apply next time
> Text: [paste]."

This turns writing into a skill-building loop rather than a one-time task.

Section 10.11: Learning for Teams - Building Training Materials That Don't Waste Time

Teams often need training but don't have time to create training.

The solution is to start from existing assets:

- SOPs
- project notes
- customer feedback

- existing decks
- onboarding checklists
- recurring errors

Then use ChatGPT to transform them into short training formats:

- One-page quick reference
- 15-minute scenario-based training outline
- Quiz and answer key
- "Common mistakes" guide
- Role-specific cheat sheets

> **Prompt: Team training kit builder**
> "Create a lightweight team training kit from the source material below.
> Rules: use the source as truth; do not add steps or policies; keep it practical.
> Output:
>
> 1-page quick reference
>
> 15-minute training outline with 3 scenarios
>
> 10-question quiz with answers
>
> Common mistakes + prevention
> Source material: [paste sanitized SOP or notes]."

This creates fast, usable training without inventing content.

Section 10.12: A Practical Research Note - What ChatGPT Can and Cannot "Research"

Professionals often use the word "research" to mean "help me understand this."

ChatGPT can help you:

- Build a conceptual model
- Identify what questions to ask
- Summarize provided materials
- Suggest frameworks and methods
- Generate hypotheses

But without reliable source access (or without you providing sources), ChatGPT cannot guarantee factual accuracy about the outside world.

So use a disciplined approach:

- Use ChatGPT for structure and questions
- Use authoritative sources for facts
- Use verification habits from Chapter 9 for claims that matter

```
Prompt: Research plan builder
"Help me research [topic] responsibly.
Goal: [decision or deliverable].
Constraints: I need reliable sources; avoid speculation.
Output:

Key questions to answer

What sources are considered authoritative in this area

A step-by-step plan to gather evidence

A template to capture findings and citations
Tone: practical."
```

This keeps "research" grounded.

Section 10.13: From Learning to Performance - Turn Knowledge into a Checklist

A professional test of learning is not "can you explain it." It's "can you do it reliably."

The fastest bridge from learning to performance is a checklist.

Example: If you're learning to run better meetings, your checklist might include:

- Purpose stated
- Desired outputs defined
- Agenda timeboxed
- Decision point identified
- Actions recorded with owners and deadlines
- Recap sent

If you're learning to write better executive updates:

- Status headline
- So what / now what
- Risks + mitigation

- Decision needed
- Next steps with owners

ChatGPT can turn any learning into a "performance checklist."

> *Prompt: Learning-to-checklist converter*
> *"Create a performance checklist for applying [topic/skill] at work.*
> *It must be: 10–15 items max, plain English, usable under time pressure.*
> *Include a short 'common mistakes' section.*
> *Context: my role is [role]."*

This is how learning becomes operational.

Practice Exercises

Use sanitized information. Treat outputs as drafts. For factual or high-stakes material, apply Chapter 9's verification habits.

Exercise 1 — Explain a topic in three layers

> *Prompt:*
> *"Explain [topic] in three layers:*
>
> *1 sentence*
>
> *1 paragraph*
>
> *A deeper explanation with one business example*
> *Rules: plain English, define jargon, keep it calm."*

Exercise 2 — Build a 90-minute get-up-to-speed packet

> *Prompt:*
> *"I need to get up to speed on [topic] for [meeting/project].*
> *My role: [role].*
> *Goal: [what you need to do].*
> *Create:*
>
> *briefing (10 key points)*
>
> *5 terms defined*
>
> *5 meeting questions*

```
3 risks/pitfalls
Then create a one-page cheat sheet and 6 practice scenarios."
```

Exercise 3 — Practice with scenarios and feedback

```
Prompt:
"Give me 6 realistic scenarios related to [topic].
Ask me what I would do.
After each answer, give feedback and a better approach.
Keep it professional and direct."
```

Exercise 4 — Teach-back coaching

```
Prompt:
"I'm going to teach back what I learned about [topic].
Correct misunderstandings, ask 5 probing questions, and give me a
simpler explanation I can use at work.
Here is my teach-back: [paste]."
```

Exercise 5 — Build a performance checklist from a new skill

```
Prompt:
"Create a 10-15 item performance checklist for applying [skill]
at work.
Include common mistakes and how to avoid them.
Context: my role is [role]."
```

Exercise 6 — Write a study plan for a skill gap

```
Prompt:
"Build a 4-week skill development plan for [skill].
My role: [role].
Time available: [minutes per week].
Output: weekly focus, 3 practice exercises per week, what 'good'
looks like, and how to measure improvement."
```

Exercise 7 — Grounded summarization of a document

```
Prompt:
"Summarize the text below.
Output: executive summary (5 bullets), key details (10 bullets),
decisions required, risks/unknowns.
Rules: do not add facts; label inferences; note ambiguous areas.
Text: [paste]."
```

Exercise 8 — Turn your work into lessons learned

Prompt:
"Turn these project notes into a lessons-learned document: what happened, what worked, what didn't, root causes (hypotheses), changes to make, and a prevention checklist.
Rules: use my notes as truth; do not invent details.
Notes: [paste]."

Exercise 9 — Writing improvement feedback loop

Prompt:
"Evaluate this writing for clarity, concision, tone, structure, and actionability.
Score each 1–10, explain why, rewrite once, and give 3 micro-lessons.
Text: [paste]."

Exercise 10 — Build team training kit from an SOP

Prompt:
"Create a lightweight team training kit from this SOP/notes.
Output: 1-page quick reference, 15-minute scenario-based training outline, 10-question quiz with answers, common mistakes guide.
Rules: use source as truth; do not add steps or policies.
Source: [paste]."

Exercise 11 — Research plan with authoritative sources

Prompt:
"Help me research [topic] responsibly.
Goal: [deliverable/decision].
Output: key questions, authoritative source types, step-by-step research plan, and a findings template with citations.
Rules: avoid speculation; label assumptions."

Exercise 12 — Convert learning into meeting readiness

Prompt:
"Based on what I learned about [topic], create:

8 meeting questions

5 talking points (concise)

3 watch-outs

```
1 short summary I can send in email
Keep it plain English and calm."
```

Skill Check

After completing this chapter, you should be able to:

- Use the learning loop (Explain → Apply → Practice → Feedback → Repeat) to build competence
- Request explanations in formats that match your time and needs (layered, busy-professional, analogy)
- Run a 90-minute get-up-to-speed plan that produces a cheat sheet, scenarios, and meeting questions
- Practice skills through role-play and scenario simulations with structured feedback
- Use teach-back to confirm understanding and correct misunderstandings
- Create a 4-week skill development program with exercises and measurable improvement
- Summarize documents in a grounded way that separates facts from inferences and unknowns
- Turn your own work into lessons learned, training materials, and performance checklists
- Approach "research" responsibly by using AI for structure and questions, and authoritative sources for facts

Chapter 11: Marketing, SEO, and Customer Communication

Marketing is not "tricks." Marketing is clarity at scale.

For many professionals and business owners, marketing feels stressful because it combines:

- Creativity (what to say)
- Strategy (who it's for and why it matters)
- Consistency (show up regularly)
- Proof (be credible)
- Constraints (time, tone, brand, compliance)

When people say, "I'm not good at marketing," they often mean: "I can't produce clear, consistent messages fast enough without feeling fake."

This chapter shows how to use ChatGPT to create marketing and customer communication that is:

- Plain-English and trustworthy
- Aligned with your real brand and values
- Consistent across channels
- Efficient to produce
- Ethical (no misleading claims)
- Built on customer needs, not hype

You will learn:

- How to clarify your brand voice in practical terms
- How to turn customer intent into useful content
- SEO fundamentals without jargon
- Writing product and service descriptions that convert without exaggeration
- Customer communication templates that preserve trust
- A repeatable content system that prevents burnout
- Guardrails for marketing claims and accuracy

This chapter is designed for non-technical professionals. You do not need to be an SEO expert to use these methods.

Section 11.1: What "Good Marketing" Means for Non-Technical Professionals

Good marketing does three things:

1. Helps the right people understand what you offer
2. Helps them trust you
3. Helps them take the next step

That's it.

Good marketing is not loud. It is not manipulative. It is not about pretending.

In professional services and business operations, the highest-value marketing is often:

- Clear positioning
- Clear benefits (not vague claims)
- Clear proof (examples, outcomes, reviews, process)
- Clear calls to action (what to do next)

ChatGPT can help you write this consistently, especially when you provide:

- Your audience
- Your offer
- Your tone
- Your constraints
- Your proof points (real ones)

Section 11.2: Brand Voice in Plain English - A "Voice Card" You Can Actually Use

Brand voice is often described with words that don't help you write: "bold," "authentic," "innovative."

A more practical approach is to create a Voice Card you can paste into prompts.

Voice Card fields:

- Audience: who we serve
- Promise: what we help them achieve
- Personality: 3–5 adjectives (calm, direct, friendly)
- Tone boundaries: what we never do (no hype, no fear, no guilt)
- Vocabulary: words we use / words we avoid
- Proof style: how we support claims (examples, process, testimonials)
- Call-to-action style: how we invite action (simple and respectful)

Figure 11.1 – Brand voice card template

Brand Voice Card

Audience

Promise

Personality

Tone boundaries

Vocabulary

Proof style

CTA style

Sample phrases

Phrases to avoid

```
Prompt: Voice Card builder
"Help me create a one-page Brand Voice Card.
Business type: [business / department].
Audience: [who].
Offer: [what you do].
Values: [3-5 values].
Tone: calm, confidence-building, practical, no hype.
Constraints: [compliance limits, sensitive topics].
Output: a Voice Card with the fields above plus 10 example
phrases in our voice and 10 phrases to avoid."
```

Once you have a Voice Card, marketing becomes easier because you stop reinventing tone and boundaries each time.

Section 11.3: Customer Intent - The Real Foundation of SEO and Content

SEO can sound technical, but the heart of it is simple: People type what they want. Search engines try to match it.

Customer intent is what a person is trying to do when they search, click, or read.

Four common intent types:

1. **Informational:** "How do I…" "What is…"
2. **Comparative:** "Best…" "X vs Y" "Which should I choose"
3. **Transactional:** "Buy…" "Order…" "Pricing…"
4. **Local/service:** "Near me" "In [city]" "Consultation"

When your content matches intent, it performs better and feels more helpful.

Figure 11.2 – Customer intent categories

Match search intent to content: examples + recommended page type

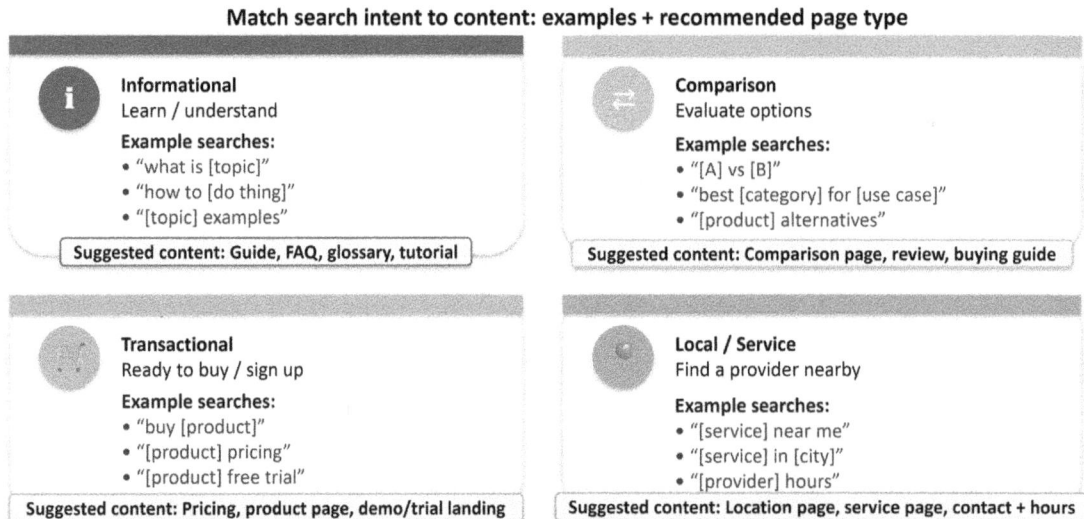

Informational
Learn / understand
Example searches:
- "what is [topic]"
- "how to [do thing]"
- "[topic] examples"

Suggested content: Guide, FAQ, glossary, tutorial

Comparison
Evaluate options
Example searches:
- "[A] vs [B]"
- "best [category] for [use case]"
- "[product] alternatives"

Suggested content: Comparison page, review, buying guide

Transactional
Ready to buy / sign up
Example searches:
- "buy [product]"
- "[product] pricing"
- "[product] free trial"

Suggested content: Pricing, product page, demo/trial landing

Local / Service
Find a provider nearby
Example searches:
- "[service] near me"
- "[service] in [city]"
- "[provider] hours"

Suggested content: Location page, service page, contact + hours

Tip: intent can shift—add internal links to guide readers from informational → comparison → transactional.

ChatGPT can help you map intent to content ideas, without forcing you into jargon.

```
Prompt: Intent-to-content mapper
"My audience is [audience].
Our offer is [offer].
Generate:

10 informational questions they would search
```

```
10 comparison questions

10 transactional keywords/phrases

10 local/service phrases (if relevant)
Then propose content ideas for each category that would genuinely
help a buyer decide.
Tone: plain English, no hype."
```

This creates a content plan that is anchored in real needs.

Section 11.4: SEO Fundamentals without Technical Overload

You do not need to know everything about SEO to benefit from it. You need a few fundamentals.

Fundamental 1: One page, one primary topic

A page should focus on one clear subject. That helps readers and search engines.

Fundamental 2: Use the language your customers use

Avoid internal jargon. Use words people actually search.

Fundamental 3: Answer the question clearly

If the page is about "custom engraved gifts," it should quickly explain:

- What it is
- Who it's for
- Options
- How to order
- What to expect

Fundamental 4: Structure matters

Clear headings, short paragraphs, lists, and FAQs help both readability and search.

Fundamental 5: Proof matters

Reviews, examples, policies, and clear process build trust.

ChatGPT can help you write pages that follow these fundamentals if you give it the topic, intent, and constraints.

> *Prompt: SEO-friendly page draft (plain English)*
> "Draft a webpage for [topic] optimized for search intent:
> [informational/comparison/transactional].
> Audience: [who].
> Primary keyword phrase: [phrase].
> Secondary phrases: [list].
>
> Constraints: calm tone, no hype, no unverified claims.
> Output:
>
> Page title (60 characters max)
>
> Meta description (155 characters max)
>
> H1
>
> Headings (H2/H3) outline with full paragraph content
>
> 5 FAQs with answers
>
> A clear call to action
> Rules: Use plain English. Avoid stuffing keywords. If a claim
> needs proof, label it as 'needs verification.'"

This prompt produces content that is structured and honest, not gimmicky.

Section 11.5: Product Descriptions That Convert without Exaggeration

Product and service descriptions often fail because they focus on features without meaning.

A professional description answers:

- What it is
- Who it's for
- What problem it solves
- What options exist
- What the process is
- What the buyer should expect
- What to do next

A calm conversion approach is to write like a confident guide.

Structure: Product description (trust-first)

1. One-sentence overview (what it is + who it's for)
2. Benefits (what it helps the buyer accomplish)
3. Key details (materials, sizes, options—fact-based)
4. Personalization or configuration options
5. Ordering process (how it works)
6. Shipping/turnaround expectations (only if verified)
7. Care/usage tips (if relevant)
8. Call to action

Figure 11.3 – Trust-first product description structure

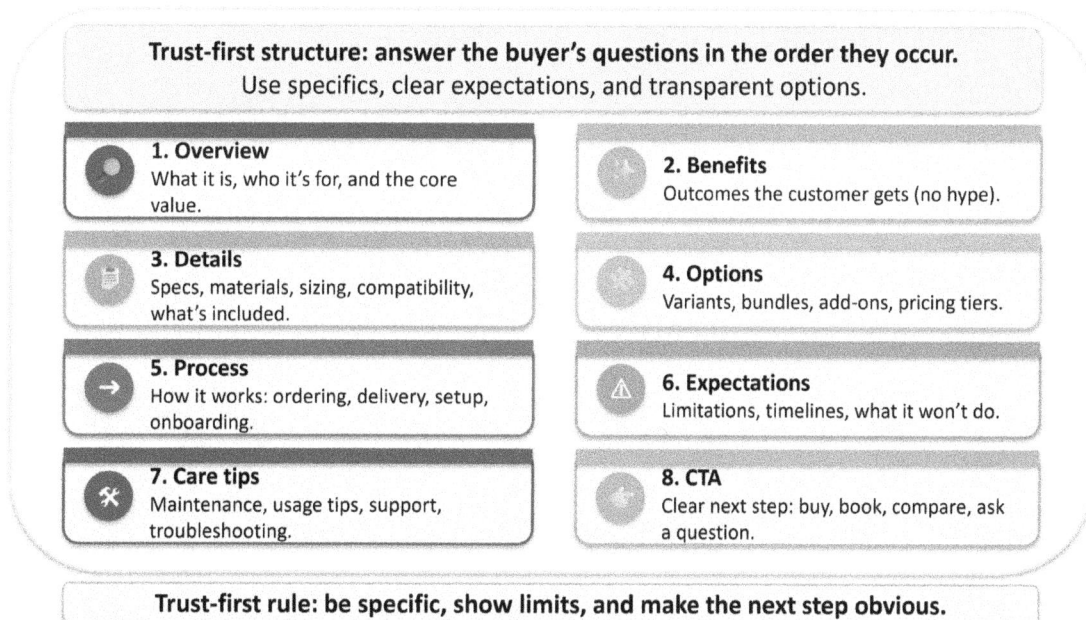

Trust-first structure: answer the buyer's questions in the order they occur.
Use specifics, clear expectations, and transparent options.

1. Overview
What it is, who it's for, and the core value.

2. Benefits
Outcomes the customer gets (no hype).

3. Details
Specs, materials, sizing, compatibility, what's included.

4. Options
Variants, bundles, add-ons, pricing tiers.

5. Process
How it works: ordering, delivery, setup, onboarding.

6. Expectations
Limitations, timelines, what it won't do.

7. Care tips
Maintenance, usage tips, support, troubleshooting.

8. CTA
Clear next step: buy, book, compare, ask a question.

Trust-first rule: be specific, show limits, and make the next step obvious.

```
Prompt: Product description builder
"Write a product description using a trust-first structure.
Product: [name].
Audience: [who].
Key facts (use as truth): [materials, sizes, options, policies].
Brand voice: [paste Voice Card].
Constraints: no hype, no guarantees, no unverified turnaround
times.
Output:

Title options (5)
```

> *Short description (2-3 sentences)*
>
> *Full description (scannable with headings)*
>
> *5 FAQs*
>
> *A 1-sentence call to action*
> *End with: 'Claims to verify' list."*

This prompt makes marketing safer and more consistent.

Section 11.6: Social Content That Doesn't Burn You Out - The "Content Triangle"

Most people fail at social content because they try to be original every day.

Figure 11.4 – The content triangle (Proof / Process / Help)

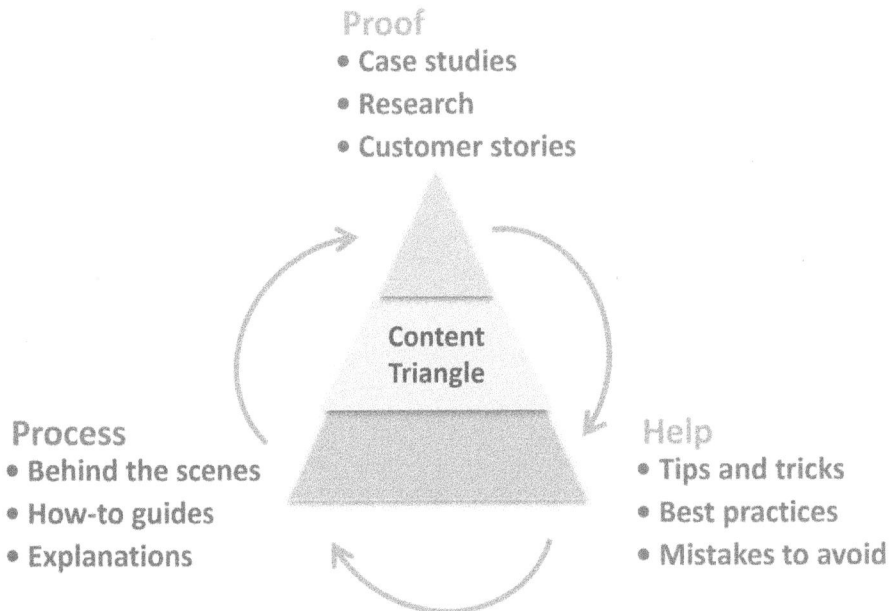

Proof
- Case studies
- Research
- Customer stories

Content
Triangle

Process
- Behind the scenes
- How-to guides
- Explanations

Help
- Tips and tricks
- Best practices
- Mistakes to avoid

Rotate weekly: Proof → Process → Help → Proof

A calmer strategy is to rotate three content types:

1. **Proof**: finished work, results, testimonials, before/after, case studies
2. **Process**: how it's made, behind the scenes, step-by-step, tools, decisions
3. **Help**: tips, FAQs, "how to choose," mistake prevention, simple education

This triangle keeps content grounded and repeatable.

ChatGPT helps by generating scripts, captions, and variations while maintaining your voice.

> **Prompt: Content triangle planner**
> "Create a 2-week content plan using the Content Triangle: Proof, Process, Help.
> Business: [type].
> Audience: [who].
> Goals: [awareness/leads/sales].
> Constraints: 3 posts/week, calm tone, no hype.
> Output:
>
> 6 post ideas (2 per category)
>
> For each: hook, main message, CTA, and caption
>
> Suggested reuse: how to repurpose each for email and a blog snippet
> Brand voice: [paste Voice Card]."

This creates consistency without requiring daily creativity.

Section 11.7: Email Marketing - The "Welcome, Value, Offer" Sequence

Email marketing works best when it is respectful and useful.

A simple sequence:

1. **Welcome:** set expectations and tone
2. **Value:** provide helpful info or a small win
3. **Offer:** invite a next step without pressure

ChatGPT can help you write emails that are consistent with your brand voice and policies.

```
Prompt: Welcome sequence builder
"Write a 3-email welcome sequence for [business].
Audience: [who].
Brand voice: [paste Voice Card].
Constraints: calm, helpful, no hype, avoid fear language.
Email 1: welcome + what to expect
Email 2: helpful guide (how to choose / FAQ)
Email 3: gentle offer + clear CTA
Output: subject lines + full emails + a compliance/claim check
list."
```

This approach builds trust and reduces unsubscribes because it respects the reader.

Section 11.8: Customer Communication as Marketing - Support is a Trust Engine

Customer communication is marketing, even if you don't call it that.

The way you respond to questions, delays, confusion, and complaints shapes your brand more than any ad.

A calm, high-trust customer message includes:

- Acknowledge and empathize (brief)
- Confirm understanding
- Provide next steps
- Set expectations carefully
- Offer options if appropriate
- Close with support

We covered the structure in Chapter 6; here we emphasize consistency across situations.

A practical professional tool is a Customer Response Library:

- Shipping/delivery questions
- Customization questions
- Pricing questions
- Refund/return policy questions
- Damaged item handling
- Delay updates
- "Can you do this?" requests

ChatGPT can help you draft and standardize this library.

```
Prompt: Customer response library builder
"Create a customer response library with 12 templates for common
situations.
Business: [type].
Policies (use as truth): [paste sanitized policy statements].
Brand voice: [paste Voice Card].
Constraints: no promises about timelines unless provided, no
blame, plain English, calm tone.
Output: for each template: subject line (if email), short
response, and an internal note listing commitments."
```

This saves time and ensures consistent quality.

Section 11.9: Claims, Proof, and Ethics - Marketing That Won't Backfire

Marketing often goes wrong when it makes claims that aren't supported.

In business communication, especially online, claims can become liabilities:

- "Best in the city"
- "Guaranteed results"
- "Fastest turnaround"
- "Always" and "never" language
- Unverified numbers

The solution is not to be timid. The solution is to be accurate and specific.

```
Instead of:
"We guarantee perfect results."

Use:
"We follow a clear process with quality checks to deliver
consistent results. If something isn't right, we'll work with you
to make it right according to our policy."

Instead of:
"Fast shipping."

Use:
"Typical turnaround is [X-Y days] (confirm current estimates at
checkout)."
```

Instead of:
"*Highest quality.*"

Use:
"*Made with [materials], finished with [process], and inspected before delivery.*"

ChatGPT can help you rewrite claims responsibly.

Prompt: Claims-to-proof rewrite
"*Rewrite this marketing text to remove unverified claims and replace them with proof-based language.*
Rules:

remove absolutes and guarantees unless explicitly policy-backed

keep it confident and clear

if a claim needs verification, label it 'Needs proof'
Text: [paste]."

This protects trust and reduces anxiety about "saying the wrong thing."

Figure 11.5 – Marketing claims guardrails (printable checklist)

Marketing Claims Guardrails
Use this before publishing: it keeps claims credible and promises controlled.

Avoid absolutes	Flag words like "always," "never," "guaranteed," "best," "perfect."
Verify timelines	Dates, shipping times, roadmaps, and "coming soon" need confirmation.
Support claims with proof	Add data, sources, examples, or customer evidence (and note limits).
Label unknowns	If you can't verify, say "TBD / depends / estimate" and explain conditions.
Keep promises controlled	Make commitments explicit (who/what/by when) or remove them.
Align with policy	Check legal/compliance rules, pricing policy, and approved terminology.

Section 11.10: SEO + Customer Communication - FAQ Pages That Do Real Work

One of the simplest, highest-value marketing assets is a good FAQ section.

FAQs:

- Reduce customer questions
- Increase confidence
- Improve search relevance
- Prevent misunderstandings
- Reduce support load

A professional FAQ is not just "what is your return policy?" It also includes:

- "How do I choose the right option?"
- "What information do you need from me?"
- "What happens if I change my mind?"
- "What does customization mean?"
- "How do you handle mistakes?"
- "What should I expect after ordering?"

ChatGPT can help you build an FAQ that is honest and helpful.

```
Prompt: FAQ generator (trust-first)
"Create an FAQ section for [product/service].
Audience: [who].
Policies: [paste sanitized policy text].
Tone: calm, helpful, plain English.
Output: 12 FAQs with short answers, plus a 'What to do next'
section.
Rules: do not invent policies; label unknowns."
```

Section 11.11: A Simple Content System - One Idea, Five Assets

Consistency becomes manageable when you reuse.

A single topic can become:

1. A short social post
2. A longer caption or story
3. A blog post section or article

4. An email newsletter section
5. A customer FAQ entry

This is how small teams create a content engine without burning out.

Figure 11.6 – One idea, five assets (repurposing map)

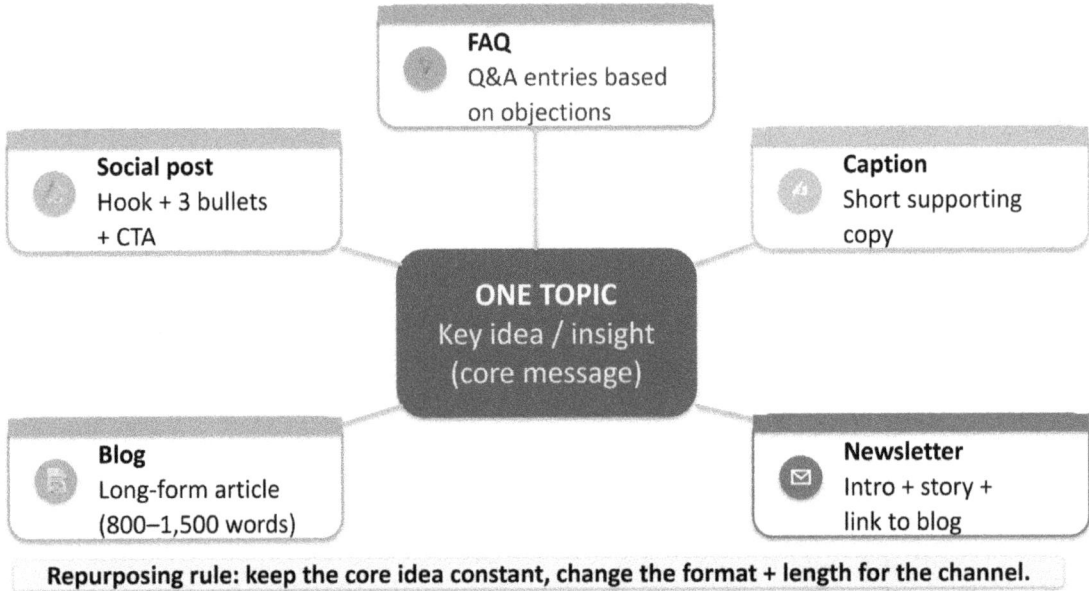

FAQ
Q&A entries based on objections

Social post
Hook + 3 bullets + CTA

Caption
Short supporting copy

ONE TOPIC
Key idea / insight (core message)

Blog
Long-form article (800–1,500 words)

Newsletter
Intro + story + link to blog

Repurposing rule: keep the core idea constant, change the format + length for the channel.

ChatGPT can help you "atomize" content.

```
Prompt: One idea → five assets
"Take this topic and turn it into five assets:

Social post (short)

Social caption (long)

Blog section (500-800 words)

Newsletter section (200-300 words)

FAQ entry (Q + answer)
Topic: [topic].
Audience: [who].
Brand voice: [paste Voice Card].
Constraints: calm tone, no hype, no unverified claims.
End with: key claims to verify."
```

This prompt creates output that is consistent and efficient.

Section 11.12: Worked Example - From Customer Intent to a Trustworthy Sales Page

Scenario (generic): You offer a customized service. Customers search for: "personalized gift for retirement" and "custom engraved award."

Step 1: Intent mapping

You identify:

- **Informational:** "What should I include on a retirement plaque?"
- **Comparison:** "wood vs metal plaques"
- **Transactional:** "custom retirement plaque order"
- **Service:** "custom engraving near me" (if local)

Step 2: Page structure

You create one page focused on "Custom Retirement Plaques" (one primary topic).

Step 3: Draft using SEO-friendly prompt

You include:

- Clear headline
- Benefits framed as outcomes (meaningful gift, lasting keepsake)
- Options (sizes, materials, personalization)
- Process (how to order, what you need from buyer)
- Proof (examples/testimonials if you have them)
- FAQs (turnaround, shipping, revisions, mistakes, care)

Step 4: Claim review

You run a claim scan:

- Any timeline mentioned must be verified
- Any "best" claims removed
- Ensure the page matches your actual capabilities

Step 5: Repurpose

You create:

- A social post: behind-the-scenes engraving
- An email: "What to include on a retirement gift"
- FAQ: "What information do we need for personalization?"

This is a sustainable content system: clear, helpful, and honest.

Practice Exercises

Use your Voice Card. Use sanitized policies. Verify claims and timelines before publishing.

Exercise 1 — Build your Brand Voice Card

> *Prompt:*
> *"Create a one-page Brand Voice Card for my business/team.*
> *Business: [type].*
> *Audience: [who].*
> *Offer: [what you provide].*
> *Values: [3-5].*
> *Tone: calm, confidence-building, practical, no hype.*
> *Output: Voice Card + 10 phrases we use + 10 phrases we avoid."*

Exercise 2 — Map customer intent for your offer

> *Prompt:*
> *"My audience is [audience].*
> *Our offer is [offer].*
> *Generate: 10 informational questions, 10 comparison questions, 10 transactional phrases, and 10 service/local phrases (if relevant).*
> *Then propose content ideas for each that would genuinely help a buyer decide."*

Exercise 3 — Draft an SEO-friendly page (plain English)

> *Prompt:*
> *"Draft a webpage for [topic].*
> *Primary keyword phrase: [phrase].*
> *Secondary phrases: [list].*
> *Intent: [informational/comparison/transactional].*
> *Brand voice: [paste Voice Card].*
> *Constraints: calm tone, no hype, no unverified claims.*
> *Output: title, meta description, H1, full page content with headings, 5 FAQs, CTA.*
> *End with claims to verify."*

Exercise 4 — Write a trust-first product/service description

> **Prompt:**
> "Write a trust-first description for [product/service].
> Key facts: [materials/options/process].
> Brand voice: [paste Voice Card].
> Constraints: no guarantees, no unverified timelines.
> Output: 5 title options, short description, full description, 5
> FAQs, CTA, claims to verify."

Exercise 5 — Create a 2-week content plan using the Content Triangle

> **Prompt:**
> "Create a 2-week content plan: 6 posts total, using
> Proof/Process/Help.
> Business: [type].
> Audience: [who].
> Goal: [awareness/leads/sales].
> Constraints: calm tone, 3 posts/week.
> Output: for each post: hook, message, CTA, caption, and reuse
> idea for email/blog."

Exercise 6 — Build a customer response library (12 templates)

> **Prompt:**
> "Create 12 customer response templates for common questions and
> issues.
> Policies (use as truth): [paste].
> Brand voice: [paste Voice Card].
> Constraints: no promises unless confirmed; calm, accountable
> tone.
> Output: templates + internal commitment notes."

Exercise 7 — Claims-to-proof rewrite

> **Prompt:**
> "Rewrite this marketing text to remove unverified claims and
> replace with proof-based language.
> Rules: remove absolutes; avoid guarantees; label 'Needs proof'
> where necessary.
> Text: [paste]."

Exercise 8 — Create an FAQ section that reduces support load

> *Prompt:*
> "Create a 12-question FAQ for [product/service].
> Policies: [paste].
> Brand voice: [paste Voice Card].
> Tone: calm and helpful.
> Rules: do not invent policies; label unknowns."

Exercise 9 — Email marketing: write a 3-email welcome sequence

> *Prompt:*
> "Write a 3-email welcome sequence for [offer].
> Audience: [who].
> Brand voice: [paste Voice Card].
> Constraints: helpful, calm, no hype.
> Email 1: welcome; Email 2: value guide; Email 3: gentle offer.
> Output: subject lines + emails + claim check list."

Exercise 10 — One idea, five assets repurposing drill

> *Prompt:*
> "Take this topic: [topic].
> Turn it into: short social post, long caption, blog section (500–800 words), newsletter section (200–300 words), FAQ entry.
> Brand voice: [paste Voice Card].
> Constraints: calm tone, no unverified claims.
> End with claims to verify."

Exercise 11 — Create a monthly content calendar skeleton

> *Prompt:*
> "Create a monthly content calendar skeleton for [business].
> Constraints: 2 posts/week + 1 email/week + 1 blog/month.
> Use the Content Triangle.
> Output: a week-by-week plan with themes and CTAs."

Exercise 12 — Build a marketing quality checklist (before publishing)

> *Prompt:*
> "Create a 15-item marketing quality checklist to run before publishing content.
> It must cover: clarity, audience fit, proof and claim accuracy, tone, CTA, policy alignment, and confidentiality.
> Keep it plain English and printable."

Skill Check

After completing this chapter, you should be able to:

- Create a practical Brand Voice Card and use it to keep messaging consistent
- Map customer intent into content ideas that help buyers decide
- Draft SEO-friendly pages in plain English with clean structure and honest claims
- Write product and service descriptions that convert through clarity and proof, not hype
- Build a sustainable content plan using the Proof/Process/Help Content Triangle
- Create a customer response library that saves time and preserves trust
- Rewrite marketing claims into proof-based language that won't backfire
- Build FAQs that reduce support load and increase customer confidence
- Repurpose one idea into five assets to scale content without burnout
- Use guardrails to verify claims and protect your brand's credibility

Chapter 12: From Chat to Systems - Automation without Coding

Most professionals do not need "automation" in the futuristic sense. They need relief from the same repeating work that drains attention every week:

- Writing the same updates in different words
- Turning meeting notes into action lists
- Rebuilding plans from scratch
- Repeating onboarding explanations
- Answering the same customer questions
- Reformatting information for different audiences
- Chasing follow-ups and status requests
- Converting messy notes into structured deliverables

You can automate much of that without writing code, not by building complex robots, but by building systems:

- Reusable prompt templates
- Standard workflows
- Input forms and checklists
- Consistent outputs
- Light "copy-paste pipelines" that remove friction
- Optional integrations later, once the workflow is stable

This chapter teaches a calm, step-by-step approach to building automation as a professional:

- Start with a repeatable workflow
- Standardize inputs
- Standardize outputs
- Create a prompt "engine" that produces those outputs
- Add guardrails for accuracy and confidentiality
- Only then, if needed, connect to tools

The goal is to turn ChatGPT from an occasional helper into a dependable operational assistant, without losing judgment or creating risk.

Section 12.1: What "Automation" Means in This Book

In plain English: **Automation is reducing repeated effort by making the same work happen the same way, faster, with fewer mistakes.**

In this book, "automation without coding" means:

- You can run it with prompts, templates, and workflows
- You don't need to write scripts
- You don't need a technical team
- You don't need to redesign your entire tool stack

We are not building software here. We are building professional systems.

A calm truth: **Most "automation" fails not because people lack tools. It fails because people automate unclear processes.**

So we begin with clarity.

Section 12.2: The Automation Rule - Standardize Before You Optimize

Here is a rule you can trust: **If you cannot do it reliably by hand, you cannot automate it reliably.**

Why? Because automation amplifies what you already do.

- If your workflow is unclear, automation produces inconsistent results faster.
- If your inputs are messy, automation produces messy outputs faster.
- If your outputs are unverified, automation spreads mistakes faster.

So the professional sequence is:

1. Clarify and document the workflow (Chapter 8)
2. Create a standard input format
3. Create a standard output format
4. Build a prompt template that connects the two
5. Add guardrails (Chapter 9)
6. Test on real examples
7. Improve through small iterations

This is calm, sustainable automation.

Section 12.3: The "Repeatability Test" - What to Automate First

Not everything should be automated. Automate what is repeatable.

A good automation candidate has these features:

- Happens often (weekly or daily)
- Has a clear input (notes, data, request)
- Has a clear output (email, summary, report, checklist)
- Has stable rules (same structure most of the time)
- Costs time or causes errors when done manually
- Is low to medium risk (Level 1 or Level 2)

Figure 12.1 – Repeatability test checklist

Repeatability Test

If most boxes are checked, it's a good candidate for a reusable prompt or SOP.

☐ Frequency	Happens often enough to justify a template (weekly/monthly).
☐ Stable rules	The rules don't change every time (clear policy/procedure).
☐ Clear inputs	You can list what information is needed up front.
☐ Clear outputs	You know what "done" looks like (format + acceptance criteria).
☐ Time cost	It takes meaningful time (≥15 minutes) without assistance.
☐ Error cost	Mistakes are expensive (rework, trust damage, delays).
☐ Risk level	Risk is understood and has matching verification steps.

Next step: turn the best candidates into a prompt + input form + review footer.

Examples of strong candidates:

- Meeting notes → decisions/action items + recap email
- Weekly status update → executive summary + risks + asks
- Customer inquiries → template responses (with policy constraints)
- SOP draft → checklists + training pack

- Brain dump → clarified tasks + daily plan
- Proposal brief → proposal draft structure

Examples of weak candidates (for non-coding automation):

- Complex forecasting requiring real-time data
- Compliance decisions without expert oversight
- Work that changes rules weekly
- Tasks involving sensitive data you cannot safely process

```
Prompt: Automation candidate selector
"Help me choose what to automate first.
Here are 10 repeating tasks I do: [list].
For each, score: frequency, time cost, error cost, clarity of
inputs, clarity of outputs, and risk level (1-3).
Then recommend the top 3 automation candidates and explain why.
Tone: practical."
```

Section 12.4: Systems Are Built From "Inputs" And "Outputs" - Define Them First

Automation begins by defining:

- The exact input you will provide
- The exact output you want

Most people fail because they ask for "help" without specifying outputs.

A strong system has a stable input form. Think of it like a mini questionnaire you fill out each time.

Example: Weekly status update system

Input form:

- Project name
- Status (on track / at risk / blocked)
- Progress (bullets)
- Risks (bullets)
- Asks/decisions needed
- Next steps (with owners if possible)
- Constraints (tone, length, audience)

Output form:

- Executive summary
- Risk list + mitigations
- Clear asks/decisions
- Next steps with owners
- Optional: stakeholder-tailored version

Once inputs and outputs are defined, the prompt becomes a "machine" you can run.

> **Prompt: Input/output SPEC builder**
> "Help me define a repeatable automation system for this workflow: [workflow].
> Output:
>
> A standard input form (fields I fill in each time)
>
> A standard output format (headings and structure)
>
> A 'definition of done' checklist
> Constraints: plain English, minimal fields, practical."

Section 12.5: Prompt Templates as "Programs" - How to Build a Reliable Prompt Engine

A prompt template is like a recipe. It works when it has:

- Role and tone constraints
- Clear inputs
- Clear outputs
- Guardrails (no invented facts, confidentiality)
- A review loop (commitments + claims scan)

Here is a reusable "Prompt Engine Template" you can adapt:

> **Prompt Engine Template (Copy-Paste)**
> Role: You are my professional assistant for [workflow].
> Audience: [who the output is for].
> Goal: Produce [output].
> Tone: calm, confident, practical, no hype.
>
> Inputs (use as truth; do not add facts):
>
> [Field 1]:

```
[Field 2]:

[Field 3]:

Output requirements:

Format: [headings / table / bullets / email]

Length: [limits]

Must include: [required sections]

Must avoid: [banned phrases or claims]

Guardrails:

Do not invent names, dates, numbers, or policy requirements

If missing information, write "Missing" and ask questions

Replace names with roles if sensitive

End with:

Commitment list (promises made)

Claims to verify (facts that must be checked)

A short verification checklist"
```

This template makes automation safe because it enforces structure and checks.

Figure 12.2 – Automation without coding: Inputs → Prompt Engine → Outputs → Review Loop

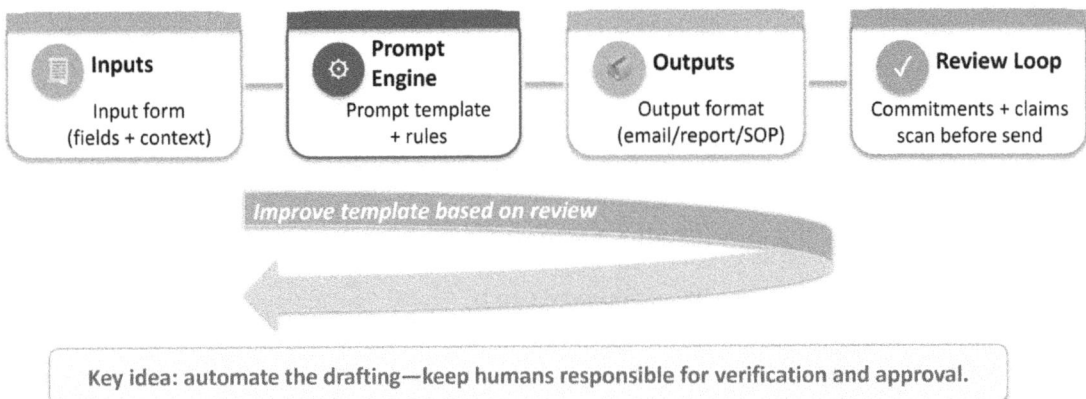

Key idea: automate the drafting—keep humans responsible for verification and approval.

Section 12.6: The "Prompt Stack" - One Workflow, Multiple Prompts

One workflow often needs multiple outputs.

Instead of cramming everything into one huge prompt, build a prompt stack:

- **Prompt A:** Convert raw notes into structured facts
- **Prompt B:** Produce the deliverable (email/report)
- **Prompt C:** Run review loops (commitment + claims scan)

This reduces errors because each prompt has one job.

Example: Meeting-to-output stack

```
Prompt A — Notes cleanup:
"Turn these notes into decisions, action items
(owner/deadline), open questions, and risks. Do not invent
details."

Prompt B — Recap email:
"Draft a recap email with purpose, decisions, action items,
and next steps. Keep it neutral."

Prompt C — Review:
"Commitment scan + claims scan. Suggest safer wording for any
risky commitments."
```

This is "automation without code": you run a small pipeline.

Figure 12.3 – Prompt stack model: Transform → Compose → Review

Transform
Turn raw inputs into structured notes (clean + organized)

Compose
Draft the output in the requested format (email, recap, memo)

Review
Scan commitments + claims, label unknowns add verification checklist

Example workflow
Meeting notes → recap email

Raw meeting notes
bullets, quotes, messy

Structured summary
decisions • actions • owners

Recap email draft
ask-first + next steps

Final send-ready
claims + commitments checked

Stack prompts to separate jobs: cleaning → drafting → trust checks. This reduces randomness and rework.

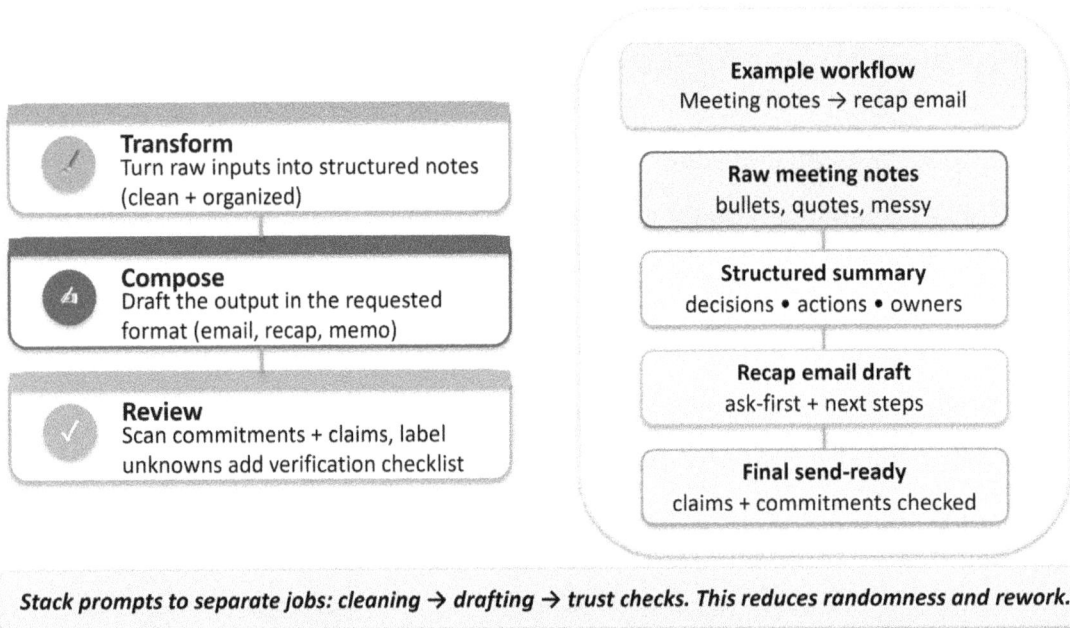

It is fast because each prompt is reusable. It is safe because review is built in.

Section 12.7: Building a Reusable Prompt Library (The Right Way)

A prompt library fails when it becomes a junk drawer.

A prompt library succeeds when it:

- Contains only prompts you actually use
- Uses consistent fields and formatting
- Has clear names and use cases
- Includes examples and guardrails
- Is easy to find and copy

A practical library structure:

- Daily planning prompts
- Writing prompts (emails, updates, proposals)
- Operations prompts (SOPs, checklists, training)
- Meeting prompts (agenda, notes → actions, recap)
- Decision prompts (frame/options/test/record)
- Marketing prompts (voice card, product descriptions, FAQs)

- Trust prompts (commitment scan, claims scan)

Figure 12.4 – Prompt library structure (categories)

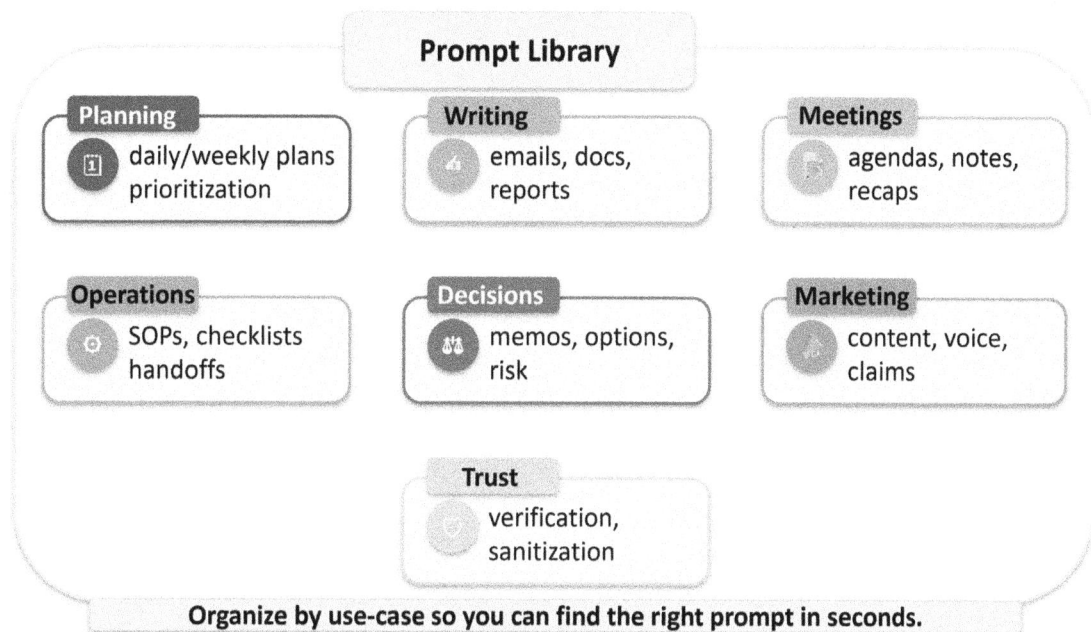

Prompt Library

Planning — daily/weekly plans prioritization

Writing — emails, docs, reports

Meetings — agendas, notes, recaps

Operations — SOPs, checklists handoffs

Decisions — memos, options, risk

Marketing — content, voice, claims

Trust — verification, sanitization

Organize by use-case so you can find the right prompt in seconds.

Start with 10 prompts maximum. Expand only when stable.

```
Prompt: Prompt library builder
"Help me build a prompt library of 10 high-value templates for my
role.
My role: [role].
My recurring workflows: [list].


Constraints: privacy, accuracy guardrails, calm tone.
Output:

Prompt name

When to use it

Copy-paste template with placeholders

Built-in guardrails and review loop."
```

Section 12.8: Automation Patterns - The Big Three You'll Use Most

Most non-coding automation falls into three patterns.

Pattern 1: Transform

Turn one form of information into another.
Examples:

- Notes → action list
- Brain dump → task plan
- SOP → checklists
- Customer feedback → themes + responses

Pattern 2: Compose

Generate a structured draft from a brief.
Examples:

- Brief → proposal
- Brief → executive update
- Brief → customer email
- Brief → training outline

Pattern 3: Review

Check and improve an existing draft.
Examples:

- Tone adjustment
- Commitment audit
- Claims verification checklist
- Bias and neutrality check

If you master these three patterns, you can automate most professional writing and operations tasks without code.

> *Prompt: Pattern selector*
> *"I have this task: [task].*
> *Classify it as Transform, Compose, or Review.*
> *Then give me a prompt template for it with guardrails and an end-of-output review loop."*

Section 12.9: Tool Connections (Optional) - When to Integrate and When Not To

Many tools advertise "AI automation" integrations. Some are helpful. Some add complexity.

A calm rule: **Only integrate after your workflow is stable with copy-paste.**

Why?

- You need to know what inputs and outputs work
- You need to know where mistakes happen
- You need to know what guardrails are required
- You need to know what you must verify

Once stable, integrations can save time.

Examples of light integrations (conceptually):

- Forms that collect input fields
- Templates stored in a shared workspace
- A standard document template for decision records
- A project management template for action items

This book stays tool-neutral. Your organization's environment determines what is allowed. The professional approach is:

Start simple. Automate the mental work first. Integrate later if justified.

Section 12.10: Safety and Governance - How to Prevent Automation from Spreading Errors

Automation amplifies both strengths and mistakes.

So you need governance, even if light.

Governance elements for non-coding automation:

- Approved prompt templates (versioned)
- Clear boundaries on what data can be used
- Built-in commitment and claims scans for external messages
- A review requirement for Level 2 and Level 3 outputs
- A quick feedback loop for improving templates

- A place to store "gold standard" examples

Figure 12.5 – Prompt governance: versioning and review by risk level

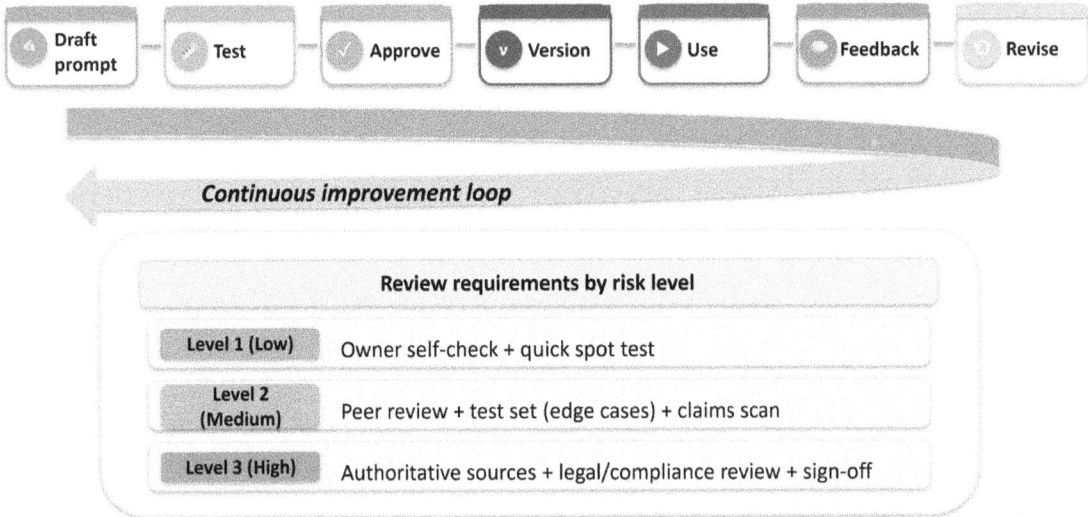

Review requirements by risk level	
Level 1 (Low)	Owner self-check + quick spot test
Level 2 (Medium)	Peer review + test set (edge cases) + claims scan
Level 3 (High)	Authoritative sources + legal/compliance review + sign-off

A practical way to govern is to treat prompts like SOPs (Chapter 8). They are operational assets.

> **Prompt: Prompt governance standard**
> "Create a lightweight governance standard for a shared prompt library.
> Include: naming conventions, version control, review requirements by risk level, what data cannot be included, and how updates are approved.
> Constraints: minimal overhead, plain English."

Section 12.11: Worked Example 1 - Automating Weekly Status Updates (Without Losing Trust)

Let's build a real system.

Figure 12.6 – Weekly status update system: input form + output template

Input form
Quick capture (5 minutes)

Project / Workstream	Name + link
This week: outcomes	3 bullets
Progress	What moved? (metrics if any)
Blockers / risks	What needs help?
Next week plan	Top 1–3 priorities
Asks	Decisions / approvals needed

Standard update
Consistent format for stakeholders

Weekly Status — [Project] — Week of [DATE]

Summary (3–5 lines)	• What changed • Why it matters • What's next
Progress	• Outcome 1 • Outcome 2 • Outcome 3
Metrics (if any)	• KPI: __ • Trend: __
Risks / blockers	• Risk: __ (mitigation) • Blocker: __ (owner)
Asks	• Decision needed: __ • Help needed from: __
Next week	• Priority 1 • Priority 2 • Priority 3

Goal: Produce a weekly status update that is executive-ready, consistent, and fast.

Step 1: Define input form

- Project name
- Status (on track/at risk/blocked)
- Progress (3 bullets max)
- Risks (3 bullets max)
- Asks/decisions (1–3 bullets)
- Next steps (with owners if possible)
- Notes (optional)

Step 2: Define output format

- Headline status
- So what / now what
- Progress
- Risks + mitigations
- Asks/decisions needed
- Next steps with owners
- Verification checklist

Step 3: Build prompt engine

- You create a template prompt that you fill in weekly.

Step 4: Add review loop

- You run commitment and claims scans before sending.

Step 5: Save and refine

Each week, you capture improvements:

- Which sections were unclear?
- Which stakeholders asked follow-ups?
- What could be preemptively clarified?

Result:

Status updates become faster, clearer, and less stressful. Leadership receives consistent communication. You reduce "surprise risk."

This is automation without coding: a stable input form + stable prompt + stable output + review loop.

Section 12.12: Worked Example 2 - Meeting Notes → Actions → Recap Email

Goal:

After a meeting, produce:

- Decisions
- Action items with owners and deadlines
- Open questions
- Recap email

Step 1: Prompt A (Transform)

> *"Turn these notes into decisions, action items (owner/deadline), open questions, and risks. Do not invent details; label unknowns as Missing."*

Step 2: Prompt B (Compose)

> *"Using the structured output, draft a recap email. Ask is in first two sentences. Tone neutral. Include next steps."*

Step 3: Prompt C (Review)

> *"Run commitment scan and claims scan. Suggest safer wording for any risky commitments."*

Step 4: Store the outputs

- Save recap emails as examples
- Save action list format
- Update prompt if needed

Result:

Meetings stop being "time spent" and become "outputs produced." This reduces rework and anxiety because responsibilities and timelines are explicit.

Section 12.13: Worked Example 3 - Customer Questions Library as a System

Goal:

Reduce time spent answering repeat customer questions and increase consistency.

Step 1: Gather common questions

List 20 questions you receive most often.

Step 2: Provide policy truth

Paste sanitized policy statements (returns, shipping, customization, etc.).

Step 3: Generate templates with constraints

- No promises unless verified
- Calm tone
- Plain English

- Internal commitments list

Step 4: Standardize a workflow

When a question arrives:

- Choose template
- Add specifics (verified)
- Run commitment scan if external
- Send
- Save any new variations

Result:

Customer communication becomes consistent and faster. Trust increases because customers receive clear, accurate responses.

Section 12.14: The Long-Term Benefit - Systems Create Calm

The biggest benefit of automation is not speed. It is predictability.

When you have:

- A daily planning system
- A writing pipeline
- SOPs and checklists
- A prompt library
- A trust workflow

You are less dependent on mood, memory, or inspiration.

You become operationally confident.

That is what "AI without the anxiety" looks like in practice: not magic, but reliable systems.

Practice Exercises

Use sanitized inputs. Apply guardrails. For external communications, always run commitment and claims scans.

Exercise 1 — Choose your first automation candidate

> **Prompt:**
> "Here are 10 repeating tasks I do: [list].
> Score each for frequency, time cost, error cost, clarity of inputs, clarity of outputs, and risk level.
> Recommend the top 3 to automate first and why."

Exercise 2 — Define inputs and outputs for one workflow

> **Prompt:**
> "Help me define a repeatable system for [workflow].
> Output:
>
> Standard input form (fields)
>
> Standard output format (headings)
>
> Definition of done checklist
> Constraints: minimal fields, plain English."

Exercise 3 — Build a Prompt Engine Template for your workflow

> **Prompt:**
> "Create a copy-paste prompt template (Prompt Engine) for [workflow].
> It must include: role, audience, goal, input fields, output requirements, guardrails, and end-of-output commitment + claims scans."

Exercise 4 — Build a prompt stack (Transform → Compose → Review)

> **Prompt:**
> "Design a prompt stack for this workflow: [workflow].
> Output: three prompts:
> A) Transform (clean and structure inputs)
> B) Compose (generate deliverable)
> C) Review (commitment scan + claims scan + safer wording)
> Constraints: no invented facts; label missing info."

Exercise 5 — Create your top 10 prompt library

> *Prompt:*
> "Build a prompt library of 10 templates for my role.
> My role: [role].
> Recurring workflows: [list].
> Constraints: calm tone, privacy guardrails, verification checklists.
> Output: prompt name, when to use, copy-paste template with placeholders."

Exercise 6 — Build a weekly status update system

> *Prompt:*
> "Create a weekly status update automation system.
> Output: input form + output template + prompt engine + review loop.
> Audience: leadership.
> Constraints: concise, neutral, no blame, no unverified claims."

Exercise 7 — Automate meeting recap outputs

> *Prompt:*
> "Create a meeting recap automation system.
> Inputs: my rough notes.
> Outputs: decisions, action items with owners/deadlines, open questions, recap email.
> Add guardrails: do not invent details; label unknowns; include commitment scan before sending."

Exercise 8 — Create a customer response library system

> *Prompt:*
> "Build a system to generate customer email responses from: question + relevant policy snippet + tone.
> Output: response email + internal commitments list + claims to verify.
> Constraints: calm, accountable, no overpromising."

Exercise 9 — Build a prompt governance standard

> *Prompt:*
> "Create a one-page governance standard for prompt templates used by a team.
> Include naming, versioning, review requirements by risk level,

prohibited data types, and feedback loop.
Keep it lightweight and plain English."

Exercise 10 — Debug an automation that produces inconsistent results

Prompt:
"My prompt template produces inconsistent outputs.
Here is the prompt: [paste].
Here are two outputs: [paste].
Diagnose why inconsistency occurs and rewrite the prompt to
enforce structure, guardrails, and output formatting.
Include a small test plan."

Exercise 11 — Create a "gold standard" example set

Prompt:
"Help me create 3 gold standard examples for [workflow] showing
what excellent output looks like.
Use placeholders where needed.
Then write a checklist that my future outputs should match."

Exercise 12 — Design a 30-day automation adoption plan

Prompt:
"Create a 30-day adoption plan for using these prompt templates
consistently.
Constraints: minimal disruption, small weekly improvements,
maintain quality.
Output: weekly focus, habits, and how to measure success."

Skill Check

After completing this chapter, you should be able to:

- Define automation in practical terms: standard inputs, standard outputs, and repeatable workflows
- Choose strong automation candidates using the repeatability test and risk levels
- Build a prompt engine that reliably produces structured deliverables without inventing facts
- Use a prompt stack (Transform → Compose → Review) to reduce errors and improve consistency
- Create a small prompt library organized by workflows that you actually use

- Add guardrails and review loops (commitment scan + claims scan) to protect trust
- Understand when to integrate with tools and when to keep automation simple
- Establish lightweight governance so templates stay accurate, safe, and effective over time

Chapter 13: Advanced Prompting Frameworks for Professionals

By now, you've learned how to write clear prompts, how to use guardrails, and how to build repeatable workflows. This chapter goes deeper.

"Advanced prompting" is not about clever tricks. It is about reliable thinking support.

Professionals don't need prompts that sound impressive. They need prompts that:

- Produce consistent outputs under time pressure
- Reduce ambiguity and rework
- Make reasoning visible
- Surface assumptions and risks
- Create decision-ready structure
- Support verification and trust

In other words: **advanced prompting is operational prompting**.

This chapter teaches a set of frameworks you can use across business contexts: planning, writing, operations, decision-making, analysis, and communication.

You will learn:

- How to choose the right prompt structure for the task
- Frameworks for clarity, analysis, and decision support
- How to force the assistant to label assumptions and unknowns
- How to handle messy inputs (notes, fragments, conflicting requirements)
- How to build "prompt stacks" that behave predictably
- Debugging prompts when outputs are inconsistent
- A professional standard for "good prompts" you can teach to others

Throughout this chapter, we maintain the core principles from earlier:

- Plain English
- No invented facts
- Human judgment stays central
- Guardrails and review loops are non-negotiable for medium and high risk

Section 13.1: The Four Functions of a Professional Prompt

Most prompts serve one or more of four functions. Knowing the function helps you structure the prompt correctly.

Figure 13.1 – The four prompt functions: Generate / Transform / Evaluate / Simulate

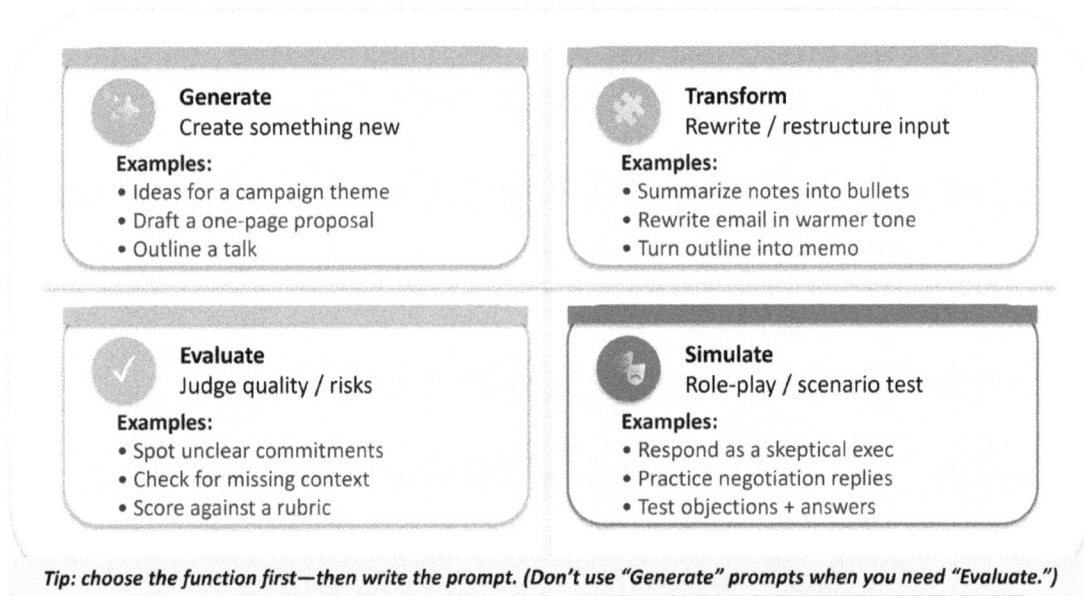

Generate
Create something new

Examples:
- Ideas for a campaign theme
- Draft a one-page proposal
- Outline a talk

Transform
Rewrite / restructure input

Examples:
- Summarize notes into bullets
- Rewrite email in warmer tone
- Turn outline into memo

Evaluate
Judge quality / risks

Examples:
- Spot unclear commitments
- Check for missing context
- Score against a rubric

Simulate
Role-play / scenario test

Examples:
- Respond as a skeptical exec
- Practice negotiation replies
- Test objections + answers

Tip: choose the function first—then write the prompt. (Don't use "Generate" prompts when you need "Evaluate.")

Function 1: Generate (Compose)

You provide a brief; the assistant drafts an output.
Examples: email, proposal, report section, SOP draft.

Function 2: Transform

You provide messy information; the assistant converts it into a structured form.
Examples: notes → action items, brain dump → tasks, raw feedback → themes.

Function 3: Evaluate (Review)

You provide a draft; the assistant critiques and improves it against criteria.
Examples: tone adjustment, clarity improvement, commitment scan, bias check.

Function 4: Simulate (Practice)

You use the assistant as a role-play partner or scenario generator.
Examples: stakeholder rehearsal, training scenarios, negotiation practice.

Advanced prompting begins by selecting the function intentionally.

```
Prompt: Function selector (fast)
"My task: [describe].
Classify it as Generate, Transform, Evaluate, or Simulate.
Then propose the best prompt structure and a copy-paste
template."
```

Section 13.2: The "SPEC" Framework - The Most Important Advanced Prompting Skill

A "SPEC" is a short specification: what you want and what you don't want.

In business, a SPEC reduces rework.

The SPEC Framework:

S — Situation: context and constraints
P — Purpose: the goal and audience
E — Expectations: output format, length, must-haves
C — Constraints: do-not list, guardrails, risk controls

Figure 13.2 – SPEC framework card (printable)

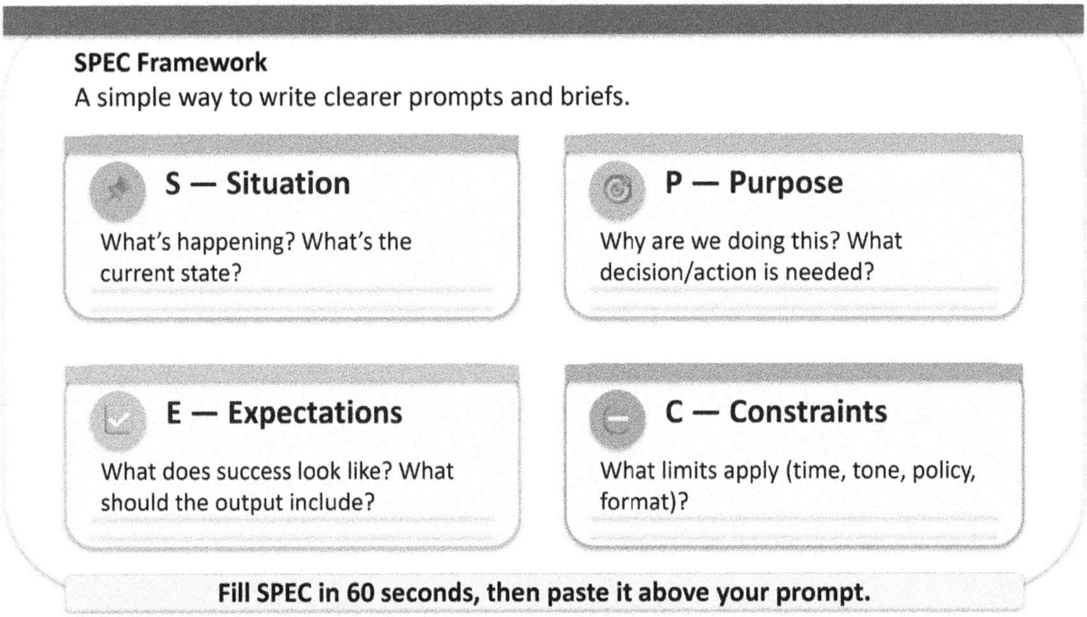

SPEC Framework

A simple way to write clearer prompts and briefs.

S — Situation

What's happening? What's the current state?

P — Purpose

Why are we doing this? What decision/action is needed?

E — Expectations

What does success look like? What should the output include?

C — Constraints

What limits apply (time, tone, policy, format)?

Fill SPEC in 60 seconds, then paste it above your prompt.

Here is a SPEC prompt template:

```
SPEC Template (Copy-Paste):
"Situation: [what's happening, key facts–sanitized]
Purpose: [what you need + who it's for]
Expectations:

Output type:

Format:

Length:

Must include:
Constraints:

Must avoid:

Do not invent facts, names, dates, or numbers

If missing info, label "Missing" and ask questions

End with: commitments + claims to verify + verification
checklist"
```

This template is "advanced" because it enforces professional control.

Most low-quality prompts fail because they skip Expectations and Constraints.

Section 13.3: The "Role + Rules + Output" Framework - Simple and Powerful

Another advanced prompt pattern is:

1. **Role:** who the assistant is acting as
2. **Rules:** how it must behave
3. **Output:** what it must produce and how

Example:

> Role: "Act as a business analyst."
> Rules: "Use only my inputs as truth; do not invent facts; label unknowns; keep it plain English."
> Output: "Executive summary + findings + options + recommendation + risks + next steps."

This framework is especially good for reports and decision memos.

```
Prompt:
"Act as a [role].
Rules:

Use my inputs as truth; do not add facts

Label unknowns as 'Missing'

State assumptions explicitly

Keep tone calm and plain English
Output:

[structured headings]
Input: [paste sanitized notes]."
```

If you only adopt one advanced technique, adopt explicit Rules. They prevent the assistant from guessing.

Section 13.4: The "Assumptions First" Framework - How to Avoid Confident Wrongness

In professional work, assumptions are often the hidden source of conflict.

A strong prompt forces assumptions into the open early.

Figure 13.3 – Assumptions first workflow

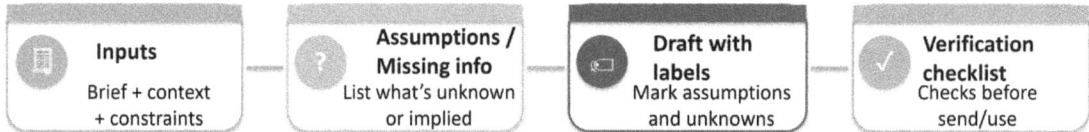

Inputs	Assumptions / Missing info	Draft with labels	Verification checklist
Brief + context + constraints	List what's unknown or implied	Mark assumptions and unknowns	Checks before send/use

Assumptions First rule:
Before drafting, surface missing info. Then label assumptions in the draft so verification is easy.

Shortcut: If you can't verify a claim now, label it and move it into the checklist.

Assumptions First prompt:
"Before you draft the output, list:

What you are assuming

What you are uncertain about

What you need from me to be accurate
Then draft with assumptions clearly labeled."

This approach is especially useful when:

- Inputs are incomplete
- Stakeholders disagree
- Requirements are unclear
- You are dealing with timelines or commitments

Prompt:
"Task: [task].
Inputs: [what you know].
Before drafting: list assumptions and missing info.
Then draft using only verified inputs, labeling assumptions inline."

This is a reliability upgrade. It prevents the assistant from filling gaps invisibly.

Section 13.5: The "Decision Memo" Framework - Options, Tradeoffs, Recommendation

Professionals often need to write memos that make decisions possible.

A decision memo needs:

- Context
- Decision to make
- Options
- Tradeoffs
- Risks
- Recommendation (with assumptions)
- Next steps

ChatGPT is very good at structuring decision memos if you provide the facts.

```
Decision memo prompt:
"Draft a decision memo for [audience].
Decision needed: [decision].
Context (facts only): [paste].
Options: [list if known; otherwise ask].
Constraints: [budget/time/policy].
Output format:

Decision statement

Context

Options (2-4)

Tradeoffs (pros/cons)

Risks and mitigations

Recommendation (state assumptions)

Next steps
Rules: do not invent facts; label missing info; keep plain
English."
```

This framework is advanced because it produces decision-ready structure consistently.

Section 13.6: The "Critique Then Rewrite" Framework - How to Get High-Quality Edits

If you ask ChatGPT, "Improve this," you may get changes you don't want.

A better approach is critique-first:

1. Identify what's wrong and why
2. Propose improvements
3. Rewrite using the improvements
4. Explain what changed (briefly)

> **Prompt:**
> "Critique this text against these criteria: [criteria].
> Then rewrite it.
> After rewriting, list the top 5 changes you made and why.
> Rules: do not add new facts; keep tone calm and professional.
> Text: [paste]."

This is especially valuable for:

- customer communications
- executive updates
- proposals
- sensitive internal messages

It makes the editing logic visible, which increases trust.

Section 13.7: The "Structure Lock" Framework - For Consistent Outputs, Every Time

In automation, inconsistency is the enemy.

A structure lock prompt forces the assistant to use the same headings and formats every time.

Figure 13.4 – Structure lock example (weekly update template)

Weekly Update — [Project] — Week of [DATE]
Structure lock: headings are fixed and each section has a word limit.

SUMMARY	≤ 60 words	3–5 lines: what changed + why it matters
PROGRESS	≤ 120 words	Bullets: outcomes delivered this week
RISKS / BLOCKERS	≤ 80 words	What might slip + what you need
ASKS	≤ 60 words	Decisions or help needed (owner + by when)
NEXT WEEK	≤ 100 words	Top 1–3 priorities + expected outputs

🔒 Structure lock benefit: consistent updates are easier to scan, compare, and act on.

> *Structure lock prompt:*
> *"Output must follow this exact structure and headings (do not add or remove sections):*
> *A) …*
> *B) …*
> *C) …*
> *Rules:*
>
> *Keep each section under X words*
>
> *Use bullet points only in sections B and D*
>
> *Use plain English*
>
> *Do not invent facts*
> *Input: [paste]."*

This is advanced prompting because it treats the output like a form, not a freeform essay.

Use structure lock when:

- You are creating recurring updates
- You are generating SOP checklists
- You are writing templates
- You need outputs to be comparable week to week

Section 13.8: The "Conflict Resolution" Framework - When Requirements Collide

Professionals often deal with conflicting requirements:

- "Make it shorter but include all details."
- "Be direct but also very warm."
- "Move fast but verify everything."
- "Keep it simple but also comprehensive."

ChatGPT can help you resolve conflict if you ask it to surface tensions.

```
Conflict resolution prompt:
"These requirements conflict.
Requirements: [list].
Task: [task].
Do three things:

Identify conflicts and why they conflict

Propose 2-3 compromise approaches

Ask me the minimum questions needed to choose an approach
Then draft using the chosen approach (label assumptions)."
```

This reduces back-and-forth. It also prevents the assistant from satisfying one requirement while silently violating another.

Section 13.9: The "Examples as Constraints" Framework - How to Teach Your Style

One of the strongest ways to get consistent outputs is to provide examples.

But examples must be used carefully. You want the assistant to follow the style and structure, not to copy content inappropriately.

Use "examples as constraints" by saying:

- "Match the structure and tone"
- "Do not reuse the specific wording"
- "Use this as a style guide"

> *Prompt:*
> *"Use the examples below as a style guide for structure and tone only.*
> *Do not copy wording.*
> *Now draft a new [deliverable] for [context].*
> *Examples: [paste 1-2 examples].*
> *Constraints: [tone, length, guardrails]."*

This framework is extremely effective for:

- executive updates
- customer response templates
- proposals
- marketing posts in a consistent voice

It is also safer than asking for "write like [famous person]," which can be ethically problematic.

Section 13.10: The "Error-Finding" Framework - Make the Assistant Look for Problems

A professional use of AI is to ask it to look for issues you might miss.

Error-finding prompt types:

- Ambiguity detection
- Missing information
- Logic gaps
- Inconsistent numbers or dates
- Stakeholder concerns
- Risk triggers
- Compliance flags (where relevant)

> *Prompt:*
> *"Act as a reviewer.*
> *Find problems in this draft: ambiguity, missing details, risky commitments, unsupported claims, and tone issues.*

```
Then propose specific fixes.
Rules: do not add new facts; keep it practical.
Text: [paste]."
```

This prompt turns ChatGPT into a "second set of eyes" (as in Chapter 6) and is one of the most reliable advanced uses.

Section 13.11: Debugging Prompts - Why Outputs Go Wrong and How to Fix Them

When outputs are inconsistent or unusable, the problem usually falls into one of these categories:

1. **Inputs are incomplete or unclear**
   Fix: add the Assumptions First step; add required fields.

2. **Output format is under-specified**
   Fix: use structure lock; specify headings, length, and section limits.

3. **Constraints are missing**
   Fix: add do-not lists, guardrails, and "do not invent facts."

4. **The task is overloaded**
   Fix: split into a prompt stack (Transform → Compose → Review).

5. **Tone is under-defined**
   Fix: use Voice Card or tone examples; add phrases to avoid.

6. **The assistant is guessing**
   Fix: require "Missing" labels and questions; require claims-to-verify list.

```
Prompt: Prompt debugger
"Here is my prompt: [paste].
Here is the output I got: [paste].
My desired output: [describe].
Diagnose why it failed (be specific), then rewrite my prompt to
enforce structure, constraints, and guardrails.
Include a small test plan with 3 example inputs."
```

This is a professional tool. It turns frustrating prompting into a solvable problem.

Figure 13.5 – Prompt debugging checklist

Prompt debugging checklist

Inputs clarity
Are the instructions clear and specific?
limit: 50 words

Output format
Is the desired response correctly structured?
limit: 50 words

Constraints
Are there any rules or restrictions?
limit: 50 words

Overload
Is the prompt too long or complex?
limit: 40 words

Tone
Does the tone match the intent?
limit: 40 words

Guessing risk
Does it rely on unstated assumptions?
limit: 40 words

Test plan
Have you tested variants and improvements?

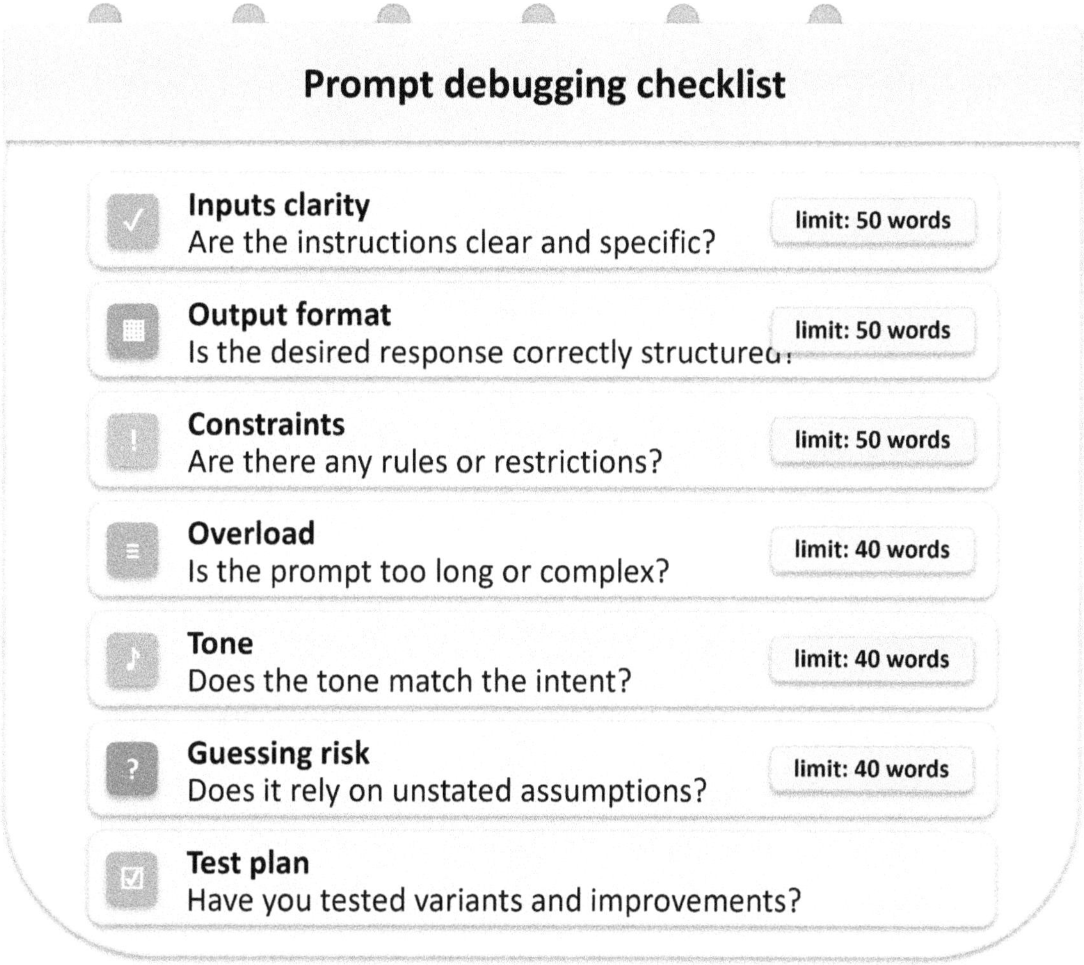

Section 13.12: Advanced Frameworks You Can Reuse Every Week (A Professional Set)

Here is a curated set of advanced frameworks you can reuse:

1. SPEC (Situation, Purpose, Expectations, Constraints)
2. Role + Rules + Output
3. Assumptions First
4. Structure Lock
5. Decision Memo
6. Critique then Rewrite

7. Prompt Stack (Transform → Compose → Review)
8. Examples as Constraints
9. Conflict Resolution
10. Error-Finding Review

These are not "hacks." They are operational patterns.

If you teach these to a team, you standardize how people work with AI, improving quality and reducing risk.

Section 13.13: Mini Case Studies - Applying Advanced Prompting in Real Work

Case Study 1: Executive update inconsistency

Problem: Updates vary by person and week. Leadership asks follow-ups.

Fix:

- Structure lock the update format
- Require "so what / now what"
- Add risks and asks
- Add commitment scan

Result: Consistent updates, fewer follow-ups.

Case Study 2: SOP drafts feel generic and untrustworthy

Problem: SOP drafts don't match reality.

Fix:

- Source-first rules
- Assumptions First step
- Exception capture prompt
- Checklist extraction

Result: SOPs become usable job aids.

Case Study 3: Marketing copy feels hyped or robotic

Problem: Tone mismatch; trust suffers.

Fix:

- Voice Card
- Examples as constraints
- Claims-to-proof rewrite
- Structure lock for product descriptions

Result: Consistent, calm marketing.

Case Study 4: Conflicting stakeholder requirements

Problem: Requirements collide; drafts never satisfy.

Fix:

- Conflict resolution prompt
- Minimum clarifying questions
- Choose compromise approach explicitly

Result: Faster alignment and less back-and-forth.

These show the power of advanced prompting: it's about reliability and coherence.

Practice Exercises

Use sanitized inputs. Apply guardrails. For external work, run commitment and claims scans.

Exercise 1 — Classify your prompt by function

```
Prompt:
"My task is: [task].
Classify it as Generate, Transform, Evaluate, or Simulate.
Then give me a best-fit prompt structure and a copy-paste
template with guardrails."
```

Exercise 2 — Rewrite a weak prompt using SPEC

> *Prompt:*
> "Here is my weak prompt: [paste].
> Rewrite it using the SPEC framework.
> Then explain what you added and why, in plain English."

Exercise 3 — Build an Assumptions First prompt

> *Prompt:*
> "Create an Assumptions First prompt template for [workflow].
> It must: list assumptions, label missing info, ask questions,
> then draft the output with assumptions labeled."

Exercise 4 — Structure lock a recurring output

> *Prompt:*
> "Create a structure-locked template for [recurring output].
> Include fixed headings, word limits per section, and rules about
> bullets/paragraphs.
> Then provide a copy-paste prompt template."

Exercise 5 — Create a decision memo from messy notes

> *Prompt:*
> "Draft a decision memo from these notes.
> Decision needed: [decision].
> Notes (facts): [paste].
> Output: decision statement, context, options, tradeoffs, risks,
> recommendation (assumptions labeled), next steps.
> Rules: do not invent facts; label missing info."

Exercise 6 — Critique then rewrite an email

> *Prompt:*
> "Critique this email against clarity, tone, and actionability.
> Then rewrite it.
> After rewriting, list the top 5 changes and why.
> Rules: do not add new facts; keep it calm.
> Email: [paste]."

Exercise 7 — Use examples as constraints (without copying)

> **Prompt:**
> "Use the examples below as a style guide for structure and tone only. Do not copy wording.
> Now draft a new [deliverable] for [context].
> Examples: [paste].
> Constraints: [tone/length/guardrails]."

Exercise 8 — Resolve conflicting requirements

> **Prompt:**
> "These requirements conflict: [list].
> Task: [task].
> Identify conflicts, propose compromise approaches, ask the minimum questions, then draft using the chosen approach.
> Label assumptions."

Exercise 9 — Build a prompt stack for a workflow

> **Prompt:**
> "Design a prompt stack (Transform → Compose → Review) for [workflow].
> Provide all three prompts with guardrails and output structure."

Exercise 10 — Error-finding review on a draft

> **Prompt:**
> "Act as a reviewer.
> Find problems in this draft: ambiguity, missing info, risky commitments, unsupported claims, and tone issues.
> Then propose specific fixes.
> Rules: do not add new facts.
> Draft: [paste]."

Exercise 11 — Debug a prompt that produces inconsistent outputs

> **Prompt:**
> "Here is my prompt: [paste].
> Here is an output that missed the mark: [paste].
> My desired output: [describe].
> Diagnose why it failed, rewrite the prompt to enforce structure and guardrails, and give a 3-case test plan."

Exercise 12 — Teach these frameworks to someone else

> *Prompt:*
> *"Create a 20-minute mini-training to teach a team advanced prompting for business use.*
> *Include: SPEC, Assumptions First, Structure Lock, and Prompt Stack.*
> *Output: outline + examples + a short practice activity."*

Skill Check

After completing this chapter, you should be able to:

- Identify whether a task is Generate, Transform, Evaluate, or Simulate and choose the correct prompt structure
- Write SPEC-based prompts that reduce rework by clarifying situation, purpose, expectations, and constraints
- Use Role + Rules + Output prompts to control behavior and avoid invented details
- Force assumptions and missing information into the open before drafting
- Lock structure for recurring outputs so they are consistent and comparable
- Use decision memo prompting to create options, tradeoffs, and recommendations with labeled assumptions
- Use critique-then-rewrite prompts to improve drafts with visible reasoning
- Build prompt stacks that separate transforming inputs, composing deliverables, and reviewing for risk
- Debug failing prompts systematically and improve them with tests
- Create a small set of advanced frameworks you can reuse and teach across your organization

Chapter 14: Personal Knowledge Management with AI

Most professionals don't have a knowledge problem. They have a retrieval problem.

You have information everywhere:

- Email threads
- Meeting notes
- Documents and spreadsheets
- Chat messages
- Project trackers
- Web pages and PDFs
- Personal reminders and to-do lists
- Ideas that show up at inconvenient times

The cost isn't only time. The cost is cognitive load.

When you can't retrieve what you already know:

- You redo work
- You hesitate to make decisions
- You lose context
- You forget commitments
- You feel behind even when you're working hard

Personal Knowledge Management (PKM) is the practice of capturing what matters, organizing it so it can be found, and using it to support decisions and action.

This chapter shows how to use ChatGPT to strengthen PKM without turning your life into a filing cabinet.

You will learn:

- A plain-English PKM system you can run with simple tools
- How to capture notes that are actually retrievable
- How to turn notes into "knowledge assets" (briefs, checklists, context packets)
- How to build a reusable personal prompt library tied to your knowledge
- How to review and maintain your knowledge system
- How to protect privacy and prevent over-sharing
- How to use AI to retrieve and apply your knowledge—not just store it

The central theme: **Your knowledge system should make your work easier next week, not harder today.**

Section 14.1: What Personal Knowledge Management (PKM) is (Without the Hype)

PKM is not about collecting information. It is about building a personal support system for thinking and work.

A practical definition:

PKM is a set of habits and tools that help you:

1. Capture valuable information quickly
2. Turn it into usable formats
3. Retrieve it when you need it
4. Apply it to decisions and deliverables
5. Maintain it with minimal overhead

The purpose is not to create a perfect archive. The purpose is to reduce rework and increase clarity.

ChatGPT supports PKM by helping you:

- Summarize notes into structured assets
- Extract action items, decisions, and risks
- Create reusable templates from one-time work
- Generate "context packets" for projects
- Build retrieval-friendly tags and titles
- Turn learning into checklists and references

But remember: **ChatGPT is not your storage system. It is your processing assistant.**

Your storage system is whatever tool you already use reliably: notes app, document folder, knowledge base, or even a single "PKM document" if you prefer simplicity.

Section 14.2: The PKM Problem in Modern Work - Context is Fragile

The hardest part of knowledge work is not doing tasks. It is preserving context.

Context includes:

- Why something matters
- What was decided

- What constraints exist
- What risks were identified
- What the next steps are
- Who is involved
- What "good" looks like

When context is lost, you rework:

- You redo analysis
- You ask the same questions again
- You revisit decisions
- You reopen closed topics
- You slow down and feel uncertain

PKM is how you protect context.

The highest-value knowledge to capture is not "everything." It is:

- Decisions
- Rationale
- Lessons learned
- Templates
- Checklists
- Definitions of done
- Stakeholder preferences
- Project status snapshots

ChatGPT can help you turn raw notes into those assets quickly.

Section 14.3: The "Capture → Condense → Connect" Model

Here is a PKM model you can actually use:

1. **Capture:** record raw notes and inputs
2. **Condense:** convert raw notes into usable summaries and assets
3. **Connect:** link knowledge to projects, tasks, and decisions so it can be retrieved

Capture

Capture should be frictionless. The goal is to get it out of your head.

Condense

Condense is where ChatGPT helps the most. Raw notes are not retrievable knowledge. Condense turns them into structured assets.

Connect

Connect is where your system becomes useful: titles, tags, and links that help the future you find the right item quickly.

This model avoids the trap of trying to organize everything perfectly at capture time.

Figure 14.1 – PKM model

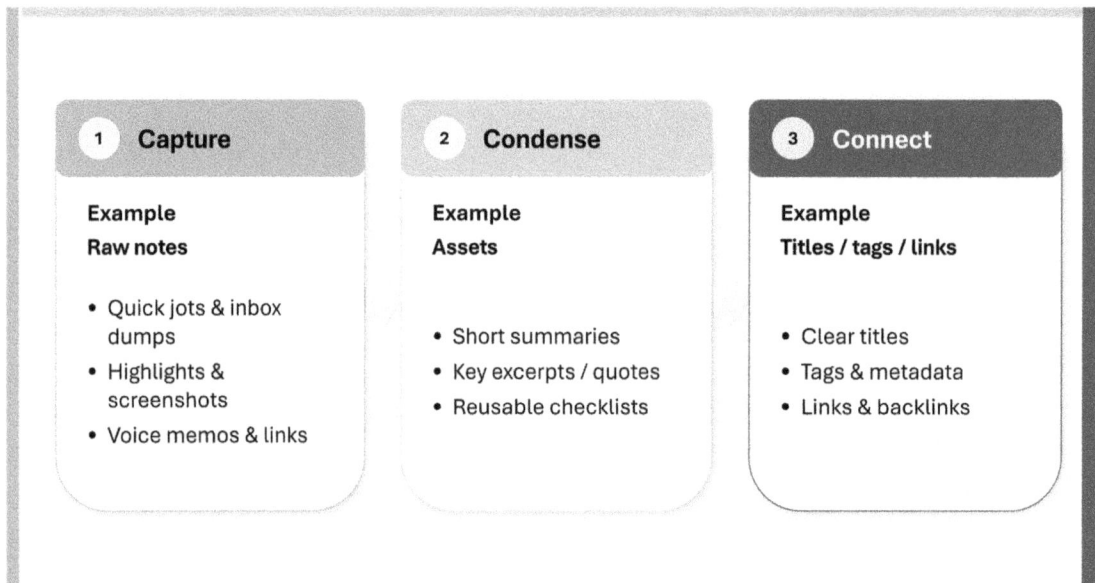

1 Capture	**2** Condense	**3** Connect
Example **Raw notes**	**Example** **Assets**	**Example** **Titles / tags / links**
• Quick jots & inbox dumps • Highlights & screenshots • Voice memos & links	• Short summaries • Key excerpts / quotes • Reusable checklists	• Clear titles • Tags & metadata • Links & backlinks

Section 14.4: The "Note Types" That Matter Most (And How to Use Them)

Most professionals benefit from standard note types. Standard note types make retrieval easier because you know what you're looking for.

Here are five high-value types:

Type 1: Meeting Note (Decisions + Actions)

Minimum content:

- Purpose

- Decisions made
- Action items (owner/deadline)
- Open questions
- Risks/concerns

Type 2: Project Snapshot (Context Packet)

Minimum content:

- Purpose
- Stakeholders (roles)
- Constraints
- Status
- Decisions
- Next steps
- Risks

Type 3: Lesson Learned

Minimum content:

- What happened
- What worked
- What didn't
- Root causes (hypotheses)
- Changes for next time

Type 4: Template

Minimum content:

- When to use
- Inputs
- Output structure
- Example

Type 5: Decision Record

Minimum content:

- Decision
- Date
- Options considered
- Rationale
- Risks
- Owner

These note types are valuable because they compress context into retrievable forms.

ChatGPT helps you convert raw notes into these standardized note types.

Figure 14.2 – Five note types

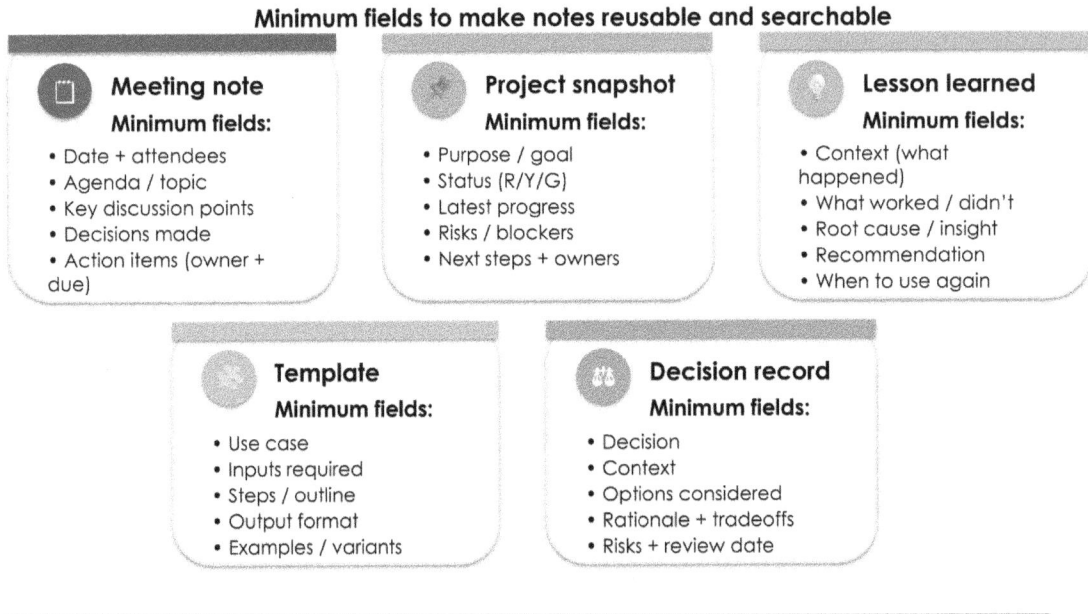

Minimum fields to make notes reusable and searchable

Meeting note
Minimum fields:
- Date + attendees
- Agenda / topic
- Key discussion points
- Decisions made
- Action items (owner + due)

Project snapshot
Minimum fields:
- Purpose / goal
- Status (R/Y/G)
- Latest progress
- Risks / blockers
- Next steps + owners

Lesson learned
Minimum fields:
- Context (what happened)
- What worked / didn't
- Root cause / insight
- Recommendation
- When to use again

Template
Minimum fields:
- Use case
- Inputs required
- Steps / outline
- Output format
- Examples / variants

Decision record
Minimum fields:
- Decision
- Context
- Options considered
- Rationale + tradeoffs
- Risks + review date

Section 14.5: Building "Knowledge Assets" - Turn Notes into Reusable Tools

A knowledge asset is a condensed piece of knowledge that saves time later.

Examples:

- A one-page briefing
- A checklist
- A "how we do this" SOP
- A customer response template
- A weekly review script
- A decision memo format
- A troubleshooting guide

Figure 14.3 – Knowledge assets map: raw notes → asset types

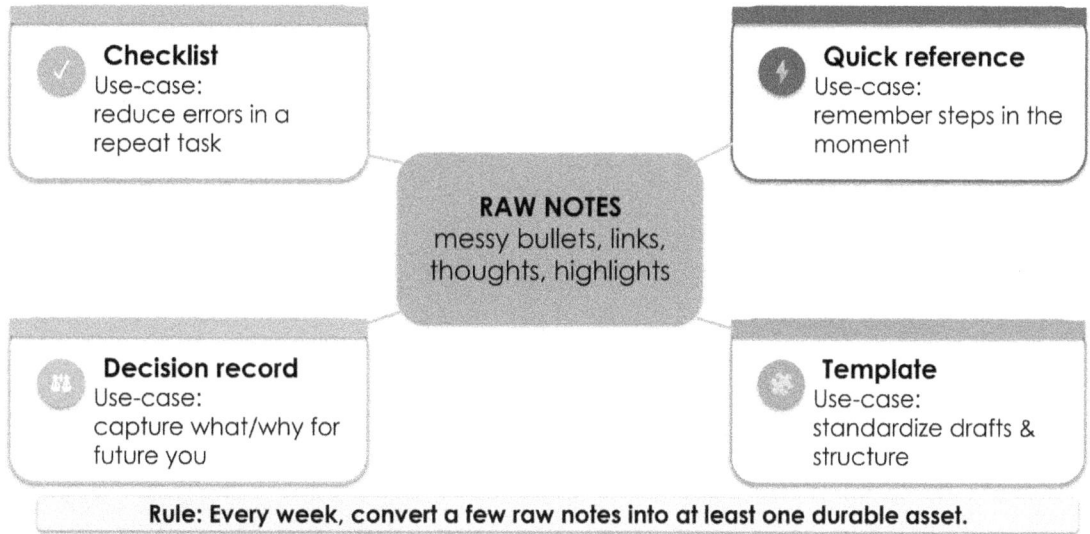

Checklist
Use-case:
reduce errors in a
repeat task

Quick reference
Use-case:
remember steps in the
moment

RAW NOTES
messy bullets, links,
thoughts, highlights

Decision record
Use-case:
capture what/why for
future you

Template
Use-case:
standardize drafts &
structure

Rule: Every week, convert a few raw notes into at least one durable asset.

The benefit is leverage: one hour of work becomes many hours saved.

ChatGPT is exceptionally good at converting notes into assets if you provide source material and enforce guardrails.

```
Prompt: Notes → Knowledge asset
"Turn these notes into a reusable knowledge asset.
Choose the best asset type: checklist, quick reference, context
packet, decision record, or template.
Rules: use my notes as truth; do not add facts; label unknowns as
Missing.
Output: the asset plus 'When to use it' and 'How to maintain it.'
Notes: [paste sanitized notes]."
```

This prompt makes your knowledge system grow through normal work.

Section 14.6: Titles, Tags, and Findability - How to Make Retrieval Easy

The biggest PKM failure is "I wrote it down but I can't find it."

Findability comes from:

- Good titles
- Consistent tags
- Short summaries at the top

- Linking to related items
- A predictable structure

Practical titling rules

A good title includes:

- Topic + purpose + date or project name (if relevant)

Examples:

- "Project Phoenix — Status Snapshot — 2026-01-05"
- "Client Onboarding — SOP Draft v1 — 2026-01-07"
- "Weekly Review Checklist — Personal System — v2"

Tags (simple and consistent)

Use 5–10 tags that match your work.

Examples:

- #project
- #meeting
- #decision
- #template
- #sop
- #customer
- #risk
- #lesson
- #weeklyreview

Avoid tag explosion. If you have 75 tags, you don't have tags. You have noise.

Figure 14.4 – Titles and tags: good vs. bad examples

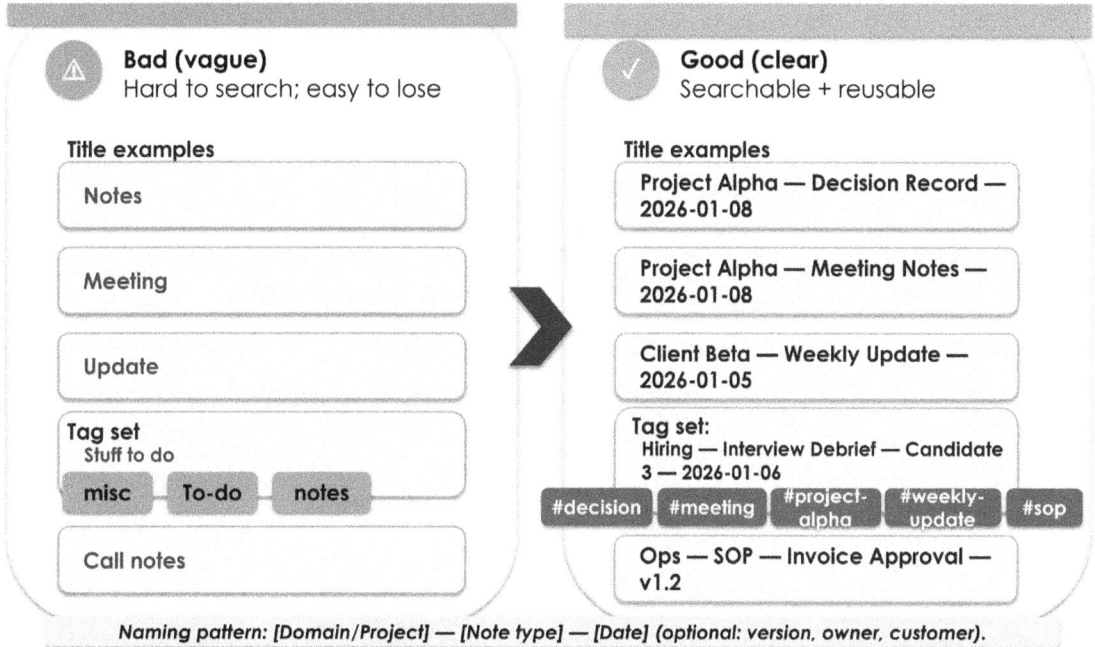

Bad (vague)
Hard to search; easy to lose

Title examples

Notes

Meeting

Update

Tag set
Stuff to do

misc   To-do   notes

Call notes

Good (clear)
Searchable + reusable

Title examples

**Project Alpha — Decision Record —
2026-01-08**

**Project Alpha — Meeting Notes —
2026-01-08**

**Client Beta — Weekly Update —
2026-01-05**

Tag set:
Hiring — Interview Debrief — Candidate
3 — 2026-01-06

#decision   #meeting   #project-alpha   #weekly-update   #sop

**Ops — SOP — Invoice Approval —
v1.2**

Naming pattern: [Domain/Project] — [Note type] — [Date] (optional: version, owner, customer).

> *Prompt: Title + tags helper*
> *"Suggest a title, short summary (2 sentences), and up to 5 tags for this note so I can find it later.*
> *Rules: keep tags consistent; avoid creating new tags unless necessary.*
> *Note: [paste]."*

This small habit improves retrieval dramatically.

Section 14.7: Personal Prompt Library + Knowledge - The "Context-Packet" Method

A powerful PKM practice is to maintain context packets for ongoing projects and roles, then pair them with prompt templates.

Example:

You maintain a context packet for a project.
When you need to write an update, you paste:

- the context packet
- the week's raw notes
- the update prompt template

This produces consistent, accurate outputs with minimal re-explaining.

Figure 14.5 – Context packet template (250 words max)

Context Packet (keep ≤ 250 words)
Sanitized: use roles + placeholders; omit identifiers and sensitive links.

PURPOSE	What are we trying to accomplish?	DELIVERABLES	What output is needed? (format)
AUDIENCE	Who will read/use this? (roles)	DECISIONS NEEDED	What decisions are required?
CONSTRAINTS	Tone, length, policy, timing	NEXT STEPS	Top 1–3 actions (owner + date)
CURRENT STATUS	What's true right now?	DO-NOT-INCLUDE	Sensitive details to omit

Here is a simple context packet format (repeated from earlier chapters because repetition builds mastery):

Context Packet (250 words max)

- Purpose
- Stakeholders (roles)
- Constraints
- Current status
- Key decisions
- Next steps
- Risks / watchlist

Then you can use it as a stable input into many prompts.

This is how you turn knowledge into output reliably.

Section 14.8: Personal Knowledge Review - The Routine That Keeps Your System Useful

A knowledge system becomes unusable if it's not maintained.

You do not need heavy maintenance. You need a lightweight review.

A weekly 20-minute PKM review:

- Clear your capture inbox (notes app, scratch docs)
- Convert raw notes into 2–3 knowledge assets
- Update 1–2 context packets
- Archive or delete low-value clutter
- Update your prompt library (if needed)

This is small, but it compounds.

```
Prompt: PKM weekly review coach
"Coach me through a 20-minute PKM weekly review.
Ask questions one at a time.
Goals: clear raw notes, convert into 2-3 knowledge assets, update
context packets, and list next week's knowledge priorities.
End with a short plan."
```

This turns PKM into a routine rather than a hobby.

Figure 14.6 – Weekly PKM review checklist (20 minutes)

Weekly PKM Review — 20 minutes
A quick reset to keep your knowledge system clean and useful.

☐	**Clear inbox**	Process raw notes, screenshots, links (≤ 5 min)
☐	**Create 2–3 assets**	Turn notes into reusable outputs (≤ 7 min)
☐	**Update context packet**	Refresh purpose/status/next steps (≤ 3 min)
☐	**Archive clutter**	Delete/merge duplicates; file old drafts (≤ 3 min)
☐	**Update templates**	Improve one prompt/checklist based on the week (≤ 2 min)

Rule: end the review with one reusable artifact (template, decision record, or lesson learned).

Section 14.9: Using ChatGPT to Retrieve Your Knowledge (Without Special Tools)

Even without fancy integrations, you can retrieve knowledge by keeping it in reusable packets and templates.

A simple retrieval workflow:

1. Search your notes for the context packet or decision record
2. Paste the relevant packet(s) into ChatGPT
3. Ask for the output you need: update, email, memo, plan
4. Run the trust workflow (commitments + claims scan)
5. Save the new output back into your system

This is not fully automated, but it is highly effective because it reduces cognitive load and rework.

ChatGPT becomes your "knowledge processor," while your notes remain the source of truth.

Section 14.10: Privacy and Safety - Keep Your Knowledge Clean and Shareable

PKM often contains sensitive information: names, problems, performance issues, customer situations. You must protect it.

A calm rule: **Store sensitive information in your secure systems. Use sanitized versions for AI-assisted processing when needed.**

Practical approach:

- Maintain "public" versions of context packets (role-based, no identifiers)
- Maintain "private" internal notes in your secure environment
- Use AI prompts on the public packet whenever possible

This separation protects you:

- If you need to share a packet with a colleague, it's already shareable
- If you need to use AI, you have a safe input prepared
- If you're audited, your practices are defensible

```
Prompt: Sanitized context packet builder
"Create a sanitized version of this context packet for AI and
cross-team sharing.
Rules: remove identifying details; replace names with roles;
remove confidential numbers; keep the meaning.
Text: [paste]."
```

Section 14.11: A Practical PKM Setup You Can Implement in One Afternoon

If you want a simple, tool-neutral setup, here is a model you can implement quickly.

PKM Setup (Simple)

Folder or note structure:

1. Inbox (raw notes)
2. Projects (context packets + key decisions)
3. Templates (prompts + writing templates + checklists)
4. Lessons learned (postmortems, improvements)

5. Reference (policies, guides, definitions)

Rules:

- Everything starts in Inbox
- Inbox is cleared weekly
- Every active project has a context packet
- Every recurring deliverable has a template
- Lessons learned are captured at the end of meaningful work

This setup is not fancy. It is durable.

ChatGPT helps by reducing the time required to convert raw notes into usable assets.

Section 14.12: Worked Example - Turning a Week of Work into a Strong Knowledge System

Scenario (generic): You have a week of meetings, tasks, and decisions. Notes are scattered.

Step 1: Capture

You dump all raw notes into "Inbox."

Step 2: Condense

You choose:

- 2 meetings to convert into decision/action records
- 1 project to update its context packet
- 1 recurring workflow to create a template

You use ChatGPT prompts:

- Notes → decisions/actions
- Notes → context packet
- Notes → template

Step 3: Connect

You title and tag:

- "Project X — Status Snapshot — date"
- "Meeting — Vendor Review — Decisions & Actions — date"
- "Template — Weekly Status Update — Version 1"

Step 4: Apply

Next week, when you need:

- a stakeholder update
- a recap email
- a decision memo

You paste the relevant packets and generate high-quality output quickly.

Result:

Your system grows through normal work. You stop rebuilding context from scratch.

Practice Exercises

Use sanitized information. Build assets that you can reuse. Keep your system small and functional.

Exercise 1 — Create your PKM structure

```
Prompt:
"Help me design a simple PKM structure using the folders: Inbox,
Projects, Templates, Lessons Learned, Reference.
My role: [role].
My main work areas: [list].
Output: recommended structure, naming conventions, and 5 tags I
should use consistently."
```

Exercise 2 — Standardize your meeting notes

```
Prompt:
"Convert these notes into a meeting note format with: purpose,
decisions, action items (owner/deadline), open questions, risks.
Rules: do not invent details; label unknowns as Missing.
Notes: [paste]."
```

Exercise 3 — Build a context packet for an active project

```
Prompt:
"Create a context packet under 250 words for this project.
Replace names with roles; remove identifying details.
Include purpose, stakeholders, constraints, current status, key
```

decisions, next steps, risks.
Notes: [paste sanitized notes]."

Exercise 4 — Turn raw notes into a knowledge asset

Prompt:
"Turn these notes into a reusable knowledge asset.
Choose the best asset type (checklist, quick reference, decision
record, template).
Rules: use my notes as truth; label unknowns as Missing; keep it
practical.
Notes: [paste]."

Exercise 5 — Improve findability with titles and tags

Prompt:
"Suggest a title, 2-sentence summary, and up to 5 tags for this
note so I can retrieve it later.
Keep tags consistent; avoid creating new tags unless necessary.
Note: [paste]."

Exercise 6 — Build a template from recurring work

Prompt:
"I do this task often: [describe].
Create a template that includes: when to use, required inputs,
output structure, and one example.
Also create a prompt engine version with guardrails and a review
loop."

Exercise 7 — Create a decision record

Prompt:
"Create a decision record from the information below.
Include: decision, date (if known), options considered,
rationale, risks, owner, next steps.
Rules: do not invent details; label unknowns as Missing.
Info: [paste]."

Exercise 8 — Run a 20-minute weekly PKM review

Prompt:
"Coach me through a 20-minute PKM weekly review. Ask questions
one at a time.
End with: 3 knowledge assets I should create next week and why."

Exercise 9 — Build a sanitized sharing packet

> **Prompt:**
> *"Create a sanitized version of this note for AI use and cross-team sharing.*
> *Rules: replace names with roles, remove identifiers and confidential numbers, keep meaning.*
> *Text: [paste]."*

Exercise 10 — Create a "gold standard" template set

> **Prompt:**
> *"Help me create 3 gold standard examples for: a context packet, a meeting decision record, and a weekly status update.*
> *Use placeholders where needed.*
> *Then provide checklists for each."*

Exercise 11 — Build a personal prompt library tied to your PKM

> **Prompt:**
> *"Create 10 prompt templates tied to my PKM system: meeting notes, context packet, lesson learned, decision record, weekly review, daily plan, status update, email rewrite, SOP checklist extraction, and claim scan.*
> *Include when to use and copy-paste templates with placeholders."*

Exercise 12 — Convert learning into a reusable checklist

> **Prompt:**
> *"From this learning summary: [paste], create a 10–15 item performance checklist and a quick reference card.*
> *Keep it plain English and usable under time pressure."*

Skill Check

After completing this chapter, you should be able to:

- Explain PKM as a practical retrieval and reuse system, not an information hoard
- Implement the Capture → Condense → Connect model with minimal overhead
- Standardize high-value note types (meeting notes, context packets, lessons learned, templates, decision records)

- Convert raw notes into reusable knowledge assets with ChatGPT while preventing invented details
- Improve findability through clear titles, small tag sets, and short top summaries
- Use context packets to reduce re-explaining and generate consistent outputs
- Run a weekly PKM review that keeps your system clean and useful
- Protect confidentiality by maintaining sanitized, shareable knowledge packets for AI-assisted work
- Build a personal prompt library that connects directly to your knowledge system and daily workflows

Chapter 15: Building Long-Term Confidence and Judgment with AI

You can learn prompts. You can build templates. You can automate workflows.

But the real goal of this book is not "using ChatGPT."

The real goal is building confidence: quiet, durable confidence in your ability to:

- Think clearly under pressure
- Use AI as a tool without being controlled by it
- Produce reliable work faster
- Verify what matters
- Communicate responsibly
- Improve your systems over time

Confidence is not bravado. Confidence is a steady relationship with reality.

And judgment is what protects that relationship.

This chapter is about making your AI use sustainable over months and years.

You will learn:

- How to build trust in your own process, not in the tool
- How to avoid dependence and preserve your voice
- How to develop calibration: knowing when outputs are likely right or wrong
- How to create habits that keep you accurate and ethical
- How to train your "AI muscle" gradually without overwhelm
- How to teach these habits to a team in a healthy way

The tone of this chapter is intentionally calm. Anxiety is often created by uncertainty and speed. Confidence is created by standards and repetition.

Section 15.1: Confidence is a Process, Not a Personality Trait

Many people believe confidence is something you either have or you don't.

In professional work, confidence is built through:

- Clear standards
- Repeatable workflows
- Evidence of competence
- Responsible correction when errors occur

- A stable sense of what you control

When you add AI into the mix, the temptation is to ask: "Can I trust this?"

But the more stable question is: "Can I trust my process?"

If your process includes:

- risk classification
- guardrails
- verification
- commitment checks
- saving final outputs
- learning from mistakes

Then your confidence becomes durable because it is not dependent on any single output.

Section 15.2: The Three Types of Confidence You Need

To use AI in modern work without anxiety, you need three distinct kinds of confidence.

Confidence Type 1: Tool confidence

You know how to get useful outputs consistently:

- You can write clear prompts
- You can structure outputs
- You can debug prompts
- You can use prompt stacks

This is practical skill.

Confidence Type 2: Judgment confidence

You can evaluate outputs accurately:

- You can identify claims
- You can detect missing info
- You can run verification
- You can spot risky commitments
- You can recognize bias or tone issues

This is professional discernment.

Confidence Type 3: Self confidence

You know that:

- Your value is not the speed of your typing
- You are responsible for decisions and communication
- You can use tools without becoming dependent on them
- You can correct and learn

Figure 15.1 – The three types of confidence: Tool, Judgment, Self

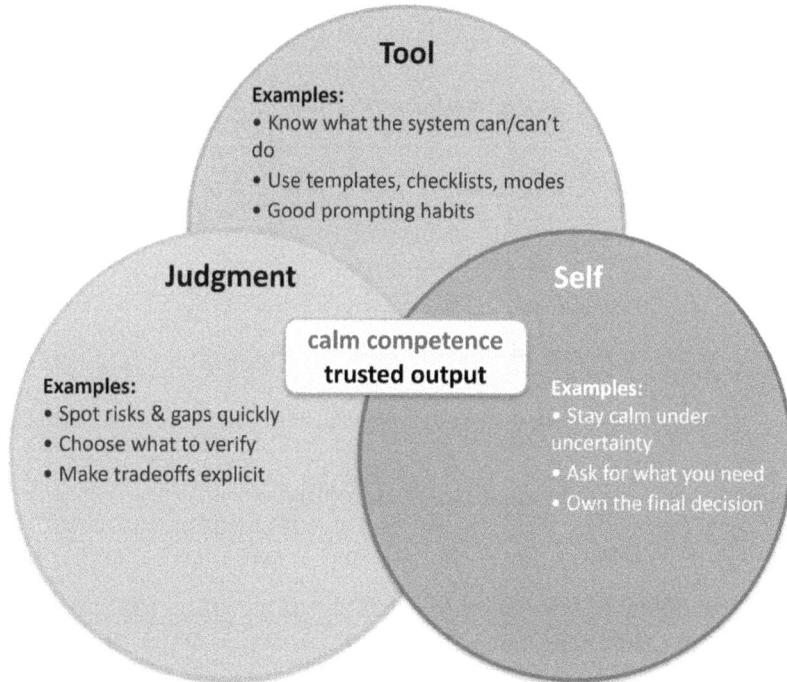

Tool

Examples:
- Know what the system can/can't do
- Use templates, checklists, modes
- Good prompting habits

Judgment

Self

calm competence
trusted output

Examples:
- Spot risks & gaps quickly
- Choose what to verify
- Make tradeoffs explicit

Examples:
- Stay calm under uncertainty
- Ask for what you need
- Own the final decision

Build all three: better tools + better judgment + better self-management.

This is psychological steadiness.

Most AI anxiety comes from a gap in Judgment confidence, not Tool confidence.

That's good news. Judgment can be trained.

Section 15.3: Calibration - Knowing When to Trust and When to Verify

Figure 15.2 – Calibration workflow: Risk Level → Claims Scan → Verification Ladder → Send/Save

① **Risk level** Low / Medium / High — ② **Claims scan** Dates • numbers • policy • promises — ③ **Verification ladder** Choose the right check level — ④ **Send / Save** Publish + store the record

Verification happens here

Self-check	Read for logic + completeness
Source-check	Confirm against source text/data
Document-check	Match to policy/SOP/contract
Cross-check	Validate with a second source
Expert-check	Escalate / peer review for high risk

Calibrate: higher risk → higher verification effort before you send or save.

Calibration means your confidence matches reality.

Overconfidence looks like:

- Accepting polished text as truth
- Sending unverified claims
- Making commitments based on drafts

Under confidence looks like:

- Refusing to use AI even for low-risk tasks
- Over checking everything until you lose speed
- Feeling paralyzed by the possibility of mistakes

Healthy calibration looks like:

- Using AI freely for low-risk drafting and organization
- Verifying proportionally for medium and high risk
- Knowing your "high-risk triggers" (the areas where errors are most costly)

A practical way to build calibration is to track where AI is most likely to fail for you.

Common failure zones:

- Dates and numbers you didn't provide
- Policy statements you didn't supply
- Industry facts that require sources
- Overgeneralizations
- Tone mismatches in sensitive contexts
- Overconfident recommendations without enough context

Your goal is to know your zones and build guardrails around them.

> **Prompt: Calibration Log**
> "Help me create a calibration log.
> When I paste an AI output I used, you will ask:
>
> What was the task risk level?
>
> What claims did we verify?
>
> What went well?
>
> What was wrong or unclear?
>
> What guardrail would prevent that next time?
> Then summarize in a short log entry."

This converts mistakes into system improvement.

Section 15.4: The "Trust Triangle" - Speed, Accuracy, and Clarity

Every professional output balances three factors:

1. **Speed:** how fast it's produced
2. **Accuracy:** how correct it is
3. **Clarity:** how understandable and usable it is

AI tends to increase speed and clarity quickly. Accuracy requires your involvement.

So the trust triangle principle is: **Use AI to accelerate speed and clarity. Use your judgment to protect accuracy.**

If you try to get all three without effort, you increase risk.

A calm professional approach is to decide explicitly which corner matters most for each task:

- A quick internal brainstorm: speed and clarity
- A customer-facing policy statement: accuracy and clarity
- A high-stakes memo: accuracy first, then clarity
- A routine recap: clarity and speed, then quick verification

This "which corner matters" decision reduces anxiety because it turns tradeoffs into choices.

Figure 15.3 – Trust triangle: Speed / Accuracy / Clarity

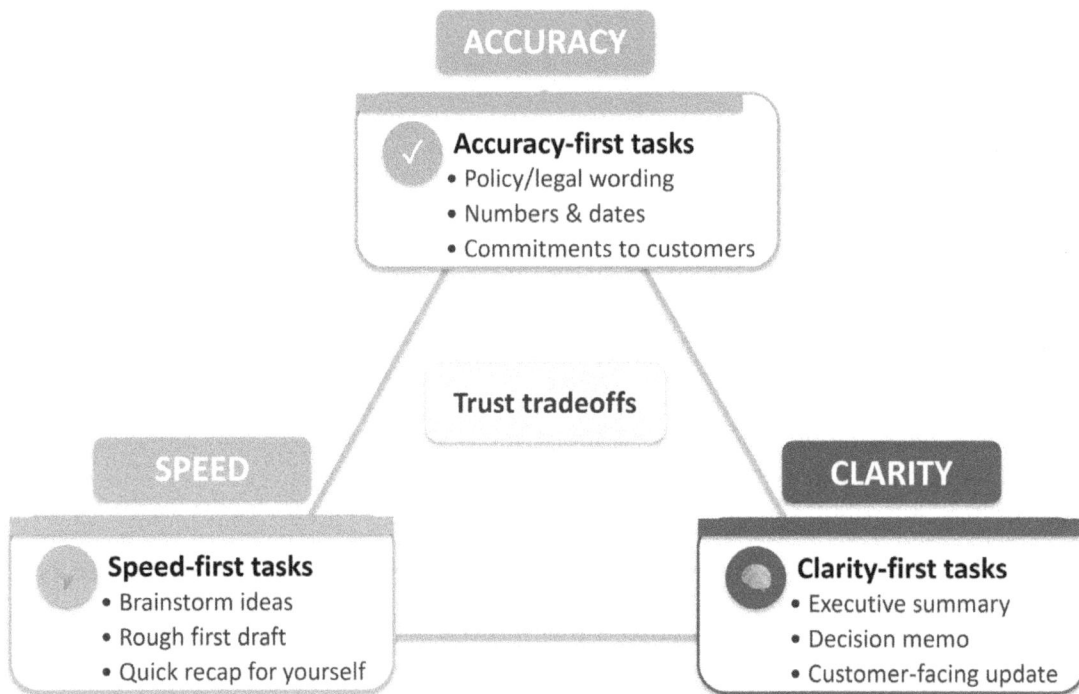

ACCURACY

✓ **Accuracy-first tasks**
- Policy/legal wording
- Numbers & dates
- Commitments to customers

Trust tradeoffs

SPEED

Speed-first tasks
- Brainstorm ideas
- Rough first draft
- Quick recap for yourself

CLARITY

Clarity-first tasks
- Executive summary
- Decision memo
- Customer-facing update

Section 15.5: How to Avoid Dependence - Keep Your Thinking in the Loop

AI is helpful, but it can create subtle dependence if you always outsource:

- First drafts
- Framing
- Decision logic
- Problem-solving steps

The solution is not to avoid AI. The solution is to keep yourself in the loop in specific ways.

Three anti-dependence habits:

Habit 1: Write a 3-line brief first

Before prompting, write:

- what you want
- who it's for
- what constraints apply

This keeps you oriented and prevents you from letting the assistant define the task.

Habit 2: Do a "teach-back" after using AI

Explain the final output in your own words:

- What are we actually saying?
- What are we committing to?
- What claims must be true?

Teach-back keeps your judgment active.

Habit 3: Alternate "AI-first" and "human-first"

For some tasks, draft a rough version yourself, then ask AI to refine.
For others, let AI draft, then rewrite key parts in your own voice.

This keeps your skills sharp and prevents you from feeling like a passenger.

```
Prompt: Human-in-the-loop discipline
"Before drafting, ask me for a 3-line brief (goal, audience,
constraints).
After drafting, ask me to teach back the output in 5 sentences.
Then run a commitment scan and claims scan."
```

This prompt forces you to stay engaged.

Section 15.6: Building a Personal "Standard of Care" for AI-Assisted Work

A professional standard of care is not fear-based. It's a minimum acceptable process.

Here is a standard you can adopt:

Standard of Care (AI-Assisted Work)

For Level 1 tasks:

- Use guardrails
- Quick review
- Save outputs only if reusable

For Level 2 tasks:

- Guardrails + structure lock
- Commitment scan before sending externally
- Claims scan and verify key facts
- Save final output and source notes

For Level 3 tasks:

- Use AI primarily for structure and clarity
- Use authoritative sources and/or expert review
- Avoid definitive claims without verification
- Follow organizational policies
- Save approvals and evidence

Figure 15.4 – Standard of care checklist (Level 1-3)

	What "good enough" looks like at each risk level			
Risk level	**Guardrails**	**Verification**	**Save outputs**	**Approvals**
Level 1 (Low)	• Use "no guessing" rule • Label unknowns • Keep it short	• Self-check • Basic claims scan	• Save only if reusable • Optional tags	• No approval needed
Level 2 (Medium)	• Add constraints + audience • Commitment scan • Use structure lock	• Source-check key claims • Cross-check 1 item • Add verification checklist	• Save draft + sources • Store decision/recap	• Peer review if external
Level 3 (High)	• Sanitize sensitive info • Strict wording • No absolutes / guarantees	• Authoritative sources • Document/policy check • Expert/peer review • Record checks done	• Save final + audit trail • Version prompt/ output • Archive supporting docs	• Manager/ legal /compliance sign-off

Rule: raise the standard of care when stakes rise—especially for commitments, money, and policy.

This standard reduces anxiety because it gives you a default process. You don't have to decide from scratch every time.

> *Prompt: Standard-of-care checklist generator*
> *"Create a one-page standard-of-care checklist for my role using risk levels 1–3.*
> *Include what I must do before using AI, what I must do before sending outputs, and what I must save for records."*

Section 15.7: Handling Mistakes - The Professional Recovery Plan

No professional avoids mistakes entirely. Professionals recover well.

If an AI-assisted output is wrong, the ethical response is:

1. Correct quickly
2. Correct clearly
3. Learn and adjust your system

A practical recovery plan:

- Identify what was wrong
- Determine impact (who saw it, what decisions it affected)
- Send correction message if needed
- Update your template or guardrails to prevent repetition
- Add a calibration log entry

A calm principle: **A correction delivered professionally often increases trust because it demonstrates integrity.**

```
Prompt: Correction message drafter
"I need to correct a mistake in a message I sent.
Context: [what was sent and to whom—sanitized].
What was wrong: [fact].
Correct fact: [fact].
Tone: accountable, calm, not overly dramatic.
Draft a correction message.
Then propose a guardrail to prevent this error next time."
```

This turns a mistake into process improvement.

Section 15.8: Building Confidence Through Gradual Exposure - A 30-Day AI Routine

Anxiety decreases when exposure is gradual and controlled.

Figure 15.5 – 30-day confidence plan (weekly ladder)

Week 4 — Systems

Build reusable templates, prompt stacks, and a review routine for consistency.

Week 3 — Controlled external

Customer-facing content with constraints + peer review (limited scope).

Week 2 — Internal deliverables

Ship internal emails, updates, SOPs with verification checklist.

Week 1 — Low-risk wins

Use AI for drafts you fully control (notes, outlines, internal summaries).

Rule: increase stakes only after you can reliably pass your verification routine.

Goal: move from "using the tool" to "trusted delivery" in 30 days.

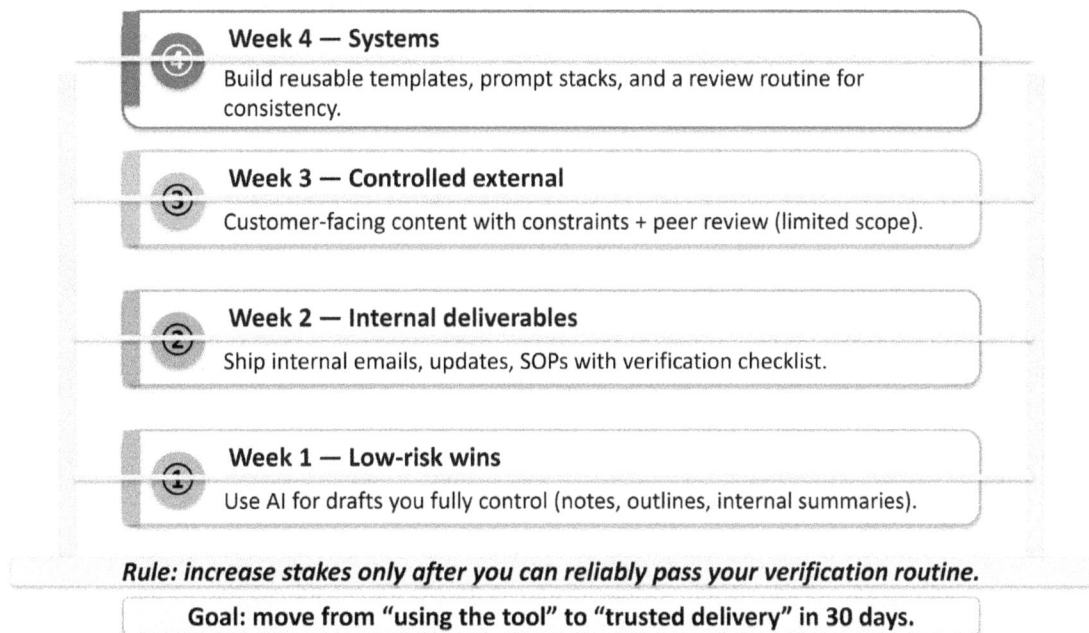

Here is a 30-day routine designed for working professionals.

Week 1: Low-risk wins

- Use AI daily for Level 1 tasks:
    - clarity rewrites
    - brainstorming
    - note structuring
    - task planning
- Keep outputs internal.
- Focus on learning prompt structure and guardrails.

Week 2: Medium-risk internal deliverables

- Use AI for:
    - meeting recaps
    - status updates
    - internal SOP drafts
- Add commitment and claims scans.
- Save templates you reuse.

Week 3: Controlled external communication

- Use AI for:
    - customer emails
    - outreach drafts
    - marketing descriptions
- Verify claims and run commitment scans before sending.

Week 4: Systems and library building

- Build:
    - prompt library (10 templates)
    - context packets for top projects
    - weekly review routine
- Audit your outputs for consistency and risk.

This routine builds confidence because it builds evidence. You see yourself using AI responsibly without harm.

```
Prompt: 30-day plan coach
"Build me a 30-day AI confidence plan based on my role: [role].
Constraints: [time].
Include daily tasks (10-15 minutes), weekly goals, and what to
save into my prompt library.
Include a weekly reflection and calibration log entry."
```

Section 15.9: Preserving Your Voice - How to Sound Like Yourself (Not Like "AI")

A common complaint is: "This sounds robotic."

That happens when:

- You accept the first draft
- You don't provide voice constraints
- You don't include examples
- You don't add your own phrasing patterns

Three ways to preserve voice:

Method 1: Voice Card + phrases to avoid

Use the Voice Card from Chapter 11.

Method 2: Provide "signature phrases"

List a few phrases you naturally use and want included occasionally.

Method 3: Human revision pass

Rewrite the first paragraph and the closing in your own words. This anchors voice.

```
Prompt: Voice preservation
"Rewrite this in my voice.
My voice characteristics: [3-5 descriptors].
Phrases I use: [list].
Phrases to avoid: [list].
Keep meaning the same. Do not add facts.
Text: [paste]."
```

Voice is not a minor detail. Voice affects trust.

Section 15.10: Team Use - How to Build a Healthy AI Culture without Pressure

If you are a leader or influence a team, how you introduce AI matters.

A healthy AI culture:

- Is opt-in, not forced
- Emphasizes guardrails and trust
- Encourages sharing templates
- Encourages learning from mistakes
- Avoids shame
- Avoids hype and fear

A practical team approach:

1. Agree on risk levels and verification ladder
2. Create a shared prompt library (10 templates)
3. Create a shared Voice Card or tone standard (if relevant)
4. Train with real scenarios
5. Encourage a "calibration log" habit
6. Review and improve templates monthly

A team that uses AI responsibly becomes:

- more consistent
- less stressed
- faster at routine work
- better at documenting decisions

> **Prompt: Team AI standard draft**
> *"Draft a one-page team standard for responsible AI use.*
> *Include: what's allowed, what's not, how to sanitize, risk levels*
> *and verification steps, requirement for commitment scans on*
> *external messages, and how to share and update templates.*
> *Tone: calm, non-punitive, practical."*

This standard builds confidence collectively.

Section 15.11: The "AI Confidence Inventory" - A Tool for Self-Awareness

Confidence grows when you know where you stand.

Inventory categories:

- Prompting skill (structure, clarity)
- Verification skill (claims scan, source checks)
- Risk awareness (when not to use AI)
- Voice control (tone, authenticity)
- System building (templates, workflows)
- Ethical boundaries (confidentiality, bias, compliance)

You can rate yourself 1–5 in each. Then choose one category to improve each month.

> **Prompt: Confidence inventory**
> *"Help me complete an AI confidence inventory.*
> *Ask me questions one at a time.*
> *Then summarize my scores, highlight my strengths, and recommend*
> *the next 2 skills to build with a 2-week practice plan."*

This makes growth manageable.

Section 15.12: The Long View - Why This Will Get Easier

The first phase of using ChatGPT feels intense because you are building new habits.

After a few weeks, the work shifts:

- You stop writing from scratch
- You reuse stable templates
- You maintain context packets
- You run the trust workflow automatically
- You spend less time on routine tasks
- You reserve your best energy for judgment and relationships

In other words, AI doesn't "replace" your work. It reallocates your energy.

When you do it responsibly, it becomes calmer, not more stressful.

Confidence is not the absence of uncertainty. It is the presence of a reliable process.

Practice Exercises

Use sanitized information. Apply your trust workflow. Focus on building durable habits.

Exercise 1 — Build your personal standard of care

> *Prompt:*
> "Create my personal standard of care for AI-assisted work using Risk Levels 1-3.
> Include: what I do before prompting, what I do before sending, and what I save.
> My role: [role].
> Constraints: privacy and accuracy."

Exercise 2 — Run a calibration log on a recent AI output

> *Prompt:*
> "Here is an AI-assisted output I used: [paste].
> Create a calibration log entry: risk level, claims verified, what went well, what was unclear or risky, and one guardrail to add next time."

Exercise 3 — Practice the trust triangle

> *Prompt:*
> *"For each task below, tell me which corner I should prioritize (speed, accuracy, clarity) and why.*
> *Tasks: [list].*
> *Then propose a workflow that matches that priority."*

Exercise 4 — Build a correction message and prevention guardrail

> *Prompt:*
> *"I need to correct a mistake.*
> *What I sent: [paste sanitized].*
> *What was wrong: [describe].*
> *Correct info: [describe].*
> *Draft a correction message (calm, accountable).*
> *Then propose a guardrail and verification step to prevent recurrence."*

Exercise 5 — Voice preservation practice

> *Prompt:*
> *"Rewrite this to sound like me.*
> *Voice: [3-5 descriptors].*
> *Phrases I use: [list].*
> *Phrases to avoid: [list].*
> *Rules: do not add facts.*
> *Text: [paste]."*

Exercise 6 — Build a 30-day confidence routine

> *Prompt:*
> *"Build a 30-day AI confidence plan for my role: [role].*
> *Time per day: [minutes].*
> *Include daily tasks, weekly goals, what to save in my prompt library, and a weekly reflection question."*

Exercise 7 — Teach-back habit for judgment

> *Prompt:*
> *"After you draft an output, ask me to teach it back in 5 sentences.*
> *Then evaluate whether my teach-back shows understanding and correct misunderstandings.*
> *Use this text: [paste]."*

Exercise 8 — Identify your high-risk triggers

Prompt:
"Help me identify my top 5 high-risk triggers when using AI (areas where errors could be costly).
My work includes: [describe].
Output: triggers, examples, and the guardrail for each."

Exercise 9 — Build a team standard (if applicable)

Prompt:
"Draft a one-page team standard for responsible AI use.
Include: allowed uses, prohibited data, risk levels and verification ladder, commitment scan requirement for external messages, and template sharing/governance.
Tone: calm and non-punitive."

Exercise 10 — Create an AI confidence inventory

Prompt:
"Help me complete an AI confidence inventory across: prompting, verification, risk awareness, voice control, system building, ethical boundaries.
Ask questions one at a time.
Then give me a 2-week plan to improve my lowest category."

Exercise 11 — Build a "human-in-the-loop" prompt footer

Prompt:
"Create a short prompt footer that forces human-in-the-loop steps: 3-line brief before drafting, teach-back after drafting, then commitment + claims scans.
Keep it copy-paste ready."

Exercise 12 — Monthly improvement loop

Prompt:
"Help me design a monthly improvement loop for my AI workflows.
Output: what to review, how to measure quality, how to update templates, and how to capture lessons learned.
Keep it lightweight."

Skill Check

After completing this chapter, you should be able to:

- Define confidence as a repeatable process rather than a personality trait
- Distinguish tool confidence, judgment confidence, and self confidence—and know which one to build
- Calibrate trust by matching verification effort to risk level
- Use the trust triangle (speed, accuracy, clarity) to choose tradeoffs intentionally
- Maintain a human-in-the-loop approach that prevents overdependence and preserves your thinking
- Apply a personal standard of care for AI-assisted work across risk levels
- Recover professionally from mistakes with correction and guardrail updates
- Build a gradual 30-day routine that increases confidence without overwhelm
- Preserve your voice with voice constraints, examples, and human revisions
- Create healthy team standards that enable responsible use without pressure or hype
- Use calibration logs and inventories to turn experience into improved judgment over time

Capstone Workbook, Part I: Your Personal AI Productivity System

This capstone is a build. Not a reading exercise.

You will construct a personal AI productivity system you can run daily and weekly, one that supports planning, writing, decision-making, and operational follow-through without turning you into a prompt hobbyist.

A calm promise: you do not need new apps. You do not need complex automation. You do not need to "optimize your life."

You need three things:

1. A small set of repeatable workflows
2. Standard inputs and outputs (so work stops feeling improvisational)
3. Guardrails that protect accuracy, confidentiality, and trust

This capstone is designed as a multi-part workbook. In Part I, you will build the foundation and implement two core workflows:

- Daily planning workflow
- Weekly review workflow

In Part II, you will build writing pipelines and decision frameworks.

In Part III, you will create a reusable prompt library, establish ethical/accuracy guardrails, and finalize your system.

The end result will be a "portable" system: a set of templates and routines you can use anywhere.

Capstone Principles

Before building, adopt these principles. They keep the system calm and sustainable.

Principle 1: You are building a system, not chasing perfection

Your goal is a system you will use when you're tired and busy.

Principle 2: Your notes are the source of truth; AI is the processor

Your system works because you keep input grounded and outputs reviewable.

Principle 3: Small is strong

A small system used consistently beats a large system used once.

Principle 4: Risk level controls verification

You will apply the standards from Chapter 9 automatically.

Principle 5: A system is only real if it produces outputs

In this capstone, you will generate tangible outputs every week: plans, reviews, drafts, and decision records.

Setup: Your "System Home" (One Place to Store Your Assets)

Choose a single place to store your system assets. This can be:

- A document folder
- A notes app
- A single "AI Productivity System" document you keep updated
- A shared workspace (if your role requires team use)

Your system home should contain five sections:

1. **Inbox** — raw notes and capture
2. **Projects** — context packets and key decisions
3. **Templates** — prompts and output templates
4. **Reviews** — weekly reviews and lessons learned
5. **Reference** — policies, voice card, standards of care

If you prefer simplicity, create one document with these headings and keep everything there. The tool matters less than the habit.

Your goal today is to create a place where you can paste outputs immediately without "filing anxiety."

Your Core Inputs: What You Will Feed Your System

A productivity system fails when inputs are vague.

You will use three input streams:

1. **Capture notes**: quick raw notes from your day
2. **Context packets**: short summaries for active projects
3. **Constraints**: time, priorities, stakeholders, policies

You will not feed your whole life into ChatGPT. You will feed structured, sanitized information that helps you act.

A practical daily capture note includes:

- What happened today (bullets)
- What must happen next (bullets)
- What is blocking progress (bullets)
- Any commitments made (bullets)

If you can capture that daily, your weekly review becomes easy.

System Asset 1: Your "Workload Map" (A Simple Inventory)

Before building workflows, you need clarity on what you're managing.

Create a workload map with three buckets:

Bucket A: Recurring responsibilities

Examples:

- weekly status updates
- customer follow-up
- payroll approvals
- content calendar
- team check-ins
- reporting

Bucket B: Active projects (3–7 max)

Examples:

- onboarding improvements
- new SOP rollout
- marketing launch
- system migration
- procurement cycle change

Bucket C: Open loops (things you worry about)

Examples:

- "I owe a response"
- "I'm unclear on next steps"
- "I need to decide"
- "I'm waiting on them"

Your workload map does not need perfect detail. It needs enough structure to build daily and weekly workflows.

> **Prompt (example-filled): Workload map builder**
> Copy-paste prompt:
> "Help me create a workload map. Use my inputs as truth. Do not invent tasks.
> Output:
>
> Recurring responsibilities (grouped by weekly/monthly)
>
> Active projects (limit to 7; list purpose + next milestone)
>
> Open loops (questions, waiting items, decisions)
> Then propose the top 3 leverage points where a simple system would reduce stress.
> My notes:
>
> Recurring: I send a weekly leadership update, run two team check-ins, handle customer escalations, and review process metrics.
>
> Projects: improving onboarding, documenting SOPs, and reducing cycle time for approvals.
>
> Open loops: waiting on vendor response, need to decide timeline, need to clarify ownership."

When you run this prompt with your real notes, you get the first output your system will store: your workload map.

Store it in your system home under "Reference" or "Reviews" as a baseline snapshot.

System Asset 2: Your "Top Three" Priority Rule (The Anxiety Reducer)

Most overwhelm is not caused by too much work. It is caused by too many competing priorities at the same time.

Your system will use a simple rule:

Each day: choose three outcomes that matter most.
Everything else becomes optional or scheduled.

These outcomes must be outcomes, not vague tasks.

Weak: "Work on the report."
Strong: "Finish the first draft of the report and send to reviewer."

Weak: "Deal with email."
Strong: "Clear the three emails that are blocking other people."

This rule reduces anxiety because it creates an achievable definition of a good day.

Your daily workflow will formalize this.

Workflow 1: Daily Planning with AI (A 10–12 Minute Routine)

You will build a daily planning workflow that has four stages:

1. Capture (2 minutes)
2. Clarify and prioritize (4 minutes)
3. Plan the day (4 minutes)
4. Commitments and risk check (1–2 minutes)

Stage 1: Capture (2 minutes)

Write a quick capture note. Keep it short.

Example capture note (plain and realistic):

- Today: client asked for revised timeline; team meeting revealed two blockers; drafted part of SOP; responded to three urgent emails.
- Next: confirm timeline options; assign owners to blockers; finalize SOP draft; send status update.
- Blockers: waiting on vendor response; unclear approval owner.
- Commitments made: told client I'd update them tomorrow.

This capture note is already a professional asset. It's not a diary. It's operational.

Stage 2: Clarify and prioritize (4 minutes)

Now use ChatGPT to convert the capture note into a plan.

Daily Planning Prompt (template + example)

```
Prompt:
"You are my executive productivity assistant.
Goal: turn my capture note into a calm, realistic daily plan.
Rules:

Use only my note as truth; do not invent tasks, dates, or
commitments
```

> *Identify risky commitments and propose safer wording*
>
> *Keep it plain English and practical*
> *Output format (use these headings exactly):*
>
> *Top 3 outcomes for today*
>
> *Task list (grouped: Deep Work / Admin / Waiting / Delegation)*
>
> *Time blocks (morning / midday / afternoon)*
>
> *Risks and blockers (with next actions)*
>
> *Commitment scan (promises I'm making today)*
>
> *Claims to verify (facts/dates/policies I must confirm)*
> *My capture note:*
> *[Paste your capture note here]"*

If your day is heavy, the system will still work because it forces you into outcomes and next actions.

Stage 3: Plan the day (4 minutes)

You will either:

- accept the time blocks
- or adjust them based on your calendar reality

The system is not meant to replace your judgment. It is meant to reduce planning friction.

A simple rule for time blocks:

- Put your Top 1 outcome first, before email.
- Put admin tasks into a single block.
- Group communication into batches.

If you do nothing else, do this: protect one deep-work block.

Stage 4: Commitments and risk check (1–2 minutes)

Before you start, run a quick self-check:

- What am I promising today?
- What must be true for these promises to hold?
- Do I need to verify anything before sending messages?

If the day includes external communication, you will use the commitment and claims scan from Chapter 9 automatically.

Daily Planning Outputs: What You Store (And Why)

You do not need to store every daily plan forever.

Store daily plans when they contain:

- a meaningful decision
- a commitment to stakeholders
- a reusable structure
- a lesson learned

Otherwise, store only the weekly review outputs.

A calm storage approach:

- Keep daily plans for one week.
- At the weekly review, extract what matters.
- Delete or archive the rest.

This prevents your system home from becoming clutter.

Workflow 2: Weekly Review with AI (A 25–35 Minute Routine)

Weekly reviews are where your system becomes real.

Without a weekly review, you will:

- forget what you learned
- repeat mistakes
- carry open loops too long
- feel behind even when you worked hard

Your weekly review has five stages:

1. Collect (5 minutes)
2. Review and extract (10 minutes)
3. Decide and plan (10 minutes)
4. Update assets (5 minutes)
5. Close loops (5 minutes)

Stage 1: Collect (5 minutes)

Gather:

- your capture notes for the week (or memory if minimal)
- your calendar highlights (meetings that mattered)

- any deliverables you produced
- any decisions that were made

You do not need perfect records. You need enough truth to extract signals.

Stage 2: Review and extract (10 minutes)

Weekly Review Prompt (template + example)

> *Prompt:*
> *"You are my weekly review coach.*
> *Goal: help me extract truth, lessons, and next priorities from my week.*
> *Rules:*
>
> *Use only the inputs I provide; do not invent accomplishments or decisions*
>
> *Keep tone calm and practical*
>
> *Label assumptions as assumptions*
> *Output format (use these headings exactly):*
>
> *Wins (what moved forward)*
>
> *Work in progress (what's unfinished and why)*
>
> *Open loops (waiting, decisions, unanswered questions)*
>
> *Risks and early warnings*
>
> *Lessons learned (what to change next week)*
>
> *Next week: top 3 outcomes*
>
> *Next week: key meetings and what I need from each*
>
> *Verification list (facts/commitments I must confirm)*
> *Inputs:*
>
> *Weekly notes: [Paste your capture notes or weekly summary]*
>
> *Calendar highlights: [List the 3-8 meetings/events that mattered]*
>
> *Deliverables shipped: [List what you sent or completed]*
>
> *Decisions made: [List decisions, even small ones]"*

This prompt produces a "weekly executive summary of your life at work"—without drama, without hype.

Stage 3: Decide and plan (10 minutes)

Your weekly review outputs become:

- your Top 3 outcomes for next week
- your project next steps
- your open loop closure plan

Here is the key practice:

Convert open loops into next actions.

Weak: "Waiting on vendor."

Strong: "Email vendor by Tuesday 10:00 a.m.; if no response by Thursday, escalate to procurement lead."

ChatGPT can help generate next actions, but you choose them.

Stage 4: Update assets (5 minutes)

Update:

- your workload map (if needed)
- your project context packets (1–2 max per week)
- your prompt library if you learned a better template

The system stays small by updating only what matters.

Stage 5: Close loops (5 minutes)

Pick 3–5 open loops and close them immediately:

- send the email
- ask the question
- schedule the conversation
- make the decision
- document the decision record

This is where anxiety reduces. Open loops are silent stress.

The "Context Packet" as a Weekly Deliverable (Your Project Anti-Friction Tool)

In Chapter 14, you learned context packets. In this capstone, they become operational.

Each week, update context packets for your top 1–2 projects.

Context packet format (keep under 250 words):

- Purpose
- Stakeholders (roles)
- Constraints
- Current status (1–3 sentences)
- Key decisions
- Next steps
- Risks / watchlist

```
Prompt: Weekly context packet update
Copy-paste prompt:
"Update this project context packet using my new notes.
Rules:

Use only provided info; do not invent dates or decisions

Keep under 250 words

Replace names with roles
Output: updated context packet + a short 'watchlist' of 3 risks
to monitor next week
Current context packet:
[Paste current packet]
New weekly notes:
[Paste notes]"
```

Context packets are how you stop re-explaining projects to yourself and others.

Your System Guardrails (Daily and Weekly)

Your capstone system includes guardrails by default:

- **No invention rule**: do not invent facts, dates, numbers, policies
- **Missing label rule**: label missing information and ask questions
- **Confidentiality rule**: sanitize inputs; replace names with roles
- **Commitment scan rule**: before external messages, list promises
- **Claims scan rule**: list facts to verify before sending
- **Save rule**: store weekly outputs and important decisions

These guardrails are what transform AI use from "helpful sometimes" to "safe and consistent."

Implementation: Your First Week Using the System

Do not wait for a perfect start. Start with a clean first week.

Day 1

- Create your system home
- Write your first capture note
- Run the daily planning prompt
- Choose Top 3 outcomes
- Do one deep work block before email (if possible)

Day 3

- Adjust your daily planning prompt if it's too long or too short
- Add one guardrail you realized you needed

Day 5

- Prepare for weekly review by collecting your notes and highlights

End of Week

- Run the weekly review prompt
- Update one context packet
- Identify one improvement to your prompt library

Your system becomes personal through iteration, not through design theory.

Capstone Workbook, Part II: Writing Pipelines and Decision Frameworks

In Part I, you built the foundation: a system home, daily planning, weekly review, context packets, and guardrails.

In Part II, you will build two high-impact systems that reduce cognitive load immediately:

1. A writing pipeline you can reuse for most professional writing
2. Decision frameworks that turn uncertainty into structured choices

The goal is not to create "perfect writing" or "perfect decisions." The goal is to create repeatable processes that:

- reduce rework
- prevent missed commitments
- improve clarity
- support verification
- preserve your voice
- produce outputs you can send with confidence

This chapter is a workbook. You will build templates and test them on real scenarios.

A Writing Pipeline is a System, Not a Prompt

Most professionals write under pressure. They start too late, draft too fast, and send with too little review.

A writing pipeline replaces improvisation with stages.

Your pipeline will have four stages:

1. **Brief** (clarify what you're writing and why)
2. **Draft** (generate the first version)
3. **Review** (commitments + claims + tone)
4. **Finalize** (short human pass; save template improvements)

This approach is calm because it separates thinking from typing.

ChatGPT supports each stage, but you remain responsible for the final output.

Pipeline Stage 1: The "3-Line Brief" (Your Writing Anchor)

Before using AI, write a 3-line brief:

1. Audience: who this is for
2. Goal: what you want them to think/do/decide
3. Constraints: tone, length, policies, what not to say

Example:

- Audience: customer who experienced delay
- Goal: acknowledge, explain next step, set expectation
- Constraints: calm and accountable, no blame, no promises unless verified

This is simple but powerful. It prevents you from outsourcing the "why" of the message.

> **Prompt: Brief assistant**
> "Help me refine this 3-line brief without changing the meaning.
> Rules: keep it short; ask questions only if necessary.
> My brief: [paste]."

Store your brief in the message draft or at the top of your working doc. Then proceed.

Pipeline Stage 2: Drafting With Structure and Guardrails

A reliable draft prompt includes:

- Role
- Audience
- Goal
- Constraints
- Source facts (what must be true)
- Output format

Here is a universal drafting prompt you can reuse for many writing tasks:

> Universal Draft Prompt:
> "You are my professional writing assistant.
> Audience: [audience].
> Goal: [goal].
> Tone: calm, confident, plain English, no hype.
> Constraints: [length, policy, what to avoid].
>
> Facts (use as truth; do not add):
>
> [fact 1]
>
> [fact 2]
> Output format: [email / memo / report section].
> Guardrails:
>
> Do not invent names, dates, numbers, or policies
>
> If info is missing, write 'Missing' and ask questions
>
> End with: commitments + claims to verify + verification checklist"

This prompt is "advanced" because it forces the assistant to stay grounded and reviewable.

Pipeline Stage 3: Review Loops (What Makes Your Writing Trustworthy)

Many professionals stop at drafting. The pipeline becomes reliable when you review.

Your review stage has three checks:

1. **Commitment scan:** what am I promising?
2. **Claims scan:** what must be verified?
3. **Tone and stakeholder impact:** how will this land?

You can do this yourself, but AI can speed it.

> *Review Prompt:*
> *"Review this draft before I send it.*
> *Do three scans:*
>
> *Commitment scan: list explicit and implied promises*
>
> *Claims scan: list factual claims that require verification*
>
> *Tone scan: identify any wording that could sound blamey,*
> *defensive, vague, or overly confident*
> *Then rewrite the draft with safer commitments and clearer*
> *Language.*
> *Rules: do not add new facts; keep it concise.*
> *Draft: [paste]."*

This is one of the most valuable prompts in the book. It preserves trust.

Pipeline Stage 4: Finalize (The Human Pass That Preserves Your Voice)

Your human pass is short. You are not rewriting everything. You are doing three things:

- Ensure the first paragraph is clear and aligned with your goal
- Ensure the ask is explicit
- Ensure the closing is human and professional

A practical trick:

Rewrite the first two sentences and the last two sentences yourself. Keep the middle mostly as drafted.

This "human anchor" preserves your voice.

After finalizing, save:

- the final version (if reusable)
- what you learned about the prompt (if it needs tuning)

Build Writing Pipeline #1: Emails That Get Results without Drama

Email is one of the biggest sources of cognitive load. The goal is not to answer everything. The goal is to move work forward.

You will build an email pipeline that produces:

- Clear subject line
- Purpose in first two sentences
- One ask or decision request
- Necessary context only
- Next steps and deadlines (only if verified)
- Polite close

Email template structure:

1. Subject: [topic + action]
2. Opening: purpose + context
3. Ask: what you need from them
4. Details: only what supports the ask
5. Close: next step + thanks

> **Prompt: Email pipeline generator**
> "Create an email using this structure: subject, opening, ask, details, close.
> Audience: [audience].
> Goal: [goal].
> Constraints: [tone, length, policy].
> Facts: [paste facts].
> Guardrails: do not invent dates; label missing info.
> End with commitments + claims to verify."

Build 5 reusable email types for your role:

- request for info
- status update
- follow-up / nudge
- escalation (calm)
- correction message

Store them in Templates.

Build Writing Pipeline #2: Updates and Reports (The Executive Format)

Executives and stakeholders do not want more detail. They want:

- What's the status
- What changed
- What risks exist
- What decisions are needed
- What happens next

A reliable update format:

- Status headline
- So what / now what
- Progress (3 bullets)
- Risks (3 bullets) + mitigation
- Asks/decisions (1–3 bullets)
- Next steps

> **Prompt: Executive update generator**
> "Draft an executive update using this structure exactly:
>
> Status headline (1 sentence)
>
> So what / now what (2-3 sentences)
>
> Progress (max 3 bullets)
>
> Risks + mitigations (max 3 bullets)
>
> Asks/decisions needed (max 3 bullets)
>
> Next steps (max 5 bullets with owners if known)
> Rules: use only my facts; do not invent; label missing info; end with commitments + claims to verify.
> Facts: [paste]."

This becomes one of your highest leverage templates.

Build Writing Pipeline #3: SOP Writing as a Pipeline (Draft → Test → Revise)

SOPs become useful when they reflect reality and are tested.

Pipeline:

1. Source notes (current process truth)
2. Draft SOP with "Missing" labels
3. Extract checklist
4. Identify exceptions and edge cases
5. Test with a real person
6. Revise and version

Prompt stack (SOP pipeline):

> *Prompt A (Draft SOP):*
> *"Draft an SOP from my source notes. Use my notes as truth. Label missing info. Include purpose, scope, steps, tools, inputs/outputs, quality checks, exceptions."*
>
> *Prompt B (Checklist):*
> *"Extract a 10-20 item checklist from the SOP. Make it usable under time pressure."*
>
> *Prompt C (Exceptions):*
> *"List the top 10 edge cases and exceptions. For each, describe what to do or what question to ask."*
>
> *Prompt D (Test plan):*
> *"Create a 15-minute test plan to validate this SOP with a new team member."*

This pipeline turns documentation into operational support.

Decision Frameworks: Why Decisions Feel Heavy (And How to Lighten Them)

Decisions feel heavy for three reasons:

1. **Unclear goals:** you don't know what "good" means
2. **Too many options:** you feel uncertain
3. **Fear of consequences:** you worry about being wrong

A decision framework reduces that weight by creating structure.

You will build three decision tools:

1. A Decision Record template
2. An Options and Tradeoffs framework
3. A Pre-mortem and risk guardrail

These tools shift decisions from "emotionally heavy" to "professionally manageable."

Decision Tool #1: The Decision Record (Your Memory and Accountability)

A decision record prevents endless revisiting.

Decision Record fields (simple):

- Decision: what are we choosing?
- Date: when decided
- Owner: who owns the decision
- Context: why it matters
- Options considered: 2–4
- Criteria: what matters most (time, cost, risk, customer impact)
- Rationale: why this option
- Risks: what could go wrong
- Mitigations: how we reduce risk
- Next steps: what happens now
- Verification list: what must be confirmed

> Prompt: Decision record generator
> "Create a decision record using the fields above.
> Rules: use only my facts; do not invent; label missing info; keep plain English.
> Facts: [paste notes]."

Store decision records in Projects. These become part of your context packets and make weekly reviews easier.

Decision Tool #2: Options And Tradeoffs (The Executive Thinking Frame)

Most decisions are tradeoffs.

A structured options framework:

- **Option A:** fast but higher risk
- **Option B:** slower but safer
- **Option C:** balanced compromise

ChatGPT can help generate options if you provide constraints, but you must validate feasibility.

> *Prompt: Options and tradeoffs builder*
> *"Help me make a decision.*
> *Decision: [decision].*
> *Constraints: [budget/time/policy/people].*
> *What matters most (rank): [criteria].*
> *Facts (use as truth): [paste].*
> *Output: 3-4 options with pros/cons, tradeoffs, key assumptions,*
> *risks, and a recommendation with assumptions labeled.*
> *Rules: do not invent facts; label unknowns."*

Use this when you need to propose options to stakeholders.

Decision Tool #3: Pre-Mortem (Find Failure Before It Happens)

A pre-mortem is a simple technique:

Imagine the plan failed in the future.
Ask: what caused the failure?

This reduces anxiety because it brings vague fear into concrete risks.

> *Prompt: Pre-mortem*
> *"We chose Option [X].*
> *Run a pre-mortem: assume this decision fails in 90 days.*
> *List 10 reasons it failed across*
> *people/process/tools/communication/timing.*
> *Then propose mitigations and early warning signs for each.*
> *Rules: keep it practical and plain English."*

Pre-mortems are especially useful for:

- launches
- process changes
- vendor selection
- timelines with dependencies
- training rollouts

They help you build guardrails into the plan.

Integrating Decisions into Your Weekly Review

In Part I, you built weekly reviews. In Part II, you add a decision layer.

Each weekly review should capture:

- Decisions made (even small ones)
- Decisions pending
- What you need to decide next week

Then you create decision records for 1–2 significant decisions per week.

This prevents decision fatigue from accumulating.

```
Prompt: Weekly decisions extractor
"From my weekly review text, extract:

Decisions made

Decisions pending

Decisions needed next week
Then propose which ones should become formal decision records
(top 2) and why.
Rules: use only my text; do not invent."
```

Implementation: Build and Test Your Pipelines This Week

This week, you will build:

- One universal drafting prompt
- One review prompt
- One email template set (5)
- One executive update template
- One decision record template

- One options/tradeoffs prompt
- One pre-mortem prompt

Then you will test them on real scenarios (sanitized as needed).

Your goal is not perfection. Your goal is "usable and repeatable."

Capstone Workbook, Part III: Prompt Library, Guardrails, and Your Final System

In Part I, you built the foundation: daily planning, weekly review, context packets, and guardrails.

In Part II, you built writing pipelines and decision frameworks.

In Part III, you will finalize your system so it becomes:

- reusable
- easy to run under stress
- safe and accurate
- consistent across months
- teachable (to yourself and others)

This chapter completes the capstone by producing four final deliverables:

1. Your personal prompt library (a curated set, not a junk drawer)
2. Your ethical and accuracy guardrails (standard of care)
3. Your system checklist (daily/weekly/monthly)
4. Your reusable prompt framework reference (quick sheet)

At the end, you will have a complete system: a practical "AI operating manual" for your own work.

Your Prompt Library: Build Small, Keep It Alive

A prompt library is not a list of clever prompts. It is a working toolkit.

A healthy library has:

- a small number of prompts you actually use
- clear naming
- consistent placeholders
- built-in guardrails
- examples or "gold standards" when possible
- a maintenance habit

Your capstone library will have 15 prompts maximum.

If you build more than that before using them, the library becomes clutter.

Your Core 15 Prompts (The Capstone Set)

Below is a professional prompt set that covers most modern knowledge work. You will customize these for your role and store them under Templates.

For each prompt, you will store:

- Prompt name
- When to use
- Copy-paste template
- Output format
- Guardrails

A short example input (optional but helpful)

PROMPT 1 — Daily Plan (Top 3 Outcomes)

When to use: start of day

```
Prompt:
"You are my executive productivity assistant.
Goal: produce a calm daily plan.
Rules: use only my note as truth; do not invent tasks; label
missing info.
Output headings:

Top 3 outcomes

Task list (Deep Work / Admin / Waiting / Delegation)

Time blocks

Risks and blockers (next actions)

Commitment scan

Claims to verify
Capture note: [paste]."
```

PROMPT 2 — Weekly Review

When to use: end of week
Prompt: (use the Capstone Workbook, Part I Weekly Review Prompt with fixed headings)

PROMPT 3 — Context Packet Creator (250 words)

When to use: new project or update

> **Prompt:**
> "Create/update a context packet under 250 words using my notes as truth. Replace names with roles.
> Include purpose, stakeholders, constraints, status, decisions, next steps, risks.
> Notes: [paste]."

PROMPT 4 — Meeting Notes → Decisions/Actions

When to use: after a meeting

> **Prompt:**
> "Convert these notes into: purpose, decisions, action items (owner/deadline), open questions, risks.
> Rules: do not invent details; label unknowns as Missing.
> Notes: [paste]."

PROMPT 5 — Recap Email (from structured notes)

When to use: meeting follow-up

> **Prompt:**
> "Draft a recap email using: purpose, decisions, action items, open questions, next steps.
> Tone: neutral, calm.
> Rules: do not add facts; if deadlines are Missing, ask.
> Structured notes: [paste].
> End with commitment scan."

PROMPT 6 — Universal Draft (Writing Engine)

When to use: any email/memo/report section
Prompt: (use Capstone Workbook, Part II Universal Draft Prompt)

PROMPT 7 — Review Loop (Commitments + Claims + Tone)

When to use: before sending anything externally
Prompt: (use Capstone Workbook, Part II Review Prompt)

PROMPT 8 — Executive Update (Structure Lock)

When to use: stakeholder updates
Prompt: (use Capstone Workbook, Part II Executive Update Structure)

PROMPT 9 — Decision Record Generator

When to use: after a significant decision
Prompt: (use Capstone Workbook, Part II Decision Record Fields)

PROMPT 10 — Options and Tradeoffs Memo

When to use: before a decision or stakeholder discussion
Prompt: (use Capstone Workbook, Part II Options Prompt)

PROMPT 11 — Pre-mortem (Risks and Early Warnings)

When to use: before launching or changing process
Prompt: (use Capstone Workbook, Part II Pre-mortem Prompt)

PROMPT 12 — SOP Draft (Source-First)

When to use: documenting a process

```
Prompt:
"Draft an SOP from source notes.
Include purpose, scope, steps, inputs/outputs, tools, quality
checks, exceptions.
Rules: use notes as truth; label missing info; do not invent
policies.
Notes: [paste]."
```

PROMPT 13 — Checklist Extractor (from SOP or Process)

When to use: make work runnable

```
Prompt:
"Extract a checklist (10-20 items) from this SOP/process.
Make it usable under time pressure.
Rules: do not add steps not in the source.
Source: [paste]."
```

PROMPT 14 — Lessons Learned (After Action)

When to use: after projects or incidents

```
Prompt:
"Create a lessons learned document from these notes: what
happened, what worked, what didn't, root cause hypotheses,
changes, prevention checklist.
Rules: do not invent details; label assumptions.
Notes: [paste]."
```

PROMPT 15 — Marketing or Customer Response (Voice + Proof)

When to use: customer communications or marketing drafts

> **Prompt:**
> "Write [email/response/description] using our Voice Card and policies.
> Voice Card: [paste].
> Policies (truth): [paste].
> Constraints: calm tone, no hype, no unverified claims.
> Output: [format].
> End with commitments + claims to verify."

This set is enough for most professionals. You can add later, but you do not need more now.

Customizing Your Library: Placeholders That Make Prompts Fast

A prompt library becomes usable when it has consistent placeholders.

Use these placeholders across all prompts:

- [Audience]
- [Goal]
- [Tone]
- [Constraints]
- [Facts: use as truth]
- [Output format]
- [Risk level]
- [Policies: truth]
- [Voice Card]
- [Missing info questions]

Standardizing placeholders reduces friction and prevents you from "starting over" every time.

> **Prompt: Placeholder standardizer**
> "Rewrite these prompt templates so they share consistent placeholders: [Audience], [Goal], [Constraints], [Facts], [Output format], [Guardrails].
> Keep meaning the same. Do not add new sections.
> Templates: [paste]."

Your Standard of Care: Ethical and Accuracy Guardrails (Final Form)

Your standard of care is the heart of "AI without the anxiety."

This is your minimum process.

Risk Level 1 (low risk; internal)

Examples: brainstorming, note cleanup, outlines, rough drafts
Minimum standard:

- sanitize if needed
- quick review for sense and alignment
- no external sending without Level 2 review

Risk Level 2 (medium risk; internal + external routine)

Examples: customer emails, routine updates, SOP drafts, marketing copy
Minimum standard:

- sanitize inputs
- structure lock if recurring
- commitment scan before sending
- claims scan and verify key facts
- save final output if reusable

Risk Level 3 (high risk; sensitive or consequential)

Examples: legal/medical/financial guidance, HR performance issues, regulatory claims, public statements with high impact
Minimum standard:

- AI for structure and clarity only
- authoritative sources or expert review required
- no definitive claims without verification
- approvals and evidence saved
- follow organizational policy strictly

Your standard of care should be written as a one-page checklist.

> **Standard of Care Prompt:**
> "AI Standard of Care — Personal Use
> Before prompting:
>
> Confirm risk level (1-3)
>
> Remove sensitive identifiers; replace names with roles
>
> List required facts and constraints
> During prompting:
>
> Use source-first rules (no invention; label Missing)
>
> Use structure lock for recurring outputs
> Before sending externally:
>
> Commitment scan (what am I promising?)
>
> Claims scan (what must be verified?)
>
> Tone scan (how will this land?)
> Verification:
>
> Verify dates, numbers, policies, and claims with authoritative sources
>
> If uncertain, revise language or delay commitments
> After sending:
>
> Save final output and key inputs if reusable
>
> Log one improvement if something felt risky or unclear"

You will customize this for your role and policies.

Your System Checklists: Daily, Weekly, Monthly

Your system becomes real when it has checklists you follow.

Daily Checklist (10–12 minutes)

1. Write capture note (today/next/blockers/commitments)
2. Run Daily Plan prompt
3. Choose Top 3 outcomes
4. Time block one deep work block
5. Run commitment scan before external messages

Weekly Checklist (25–35 minutes)

1. Collect weekly notes + calendar highlights
2. Run Weekly Review prompt
3. Identify open loops and convert to next actions
4. Update 1–2 context packets
5. Create 1–2 decision records (if needed)
6. Close 3–5 open loops immediately
7. Save weekly review and key outputs

Monthly Checklist (30–45 minutes)

1. Review your prompt library: keep, revise, delete
2. Review your calibration log for recurring errors
3. Update gold standard examples
4. Identify one skill to build next month
5. Update your standard of care if needed

These checklists protect your system from drift.

Your Final System Map: How it All Works Together

Your system is a loop:

Inputs:

- capture notes
- project context packets
- policies and voice card
- facts and constraints

Workflows:

- daily planning
- weekly review
- writing pipeline
- decision frameworks
- SOP and checklist creation

Outputs:

- daily plan (Top 3 outcomes)
- weekly review summary
- context packet updates
- decision records
- polished communications
- reusable templates

Guardrails:

- risk levels
- no invention
- commitment and claims scans
- verification ladder
- sanitization practices

Maintenance:

- weekly asset updates
- monthly library review

This is what "systems" look like without coding: stable inputs, stable outputs, repeatable workflows, and safety standards.

Your "AI Operating Manual" (One Page You Can Print)

Below is a one-page operating manual you can adapt. It is intentionally simple.

AI OPERATING MANUAL (Draft)

1. Decide risk level:

   - Level 1 = internal drafting and organization
   - Level 2 = routine external communications (verify)
   - Level 3 = high-stakes (AI for structure only; expert/source required)

2. Prepare inputs:

   - sanitize; replace names with roles
   - list facts and constraints
   - define audience and goal

3. Run the right template:

   - daily plan / weekly review / writing engine / review loop / decision record

4. Before sending:

   - commitment scan
   - claims scan
   - tone scan
   - verify dates, numbers, and policies

5. Save what matters:

   - weekly review
   - context packets
   - decision records
   - reusable templates
   - gold standards

6. Improve monthly:

   - delete unused prompts
   - strengthen guardrails
   - track calibration mistakes and fixes

This manual is your confidence tool. It turns AI use into a routine with standards.

Final Validation: Prove Your System Works (A 7-Day Test)

A system is real when it survives a normal week.

Run this 7-day test:

Day 1–5:

- daily planning workflow each morning
- writing pipeline for at least 2 messages
- review loop before at least 1 external message

Day 6 or 7:

- weekly review workflow
- update one context packet
- create one decision record
- close five open loops

Success criteria:

- You produced tangible outputs
- You reduced rework

- You reduced "open loop stress"
- You did not overpromise
- You verified key facts before sending
- You improved one template based on experience

If it didn't work, you do not throw it away. You debug it like a process.

Expanded Glossary for Business Users

This glossary is written for working professionals. Each term is defined in plain English, with a business-use example. When a term is debated or used differently across organizations, the definition here reflects how it is used in this book.

A

Accuracy ladder (Verification ladder)
A step-by-step way to decide how much checking an AI output needs. Low-risk tasks get quick checks; medium-risk tasks get claims verification; high-risk tasks require authoritative sources and/or expert review.
Example: You verify dates and policy statements before sending a customer email.

Action item
A specific, owned next step that moves work forward. A good action item has an owner and a due point (date or event).
Example: "Alex drafts the SOP by Thursday 3 p.m." (not "Work on SOP.")

Agent (AI agent)
A system that can take steps toward a goal (often across tools) with minimal prompts from a person. In this book, you do not need agents to get real productivity gains.
Example: An "agent" that drafts and routes updates automatically—useful only after your workflow is stable.

Ambiguity
Language that can be interpreted multiple ways, which creates rework and conflict. AI can reduce ambiguity when you demand clear structure and explicit assumptions.
Example: "Soon" is ambiguous; "by Friday at noon" is not.

Assumption
A statement you treat as true without direct confirmation. In professional AI use, assumptions must be labeled so they can be verified or revised.
Example: "Assumption: the stakeholder wants a one-page summary."

Assumptions First

A prompt practice where the assistant lists assumptions and missing information before drafting. This reduces confident wrongness and improves trust.
Example: "Before drafting, list what you assume, what you don't know, and what you need from me."

Audience

The person or group your output is for. Audience drives tone, format, and level of detail.
Example: An executive update is different from a team working note.

B

Bias (in outputs)

A tendency toward one viewpoint or framing that may not be justified by evidence or context. Bias can show up as overly certain recommendations, one-sided tradeoffs, or tone that favors one stakeholder.
Example: A draft that assumes one department is at fault without evidence.

Brief (3-line brief)

A short writing anchor: audience, goal, constraints. It keeps you in control of "why" before AI drafts "how."
Example: "Audience: customer. Goal: set expectation. Constraints: no promises unless verified."

Business-focused PKM (Personal Knowledge Management)

Your system for capturing, condensing, and retrieving work knowledge (decisions, context, lessons, templates). AI helps process; your storage remains the source of truth.
Example: Keeping a project context packet updated weekly.

C

Calibration

Your ability to match confidence to reality—knowing when to trust an output and when to verify more. Calibration improves through logs and review loops.
Example: You learn that AI is error-prone on dates unless you supply them.

Capture note

A short operational note (today/next/blockers/commitments) that preserves context and feeds planning workflows.
Example: "Blocker: waiting on vendor. Commitment: promised update tomorrow."

Chain-of-thought (internal reasoning)

The model's internal reasoning process. You do not need access to it to work effectively. In this book, you use visible structure: assumptions, missing info, and verification lists.

Example: Asking for "assumptions and claims to verify" instead of hidden reasoning.

Claims scan

A review step that lists factual statements that require verification (dates, numbers, policies, results).

Example: "Claim: turnaround time is 3–5 days" → verify before publishing.

Cognitive load

The mental effort required to hold and process information. AI reduces cognitive load when it structures and summarizes—not when it adds noise.

Example: Turning messy notes into decisions and action items.

Commitment

Any promise you make, explicit or implied. Commitments create expectations and risk when they aren't controlled.

Example: "I'll send the final draft tomorrow" is a commitment.

Commitment scan

A review step that lists promises in a draft so you can revise risky wording before sending.

Example: Changing "I guarantee" to "I will do X by Y if Z holds."

Compliance (work context)

Rules your organization must follow (legal, regulatory, contractual, policy). AI use must align with compliance rules—especially around confidentiality and claims.

Example: Not pasting confidential customer data into unapproved tools.

Compose (Generate)

A prompt function: you provide a brief and the assistant drafts an output.

Example: Drafting a proposal section from a structured brief.

Confidentiality

Protecting sensitive information from improper disclosure. In AI workflows, confidentiality often means sanitizing inputs and using approved tools.

Example: Replacing names with roles in context packets.

Constraint

A boundary that limits what the output can do: length, tone, policy, what must not be claimed, what must be included.

Example: "No hype, no fear language, no unverified timeline promises."

Context packet

A short, reusable summary of a project or situation (purpose, stakeholders, constraints, status, decisions, next steps, risks). It prevents re-explaining and supports consistent outputs.

Example: A 250-word project snapshot pasted into updates and emails.

Corrective action

A change made to prevent a problem from recurring, often after a mistake. In AI workflows, corrective action is usually a new guardrail or template revision.

Example: Adding a "do not invent dates" rule after a date error.

Critique then rewrite

A prompt pattern: evaluate a draft against criteria, then rewrite it, then list changes. It makes edits visible and trustworthy.

Example: "Critique for clarity and tone, then rewrite, then list top 5 changes."

D

Decision record

A structured note capturing a decision, rationale, options considered, risks, and next steps. Decision records reduce revisiting and preserve context.

Example: "We chose Vendor B because... Risks... Mitigations..."

Decision memo

A decision-ready document: decision needed, context, options, tradeoffs, recommendation (with assumptions), and next steps.

Example: A one-page memo to leadership proposing three timeline options.

Definition of done

A clear description of what "finished" means for a deliverable. This prevents endless revision and unclear expectations.

Example: "Done means: approved by legal, posted on site, stored in templates."

Delegation

Assigning work to someone else with clear ownership and expectations. AI helps create clear delegation messages and task definitions.

Example: "Owner, deliverable, due date, success criteria."

Dependency

A condition that must occur before work can proceed. Dependencies are a major source of schedule risk.

Example: "Cannot finalize report until finance confirms numbers."

Draft

A working version meant to be reviewed and improved. AI is excellent at drafts; humans are essential for verification and final judgment.

Example: First version of a customer email before the commitment scan.

E

Edge case

An uncommon situation that breaks the "normal process." SOPs become reliable when edge cases are identified and handled.

Example: "What if the customer requests a change after production starts?"

Evaluate (Review function)

A prompt function: you provide a draft and criteria; the assistant checks and improves it.

Example: Reviewing an email for tone, promises, and unclear asks.

Exception

A scenario where the standard process does not apply. Documenting exceptions reduces confusion and errors.

Example: "Urgent orders follow an expedited path with approval."

Executive update

A concise stakeholder update that prioritizes what matters: status, risks, decisions needed, and next steps.

Example: "On track; risk: vendor delay; ask: approve option B."

F

Fact vs. inference

A fact is directly known or verified. An inference is a conclusion drawn from facts. Good AI workflows separate them clearly.

Example: Fact: "Vendor hasn't replied." Inference: "They may be delayed."

Failure mode
A way a process or plan can break. Pre-mortems identify failure modes before launching.
Example: "Training fails because managers don't adopt the checklist."

Findability
How easily you can retrieve what you already captured. Findability improves through titles, tags, summaries, and consistent note types.
Example: "Project Alpha — Decision Record — 2026-01-08."

Framework
A reusable structure for thinking or writing that reduces rework.
Example: SPEC, decision memos, prompt stacks.

G

Garbage in, garbage out
If your inputs are unclear or wrong, your outputs will be too—faster. AI amplifies input quality.
Example: Vague notes → vague plan.

Gold standard example
A saved example of excellent output used as a style and quality reference.
Example: Your best executive update becomes a model for future updates.

Governance (prompt governance)
Light rules for managing shared templates: versioning, review requirements, prohibited data, and update process.
Example: "All external email prompts require a commitment scan by default."

Guardrail
A rule that prevents common failure: no invention, label missing info, verify claims, sanitize inputs, avoid absolute promises.
Example: "If a timeline isn't provided, mark it Missing."

H

Hallucination (AI output)
When an AI produces plausible-sounding information that is not grounded in your inputs or verified sources. The cure is guardrails and verification.
Example: Inventing a policy clause you never provided.

Human-in-the-loop

A workflow where a person reviews, verifies, and approves AI outputs before they are used. This is essential for medium and high-risk work.
Example: Draft → claims scan → verify → send.

I

Intent (customer intent)

What a person is trying to accomplish (learn, compare, buy, resolve). Marketing works better when content matches intent.
Example: "How to choose" content for comparison intent.

Input form

A standard set of fields you fill in each time so a prompt produces consistent outputs.
Example: Status update input: progress, risks, asks, next steps.

Iteration

A small improvement cycle: run the workflow, observe errors/friction, adjust the template, test again.
Example: Tightening headings to reduce rambling drafts.

K

Key risk indicator (early warning sign)

A measurable or observable sign that a risk is becoming real.
Example: "No vendor response within 48 hours" signals schedule risk.

Knowledge asset

A condensed, reusable piece of knowledge that saves time later: checklist, template, quick reference, context packet, decision record.
Example: A reusable customer response library.

L

Label "Missing"

A disciplined practice: when information is not provided, the assistant must mark it as Missing instead of guessing.
Example: "Missing: due date. Question: when must this be delivered?"

Lesson learned

A short record of what worked, what didn't, and what you will change. Lessons become checklists and improved SOPs.
Example: "We missed approval owner—add owner field to intake form."

Level 1/2/3 risk

A simple risk scale used throughout the book. Level 1 is low-risk internal work; Level 2 is routine external or medium-risk internal; Level 3 is high-stakes or sensitive.
Example: A public policy statement is Level 3.

M

Meta description (SEO)

A short description that appears in search results. It should be clear and accurate, not stuffed with keywords.
Example: "Custom engraved gifts with proof-based details and clear ordering steps."

Metric (process metric)

A measurable indicator of performance (cycle time, error rate, throughput). AI can help interpret metrics but should not invent them.
Example: Summarizing trends from provided numbers.

Model (AI model)

The underlying system that generates outputs from prompts. Different versions have different capabilities and error patterns. Your process protects you regardless of model.
Example: You rely on verification, not on "it sounds right."

N

Neutral tone

Language that avoids blame and emotional escalation while staying direct and clear. Useful in conflict, customer support, and cross-team updates.
Example: "We observed X; next step is Y" rather than "You failed to do X."

No invention rule

A guardrail: do not add facts, names, dates, numbers, or policies not supplied. When missing, ask.
Example: Prevents invented turnaround times.

O

Open loop
A task, question, or unresolved item that stays in your mind and creates stress. Good systems convert open loops into next actions.
Example: "Waiting on approval" → "Ping approver by Tuesday."

Options analysis
A structured comparison of choices with tradeoffs, risks, and assumptions.
Example: "Option A faster/higher risk; Option B slower/safer."

Output format
The required structure of the deliverable: headings, bullets, length, tone. Clear formats reduce rework.
Example: "Six-section executive update with bullet limits."

P

Personal prompt library
A curated set of templates you actually use. Quality beats quantity.
Example: 10–15 prompts covering planning, writing, decisions, operations.

PKM (Personal Knowledge Management)
Your system for capturing and retrieving what matters so you stop redoing work. AI helps condense; your notes store truth.
Example: Weekly context packet updates.

Plain English
Writing that avoids unnecessary jargon and explains any technical term used. Plain English is faster to read and reduces errors.
Example: "Turnaround time" explained as "how long it takes from order to shipment."

Pre-mortem
A technique: assume a plan failed, list reasons, then add mitigations and early warning signs.
Example: "If rollout fails, why?" → training gaps, unclear ownership, tool friction.

Prompt
The instructions and inputs you provide to the assistant. In business use, good prompts behave like SPECs: clear expectations and constraints.
Example: A structure-locked status update prompt.

Prompt stack

A workflow using multiple prompts in sequence, each with one job (Transform →
Compose → Review). This improves reliability.
Example: Notes cleanup → recap email → commitment scan.

Proof-based language

Claims supported by facts, process, examples, or policy—without exaggerated
guarantees.
Example: "Inspected before shipping" vs. "Flawless every time."

Q

Quality check

A step that prevents errors before delivery. AI outputs can include quality checks
(commitments, claims, tone) but humans verify.
Example: Verifying policy language before publishing.

R

Repeatability test

A test for automation candidates: frequent, clear inputs, clear outputs, stable rules,
manageable risk.
Example: Weekly updates pass; one-off crisis response may not.

Retrieval

Finding what you already captured when you need it. Retrieval is the practical
purpose of PKM.
Example: Quickly finding the last decision record before a meeting.

Risk

The chance of harm or cost if something goes wrong. In AI-assisted work, risk often
comes from wrong facts, wrong commitments, or confidentiality breaches.
Example: Incorrect pricing info in customer messaging.

S

Sanitization

Removing or abstracting sensitive details before using AI: replace names with
roles, remove identifiers, remove confidential numbers.
Example: "Customer A" instead of a real name.

Scope

What a deliverable or process includes—and what it does not include. Clear scope prevents "creep" and missed expectations.
Example: "This SOP covers onboarding steps 1–5 only."

SEO (Search Engine Optimization)

Making content easier to find in search by matching intent, using clear structure, and answering questions honestly. In this book, SEO is clarity and usefulness, not tricks.
Example: A page that answers "how to choose" with real options.

Simulation (Practice function)

Using AI for role-play or rehearsal, not for factual authority.
Example: Practicing a stakeholder conversation.

SOP (Standard Operating Procedure)

A documented, repeatable process for doing work consistently. SOPs work best when paired with checklists and edge-case notes.
Example: "How we process customer customization requests."

SPEC framework

Situation, Purpose, Expectations, Constraints—a prompt structure that reduces ambiguity and rework.
Example: Defining format, length, must-haves, and do-nots before drafting.

Stakeholder

Anyone affected by the work: leaders, peers, customers, partners, compliance, team members. Stakeholders determine what "good" means.
Example: Finance cares about accuracy; customers care about clarity and timeliness.

Structure lock

A prompting method that forces consistent headings and formatting across outputs.
Example: Weekly update must follow six headings exactly.

Style guide (Voice Card)

A short, practical reference for tone, vocabulary, proof style, and phrases to avoid.
Example: "Calm, confident, no hype, no fear language."

T

Template
A reusable structure for outputs or prompts. Templates reduce cognitive load and improve consistency.
Example: A recurring "status update" template.

Tone scan
A review step that checks whether language could sound blamey, vague, overly confident, or robotic.
Example: Removing "obviously" and "as I already said."

Tradeoff
A choice where you gain something and give up something. Naming tradeoffs reduces conflict and builds alignment.
Example: Faster launch vs. more testing.

Transform (Prompt function)
Converting messy inputs into structured outputs.
Example: Notes → decisions/actions/open questions.

Trust workflow
Your standard process for safe outputs: risk level → structure → commitment scan → claims scan → verification → send/save.
Example: Running a claims scan before posting marketing copy.

U

Uncertainty
What you do not know yet. In professional AI use, uncertainty is not hidden; it is labeled and managed.
Example: "Missing: final approval owner."

V

Verification
Checking claims against authoritative sources or your trusted internal records. Verification is how you keep AI outputs grounded.
Example: Confirming policy language from your official policy document.

Voice

The consistent personality and tone of your communication. Voice builds trust when it's steady and human.

Example: Calm, clear, respectful, direct.

W

Weekly review

A routine that extracts wins, open loops, risks, and next priorities from the week. It keeps your system alive and reduces anxiety.

Example: Converting "waiting items" into explicit next actions.

Workload map

A simple inventory of recurring responsibilities, active projects, and open loops. It makes work visible and manageable.

Example: Three-bucket list updated weekly.

Printable Productivity Cheat Sheets

These cheat sheets are designed to be printed or copied into your notes system. Each is written as a quick reference you can use during real work. They are intentionally short and operational.

Cheat Sheet 1 — The Trust Workflow (Desk Version)

Use this before you send anything that matters.

1. **Choose risk level (1–3)**
   - Level 1: internal drafts and organization
   - Level 2: routine external communication or medium-impact internal work
   - Level 3: high-stakes, sensitive, regulated, or high-impact public work

2. **Sanitize inputs**
   - Remove identifiers
   - Replace names with roles
   - Remove confidential numbers unless approved

3. **Lock structure (if recurring)**
   - Use fixed headings and limits

4. **Draft with guardrails**
   - No invention
   - Label Missing info
   - Plain English

5. **Commitment scan**
   - What am I promising (explicit or implied)?

6. **Claims scan**
   - What facts must be true (dates, numbers, policies, results)?

7. **Verify**
   - Check claims against authoritative sources or trusted records

8. **Tone scan**
   - Does it sound calm, clear, respectful, and direct?

9. **Send**
   - Only after verification for Level 2/3

10. **Save what matters**
    - Save final version + key inputs (if reusable)
    - Log one improvement if something felt risky

Cheat Sheet 2 — Daily Planning (10–12 Minutes)

Goal: calm clarity, not perfection.

Step 1: Capture (2 minutes)

Write 4 lines:

- Today:
- Next:
- Blockers:
- Commitments:

Step 2: Top 3 outcomes (2 minutes)

Choose outcomes, not vague tasks.

Step 3: Time blocks (4 minutes)

- One deep work block first
- One admin block
- One communication block

Step 4: Risk check (2 minutes)

- What could derail the Top 3?
- What is the next action on each blocker?

Step 5: Pre-send rule (2 minutes)

If anything is going outside your team:

- commitment scan
- claims scan
- verify

Cheat Sheet 3 — Weekly Review (25–35 Minutes)

1. **Collect (5 minutes)**
   - capture notes
   - calendar highlights
   - deliverables shipped
   - decisions made

2. **Extract (10 minutes)**
   - Wins
   - Work in progress
   - Open loops
   - Risks
   - Lessons learned

3. **Decide (10 minutes)**
   - Next week Top 3 outcomes
   - Key meetings: what you need from each
   - Next actions for open loops

4. **Update assets (5 minutes)**
   - update 1–2 context packets
   - create 1–2 decision records (if needed)
   - update one template if it caused friction

5. **Close loops (5 minutes)**
   - resolve 3–5 open loops immediately

6. **Save**
   - weekly review summary
   - updated context packets
   - decision records

Cheat Sheet 4 — The 3-Line Brief (Writing Anchor)

Before drafting anything important, write:

1. Audience:
2. Goal:
3. Constraints:

Examples:

- Audience: leadership. Goal: approve option B. Constraints: one page, neutral tone, no unverified dates.
- Audience: customer. Goal: clarify next step. Constraints: calm, accountable, no promises unless verified.

If the brief is unclear, the writing will be unclear.

Cheat Sheet 5 — Universal Draft Prompt (Copy-Paste)

Use this as your default writing engine.

```
"You are my professional writing assistant.
Audience: [Audience].
Goal: [Goal].
Tone: calm, confident, plain English.
Constraints: [Constraints].
Facts (use as truth; do not add):

[Fact 1]

[Fact 2]
Output format: [Email/Memo/Report section].
Guardrails:

Do not invent names, dates, numbers, or policies

If info is missing, write 'Missing' and ask questions

End with: commitments + claims to verify + verification
checklist."
```

Cheat Sheet 6 — Review Prompt (Commitments + Claims + Tone)

Use this before sending external messages.

> *"Review this draft before I send it.*
>
> *Commitment scan: list explicit and implied promises*
>
> *Claims scan: list factual claims requiring verification*
>
> *Tone scan: identify wording that could sound blamey, vague,*
> *defensive, or overly confident*
> *Then rewrite with safer commitments and clearer language.*
> *Rules: do not add new facts; keep concise.*
> *Draft: [paste]."*

Cheat Sheet 7 — Structure Lock (For Consistent Outputs)

Use when you want the same format every time.

> *"Output must follow this exact structure (do not add/remove*
> *sections):*
> *A)*
> *B)*
> *C)*
> *Limits:*
>
> *Each section under [X] words*
>
> *Bullets only in sections [B, D]*
> *Rules: do not invent facts; label Missing.*
> *Input: [paste]."*

Cheat Sheet 8 — Context Packet (250 Words Max)

Purpose: stop re-explaining; improve consistency.

Context Packet Template:

- Purpose:
- Stakeholders (roles):
- Constraints:
- Current status:

- Key decisions:
- Next steps:
- Risks / watchlist:

Rules:

- Replace names with roles
- Remove identifiers and confidential numbers
- Keep under 250 words

Cheat Sheet 9 — Decision Record (One Page)

Decision Record Fields:

- Decision:
- Date:
- Owner:
- Context:
- Options considered:
- Criteria (rank):
- Rationale:
- Risks:
- Mitigations:
- Next steps:
- Verification list:

Use decision records to reduce revisiting and preserve rationale.

Cheat Sheet 10 — Options And Tradeoffs (Decision Support)

When you're stuck, structure the choice:

- What decision are we making?
- What matters most (rank criteria)?
- What constraints exist (time, budget, policy)?
- What options are available (2–4)?
- What tradeoffs are we accepting?
- What risks exist and how do we reduce them?
- What assumptions must be true?

Cheat Sheet 11 — Pre-Mortem (Risk-Finding Before Launch)

Prompt you can run quickly:

> "We chose Option [X].
> Assume this fails in 90 days.
> List 10 reasons it failed
> (people/process/tools/communication/timing).
> For each: mitigation + early warning sign."

Use pre-mortems for launches, process changes, and timelines with dependencies.

Cheat Sheet 12 — SOP Quick Template (Source-First)

SOP Template:

- Purpose:
- Scope (what's included/excluded):
- Inputs:
- Tools:
- Steps (numbered):
- Quality checks:
- Exceptions / edge cases:
- Outputs:
- Owner / version / last updated:

Rule: Draft from source notes only. Label Missing. Test with a real person.

Cheat Sheet 13 — Lessons Learned (After Action)

Questions:

- What happened?
- What worked?
- What didn't?
- What do we think caused issues?
- What will we change next time?
- What checklist item would prevent this?

This turns experience into improvement instead of stress.

Cheat Sheet 14 — Prompt Stack (Transform → Compose → Review)

Use when tasks feel too complex.

1. **Transform:** clean and structure inputs
2. **Compose:** draft the deliverable
3. **Review:** commitments + claims + tone

Example:

- Notes → decisions/actions
- Decisions/actions → recap email
- Recap email → commitment + claims scan rewrite

Cheat Sheet 15 — AI Operating Manual (One Page)

1. Choose risk level
2. Sanitize inputs
3. Define audience + goal + constraints
4. Use the right template
5. Run commitment + claims scans
6. Verify what matters
7. Tone check
8. Send
9. Save reusable outputs
10. Improve one template monthly

Prompt Frameworks Reference

This chapter is a reference section you can return to when you need a prompt that behaves predictably. Each framework includes:

- What it is
- When to use it
- The template (copy-paste)
- A short example
- Common failure modes and fixes

These frameworks are consistent with the book's standards: plain English, no hype, no invented facts, and human judgment remains central.

SPEC: Situation, Purpose, Expectations, Constraints

What it is

A short "specification" you include in your prompt to reduce ambiguity and rework.

When to use it

- Anything you'll send to someone else
- Any recurring deliverable
- Any task where requirements are unclear

Prompt (Copy-Paste)

```
"Situation: [context + facts]
Purpose: [goal + audience]
Expectations:

Output type:

Format/headings:

Length:

Must include:
Constraints:

Must avoid:

Do not invent facts, names, dates, or numbers
```

```
If info is missing, label 'Missing' and ask questions
End with: commitments + claims to verify + verification
checklist"
```

Example (Short)

Situation: "Customer requested an update; we are waiting on a vendor shipment."
Purpose: "Email the customer to set expectation and keep trust."
Expectations: "Email; under 180 words; includes next step and timing if verified."
Constraints: "No blame; no promises unless verified."

Failure modes and fixes

- **Too vague:** Add concrete "must include" fields.
- **Still inventing facts:** Add "Use only my facts as truth."
- **Too long:** Add word limits per section.

Role + Rules + Output

What it is

A prompt structure that controls behavior by making expectations explicit.

When to use it

- Reports and memos
- Analytical tasks
- SOP drafting
- Any task where you want predictable structure

Prompt (Copy-Paste)

```
"Role: Act as a [role].
Rules:

Use only my inputs as truth; do not add facts

Label unknowns as 'Missing'

State assumptions explicitly

Keep plain English
Output:

[Headings you want]
Input: [paste]."
```

Example (Short)

Role: "Act as a business analyst."
Output: "Executive summary, findings, options, recommendation, risks, next steps."

Failure modes and fixes

- **Output drifts:** Add "Use these headings exactly; do not add/remove sections."
- **Too verbose:** Add section word limits.

Assumptions First

What it is

A disciplined way to prevent the assistant from filling gaps invisibly.

When to use it

- Incomplete notes
- Conflicting requirements
- Medium/high-risk tasks

Prompt (Copy-Paste)

```
"Task: [task]
Inputs: [facts]
Before drafting:

List assumptions you would otherwise make

List what is uncertain or missing

Ask the minimum questions needed
Then draft using only verified inputs, labeling assumptions
inline."
```

Example (Short)

"Before drafting the project update, list missing dates and owners."

Failure modes and fixes

- **Too many questions:** Ask for "minimum questions only."
- **Still guessing:** Require "If missing, write Missing—do not infer."

Structure Lock

What it is

A method to force consistent headings and formatting across outputs.

When to use it

- Weekly updates
- Meeting recaps
- SOP checklists
- Any recurring deliverable

Prompt (Copy-Paste)

```
"Output must follow this exact structure (do not add/remove
sections):
A) …
B) …
C) …
Limits:

Each section under [X] words

Bullets only in sections [B, D]
Rules:

Do not invent facts

Label missing info as 'Missing'
Input: [paste]."
```

Example (Short)

1. Status headline
2. Progress (3 bullets)
3. Risks (3 bullets)
4. Asks (2 bullets)

Failure modes and fixes

- **Still inconsistent:** Reduce degrees of freedom: fewer sections, stricter limits.

Prompt Stack: Transform → Compose → Review

What it is

A multi-step approach that improves reliability by giving each prompt one job.

When to use it

- Complex tasks
- Messy notes
- High rework situations

Prompt (Copy-Paste)

```
Prompt A (Transform):
"Convert this into structured notes: decisions, actions,
questions, risks. Do not invent."

Prompt B (Compose):
"Draft [deliverable] from structured notes using fixed headings.
Do not invent."

Prompt C (Review):
"Run commitment scan, claims scan, tone scan. Rewrite safely. Do
not add facts."
```

Example (Short)

Meeting notes → recap email → commitment/claims scan.

Failure modes and fixes

- **Too slow:** Use stack only for medium/high risk.
- **Still unclear:** Add Assumptions First to step A.

Critique Then Rewrite

What it is

A structured editing method that makes improvements visible.

When to use it

- Customer emails
- Sensitive internal messages
- Proposals and reports

Prompt (Copy-Paste)

> *"Critique this text against: [criteria].*
> *Then rewrite it.*
> *After rewriting, list the top 5 changes you made and why.*
> *Rules: do not add new facts; keep plain English.*
> *Text: [paste]."*

Example criteria

Clarity, tone, actionability, risk, length, and alignment with constraints.

Failure modes and fixes

- **Over-editing:** Add "keep 80% of meaning and structure; adjust only what's needed."

Decision Memo

What it is

A decision-ready structure that turns uncertainty into options and tradeoffs.

When to use it

- Planning discussions
- Stakeholder approvals
- Any decision with tradeoffs

Prompt (Copy-Paste)

> *"Draft a decision memo.*
> *Decision needed: [decision].*
> *Context (facts only): [paste].*
> *Constraints: [time/budget/policy].*
> *Output format:*
>
> *Decision statement*
>
> *Context*
>
> *Options (2–4)*
>
> *Tradeoffs (pros/cons)*
>
> *Risks + mitigations*
>
> *Recommendation (assumptions labeled)*

```
Next steps
Rules: do not invent facts; label missing info."
```

Failure modes and fixes

- **Recommendations too confident:** Add "recommendation must list assumptions and uncertainties explicitly."

Options and Tradeoffs (Short Form)

What it is

A compact comparison prompt for quick choices.

When to use it

- When you're stuck and need structure fast

Prompt (Copy-Paste)

```
"Decision: [decision]
Criteria (rank): [criteria]
Constraints: [constraints]
Facts: [facts]
Output: 3 options, each with pros/cons, tradeoffs, risks, key
assumptions.
Then recommend one with assumptions labeled.
Rules: do not invent facts."
```

Pre-Mortem

What it is

A risk-finding method: assume failure, list reasons, add mitigations.

When to use it

- Launches, rollouts, process changes, vendor choices

Prompt (Copy-Paste)

```
"We chose Option [X].
Assume this fails in 90 days.
List 10 reasons it failed across
people/process/tools/communication/timing.
```

> *For each: mitigation + early warning sign.*
> *Keep it practical."*

Failure modes and fixes

- **Too abstract:** Ask for "specific early warning signs I can observe this week."

Error-Finding Review (Second Set of Eyes)

What it is

A prompt that asks the assistant to look for problems rather than produce new content.

When to use it

- Before sending externally
- Before publishing
- Before finalizing SOPs or reports

Prompt (Copy-Paste)

> *"Act as a reviewer.*
> *Find problems: ambiguity, missing info, risky commitments,*
> *unsupported claims, logic gaps, tone issues.*
> *Then propose fixes.*
> *Rules: do not add facts.*
> *Text: [paste]."*

Sanitization Transform

What it is

A method to remove sensitive details while keeping meaning.

When to use it

- When you want to use AI with work information responsibly
- When you want a shareable packet

Prompt (Copy-Paste)

> *"Create a sanitized version of this text for AI use and cross-*
> *team sharing.*
> *Rules: remove identifiers; replace names with roles; remove*

```
confidential numbers; keep meaning.
Text: [paste]."
```

Tone and Voice Card Enforcer

What it is

A way to preserve your voice and prevent robotic or hyped language.

When to use it

- Marketing
- Customer communication
- Leadership updates
- Any place where trust matters

Prompt (Copy-Paste)

```
"Rewrite this to match my Voice Card.
Voice Card: [paste].
Phrases to use occasionally: [list].
Phrases to avoid: [list].
Rules: do not add facts; keep meaning.
Text: [paste]."
```

Prompt Debugger

What it is

A method for fixing prompts that produce inconsistent or wrong outputs.

When to use it

- When you keep reworking outputs
- When outputs drift or invent details
- When your team needs a stable template

Prompt (Copy-Paste)

```
"Here is my prompt: [paste].
Here is the output I got: [paste].
My desired output: [describe].
Diagnose why it failed (be specific).
Rewrite the prompt with structure lock, guardrails, and
```

```
placeholders.
Then provide a 3-case test plan."
```

Final Word and Next Steps

You have now built more than "skill with a tool."

You have built:

- a calm way to think about AI in professional life
- a set of repeatable workflows for planning, writing, operations, and decisions
- a verification and ethics standard that protects trust
- a personal system that reduces cognitive load
- a prompt library you can maintain without overwhelm

If you take nothing else from this book, take this:

Confidence does not come from trusting AI. Confidence comes from trusting your process.

This final chapter is short by design. It is intended to be read once now, then returned to when you want a reset.

The Most Important Shift: From "Prompts" To "Practice"

At the beginning, ChatGPT can feel like a question: "How do I talk to it?"

Over time, it becomes a practice: "How do I work with it responsibly?"

That shift matters because prompts are not stable by themselves. Situations change, teams change, tools change, and your role changes.

Practice is what stays.

Your practice is a set of habits:

- brief first
- structure lock when recurring
- no invention rule
- label Missing
- commitment scan
- claims scan
- verify
- save what matters

- improve one thing each month

That list is not "extra." It is what makes AI use calm.

What To Do Tomorrow Morning (A Very Small Start)

If you are unsure how to carry this forward, do not start big.

Tomorrow morning, do this:

1. Write a 4-line capture note (today/next/blockers/commitments).
2. Run your Daily Plan prompt.
3. Choose Top 3 outcomes.
4. Protect one deep-work block.
5. Before you send any external message, run the Review Prompt.

That's it.

You do not need a perfect system. You need a first repetition.

What To Do Next Week (The Weekly Loop That Builds Relief)

Next week, do one thing that most professionals skip:

Run your weekly review.

A weekly review is where:

- open loops become next actions
- wins become evidence
- decisions become records
- lessons become checklists
- context packets become stable

If you do weekly reviews, your stress profile changes because your brain stops acting like your only storage system.

What To Do Next Month (The Maintenance Habit That Prevents Drift)

A system decays unless you maintain it. The maintenance here is lightweight.

Once a month:

- delete prompts you didn't use

- revise one prompt that caused friction
- update one gold standard example
- review your calibration log for recurring errors
- choose one skill to build next

This is how you keep your system alive without making it another job.

How To Teach This to Others (Without Pressure)

If you lead people, you may want to share this approach.

A calm way to teach:

1. Teach the trust workflow first.
2. Share 3 templates, not 30.
3. Use real scenarios (sanitized).
4. Invite improvements and shared ownership.
5. Normalize "we verify and we correct."

The goal is not to turn your team into "AI power users." The goal is to reduce rework and improve clarity safely.

A Final Reminder About Ethics and Professionalism

Ethical AI use is not complicated. It is consistent:

- protect confidentiality
- don't misrepresent certainty
- don't outsource responsibility
- verify what matters
- communicate with respect
- correct mistakes promptly
- leave an evidence trail when needed

Professional trust is difficult to earn and easy to lose. Your standards protect it.

What This Book Is Really Offering

This book is not offering you speed at any cost.

It is offering you a way to work, that is:

- more structured
- less mentally noisy
- more consistent
- more ethical
- more reliable under pressure

AI is a tool. It can help. It can also distract.

Your system ensures it helps.

Acknowledgments and Author's Note

This book is practical by design. It's meant to be used, marked up, and lived with, not admired from a distance. If you're reading this, you've done something that matters: you've chosen to approach a loud topic with quiet intention.

That choice deserves respect.

Acknowledgments

A book like this is never created in isolation, even when the writing happens alone.

It relies on:

- the working professionals who asked for clarity instead of hype
- the managers who wanted guardrails, not shortcuts
- the entrepreneurs who needed calm support in the middle of real operational pressure
- the readers who are willing to learn a new tool without surrendering their judgment

This book is also shaped by countless everyday moments in modern work:

- meetings where clarity is needed more than cleverness
- inboxes that feel like a second job
- projects where the real challenge is not work, but the coordination
- decisions made under imperfect information
- the quiet stress of open loops that follow people home

If you've lived any of that, you already understand the purpose of this book.

Thank you for bringing your real work into the learning process.

Author's Note

You do not need to become an "AI person" to benefit from AI.

You need only two things:

1. a clear definition of what you want the tool to do
2. a process that keeps you accurate and responsible

Everything in this book points back to that idea.

If you feel hesitant or skeptical, that's not a flaw. That's discernment. The goal is not blind adoption. The goal is capable use.

The approach in this book is intentionally steady:

- no fear language
- no hype
- no claims that you must use AI to stay relevant
- no suggestion that AI is an authority

Instead, you are offered something more useful:

a set of repeatable, plain-English practices that reduce cognitive load and increase clarity while protecting trust.

How To Get the Most Out of This Book After Finishing It

The fastest way to forget what you read is to treat it like information.

The fastest way to keep it is to treat it like training.

Here is a simple rhythm:

- Use the daily planning prompt for two weeks
- Run weekly reviews for one month
- Build one SOP and checklist for a recurring task
- Save three gold standard examples
- Review and maintain your prompt library once a month
- Keep a lightweight calibration log when something feels off

That's enough to build lasting confidence.

A Quiet Measure of Success

Success here is not "how many prompts you know."

Success is:

- fewer open loops
- fewer rewrites
- fewer unclear emails
- more reliable follow-through
- more time spent on judgment and relationships
- less mental noise at the end of the day

If your work becomes calmer and more consistent, the book did its job.

Appendix I: Complete Prompt Library (Copy-Paste Version)

This appendix is a clean, copy-paste prompt library designed for daily use. It consolidates the "Core 15" prompts from the capstone and expands them into a complete, ready-to-run set with consistent placeholders and built-in guardrails.

Use this appendix as your working toolkit. Customize once, then reuse.

Important usage rule: **Replace bracketed placeholders (like [Audience]) with your real input. If you do not know something, do not guess—write "Missing" and ask.**

Standard Placeholders (Use These Everywhere)

- [Risk level] = 1 (low), 2 (medium), 3 (high)
- [Audience] = who the output is for
- [Goal] = what you want them to think/do/decide
- [Tone] = calm, confident, plain English (customize if needed)
- [Constraints] = length, policy, what to avoid, must-include
- [Facts] = facts you provide as truth (no invention)
- [Output format] = email, memo, report section, checklist, SOP, etc.
- [Voice Card] = your style guide (if using)
- [Policies] = authoritative policy language you provide (if relevant)

Global Guardrails (Paste into Any Prompt)

Copy-paste this block at the end of any prompt:

> "Guardrails:
>
> Use only my inputs as truth; do not invent names, dates, numbers, policies, or results
>
> If information is missing or uncertain, label it 'Missing' and ask the minimum questions needed
>
> Separate facts from assumptions; label assumptions explicitly
>
> Keep plain English; explain any technical term

For any draft that may be sent externally: include a Commitment Scan and Claims Scan before final text

End with: (1) Commitments, (2) Claims to verify, (3) Verification checklist"

Prompt 1 — Daily Capture → Daily Plan (Top 3 Outcomes)

When to use: Start of day
Risk level: Usually 1

Copy-paste prompt:

"You are my executive productivity assistant.
Goal: turn my capture note into a calm, realistic daily plan.
[Risk level]: 1
Output format: Use these headings exactly:

Top 3 outcomes for today

Task List (grouped: Deep Work / Admin / Waiting / Delegation)

Time blocks (morning / midday / afternoon)

Risks and blockers (with next actions)

Commitment scan (promises I'm making today)

Claims to verify (facts/dates/policies I must confirm)
Capture note (truth):

Today: [paste]

Next: [paste]

Blockers: [paste]

Commitments: [paste]
Guardrails:

Use only my note as truth; do not invent tasks, dates, or commitments

If anything is missing, label 'Missing' and ask"

Prompt 2 — End Of Day: Close Loops and Reset

When to use: End of day
Risk level: 1

Copy-paste prompt:

> "Help me close loops and reset for tomorrow.
> Inputs (truth):
>
> What I did today: [paste]
>
> What is unfinished: [paste]
>
> What I'm worried I'll forget: [paste]
> Output format:
>
> Closed loops (what's done)
>
> Open loops (converted into next actions)
>
> Tomorrow's Top 3 candidate outcomes
>
> Draft capture notes for tomorrow
> (today/next/blockers/commitments)
> Rules: do not invent details; label Missing."

Prompt 3 — Weekly Review (Executive Summary)

When to use: End of week
Risk level: 1–2

Copy-paste prompt:

> "You are my weekly review coach.
> [Risk level]: 1-2
> Goal: extract truth, lessons, and next priorities from my week.
> Rules: use only the inputs I provide; do not invent
> accomplishments or decisions; label assumptions.
> Output format (use headings exactly):
>
> Wins (what moved forward)
>
> Work in progress (what's unfinished and why)
>
> Open loops (waiting, decisions, unanswered questions)

Risks and early warnings

Lessons learned (what to change next week)

Next week: Top 3 outcomes

Next week: key meetings and what I need from each

Verification list (facts/commitments I must confirm)
Inputs (truth):

Weekly notes: [paste]

Calendar highlights: [paste]

Deliverables shipped: [paste]

Decisions made: [paste]"

Prompt 4 — Workload Map (Recurring / Projects / Open Loops)

When to use: Weekly or when overwhelmed
Risk level: 1

Copy-paste prompt:

"Create a workload map from my notes. Use only my notes as truth.
Output:

Recurring responsibilities (weekly/monthly)

Active projects (max 7; purpose + next milestone)

Open loops (waiting items, decisions, unanswered questions)

Top 3 leverage points to reduce stress
Notes: [paste]
Rules: do not invent tasks; label Missing."

Prompt 5 — Context Packet (Create or Update, 250 Words)

When to use: Active projects
Risk level: 1–2

Copy-paste prompt:

> *"Create/update a project context packet under 250 words using my notes as truth.*
> *Replace names with roles. Remove identifiers and confidential numbers.*
> *Include: purpose, stakeholders (roles), constraints, current status, key decisions, next steps, risks/watchlist.*
> *Notes (truth): [paste]*
> *Rules: do not invent dates or decisions; label Missing."*

Prompt 6 — Meeting Notes → Decisions / Actions / Questions / Risks

When to use: After meetings
Risk level: 1–2

Copy-paste prompt:

> *"Transform these meeting notes into structured output.*
> *Output format:*
>
> *Purpose*
>
> *Decisions (if any)*
>
> *Action items (owner, due point; if missing, label Missing)*
>
> *Open questions*
>
> *Risks / dependencies*
> *Notes (truth): [paste]*
> *Rules: do not invent; label Missing."*

Prompt 7 — Recap Email (From Structured Notes)

When to use: Meeting follow-up
Risk level: 2

Copy-paste prompt:

> "Draft a recap email from these structured notes.
> Audience: [Audience]
> Goal: confirm decisions and next steps
> Tone: neutral, calm, direct
> Constraints: keep under [X] words; no blame; no invented deadlines
> Structured notes (truth): [paste]
> Output: subject + email body
> Then include: Commitment scan + Claims scan
> Rules: do not add facts."

Prompt 8 — Universal Draft (Email / Memo / Report Section)

When to use: Any writing task
Risk level: 1–3

Copy-paste prompt:

> "You are my professional writing assistant.
> [Risk level]: [1/2/3]
> Audience: [Audience]
> Goal: [Goal]
> Tone: [Tone]
> Constraints: [Constraints]
> Facts (use as truth; do not add):
>
> [Fact 1]
>
> [Fact 2]
> Output format: [Output format]
> Before drafting: list assumptions and Missing info questions (minimum only).
> Then draft.
> End with:
>
> Commitment scan

```
Claims scan

Verification checklist
Rules: do not invent facts."
```

Prompt 9 — Review Loop (Commitments + Claims + Tone) + Safer Rewrite

When to use: Before sending externally
Risk level: 2–3

Copy-paste prompt:

```
"Review this draft before I send it.
Do three scans:

Commitment scan: list explicit and implied promises

Claims scan: list factual claims requiring verification

Tone scan: identify wording that could sound blamey, vague,
defensive, or overly confident
Then rewrite the draft with safer commitments and clearer
language.
Rules: do not add new facts; keep plain English; keep concise.
Draft: [paste]"
```

Prompt 10 — Executive Update (Structure Lock)

When to use: Weekly leadership updates, stakeholder updates
Risk level: 2

Copy-paste prompt:

```
"Draft an executive update using this structure exactly (do not
add/remove sections):

Status headline (1 sentence)

So what / now what (2-3 sentences)

Progress (max 3 bullets)
```

Risks + mitigations (max 3 bullets)

Asks/decisions needed (max 3 bullets)

Next steps (max 5 bullets; owners if known)
Rules: use only my facts; do not invent; label Missing; end with
commitments + claims to verify.
Facts (truth): [paste]"

Prompt 11 — Decision Record (One Page)

When to use: After a significant decision
Risk level: 2

Copy-paste prompt:

"Create a decision record in plain English using my notes as
truth.
Fields: decision, date (if known), owner, context, options
considered, criteria (rank), rationale, risks, mitigations, next
steps, verification list.
Notes (truth): [paste]
Rules: do not invent; label Missing."

Prompt 12 — Options And Tradeoffs (Decision Support)

When to use: Before deciding
Risk level: 2–3

Copy-paste prompt:

"Help me decide.
Decision: [decision]
Constraints: [time/budget/policy]
Criteria (rank): [criteria]
Facts (truth): [paste]
Output: 3-4 options with pros/cons, tradeoffs, risks, key
assumptions, and a recommendation with assumptions labeled.
Rules: do not invent facts; label Missing; keep practical."

Prompt 13 — Pre-Mortem (Failure Reasons → Mitigations → Early Warnings)

When to use: Before launch or process change
Risk level: 2–3

Copy-paste prompt:

> "We chose Option: [option]
> Assume this fails in 90 days.
> List 10 reasons it failed across
> people/process/tools/communication/timing.
> For each reason, provide: mitigation + early warning sign.
> Constraints: keep it practical; no speculation beyond these
> categories.
> Facts (truth): [paste any relevant facts]"

Prompt 14 — SOP Draft (Source-First)

When to use: Documenting operations
Risk level: 1–2

Copy-paste prompt:

> "Draft an SOP from my source notes. Use only my notes as truth.
> Include: purpose, scope, inputs, tools, steps (numbered), quality
> checks, exceptions/edge cases, outputs, owner, version, last
> updated.
> Label Missing information clearly.
> Source notes (truth): [paste]"

Prompt 15 — SOP → Checklist (10–20 Items)

When to use: Make process runnable
Risk level: 1–2

Copy-paste prompt:

> "Extract a checklist (10-20 items) from this SOP/process.
> Make it usable under time pressure.
> Rules: do not add steps not in the source; keep items actionable.
> Source: [paste]"

Prompt 16 — SOP Edge Cases / Exceptions

When to use: Strengthening SOP reliability
Risk level: 1–2

Copy-paste prompt:

> *"List the top 10 edge cases and exceptions for this SOP/process.*
> *For each: what happens, what to do, what to ask, and what to document.*
> *Rules: base only on the source; label assumptions.*
> *Source: [paste]"*

Prompt 17 — SOP Test Plan (15-Minute Validation)

When to use: Testing SOP usability
Risk level: 1

Copy-paste prompt:

> *"Create a 15-minute test plan to validate this SOP with a new team member.*
> *Include: tasks to perform, what success looks like, where confusion may occur, and what to revise.*
> *Rules: keep it practical; no invention beyond reasonable test steps.*
> *SOP: [paste]"*

Prompt 18 — Lessons Learned (After Action)

When to use: After projects, incidents, rollouts
Risk level: 1–2

Copy-paste prompt:

> *"Create a lessons learned document from these notes.*
> *Output: what happened, what worked, what didn't, root cause hypotheses (label as hypotheses), changes to make, prevention checklist (5-10 items).*
> *Rules: do not invent details; keep plain English.*
> *Notes: [paste]"*

Prompt 19 — Sanitize Text for AI or Sharing

When to use: Protect confidentiality
Risk level: 2–3

Copy-paste prompt:

> *"Create a sanitized version of this text for safe AI use and cross-team sharing.*
> *Rules: remove identifiers; replace names with roles; remove confidential numbers; keep meaning; label any removed categories.*
> *Text: [paste]"*

Prompt 20 — Voice Card Enforcer (Sound Like You)

When to use: Customer comms, marketing, leadership tone
Risk level: 2

Copy-paste prompt:

> *"Rewrite this to match my Voice Card.*
> *Voice Card: [paste]*
> *Phrases to use occasionally: [list]*
> *Phrases to avoid: [list]*
> *Rules: do not add facts; keep meaning; keep it human and plain English.*
> *Text: [paste]"*

Prompt 21 — Error-Finding Review (Second Set of Eyes)

When to use: Final check on important docs
Risk level: 2–3

Copy-paste prompt:

> *"Act as a reviewer. Find problems: ambiguity, missing info, risky commitments, unsupported claims, logic gaps, tone issues.*
> *Then propose fixes.*
> *Rules: do not add facts.*
> *Text: [paste]"*

Prompt 22 — Prompt Debugger (Fix A Template)

When to use: Prompts drift, invent, or produce rework
Risk level: 1

Copy-paste prompt:

> *"Here is my prompt: [paste]*
> *Here is the output I got: [paste]*
> *My desired output: [describe]*
> *Diagnose why it failed (specific).*
> *Rewrite the prompt with structure lock, guardrails, and placeholders.*
> *Then provide a 3-case test plan."*

Appendix II: Voice Card Templates for Professional Use

A Voice Card is a one-page style guide you paste into prompts to keep outputs consistent, human, and aligned with your standards. It is not branding fluff. It is operational.

Voice Cards matter because AI outputs tend to drift toward:

- generic corporate tone
- overconfidence
- unnecessary buzzwords
- robotic phrasing
- inconsistent formality

A Voice Card prevents drift. It also makes teamwork easier when multiple people use the same templates.

This appendix provides three Voice Card templates you can use immediately:

1. Business professional (calm, direct)
2. Customer-first support (warm, accountable)
3. Marketing (proof-based, no hype)

You can copy one as-is or combine elements.

Voice Card 1 — Business Professional (Calm, Direct, Executive)

Voice identity: Calm, competent, plain-English, action-oriented.

Tone:

- Confident, not certain beyond evidence
- Direct, not harsh
- Neutral, not blamey
- Helpful, not overly enthusiastic

Default posture:

- Lead with purpose and the "ask"
- Provide minimal context needed to act
- Name risks and next steps clearly
- Avoid drama; stay professional

Sentence style:

- Short to medium sentences

- Prefer active voice
- Avoid stacked clauses and hedging

Preferred words and phrases:

- "Here's what we need next..."
- "To keep this moving..."
- "The decision needed is..."
- "The risk is..."
- "Next step..."
- "If we confirm X, then we can..."
- "Missing information:" (when needed)

Words and phrases to avoid:

- "Obviously," "clearly," "as you know"
- "Just" (minimizes)
- "Guarantee," "always," "never" (unless truly true)
- Buzzwords: "synergy," "leverage" (unless required)
- Emotional escalation: "frustrating," "unacceptable" (unless carefully warranted)

Formatting preferences:

- Use headings for longer messages
- Use bullets for lists (max 5 per section)
- One clear ask per message when possible
- End with next step + owner (if known)

Proof and accuracy rules:

- Never invent dates, numbers, policies, or results
- Label Missing info and ask questions
- For external messages: include commitment and claims scans

Example closing lines:

- "If you confirm [Missing item], I'll proceed with [next step]."
- "Thanks—once approved, we'll move to [step]."

Voice Card 2 — Customer-First Support (Warm, Accountable, Clear)

Voice identity: Warm, respectful, calm, solutions-focused.

Tone:

- Empathetic without over-apologizing
- Accountable without blame
- Clear about next steps and timing (only if verified)
- Human, not robotic

Default posture:

- Acknowledge the customer's experience
- State what you can do now
- Set expectations honestly
- Offer one simple next step

Sentence style:

- Short sentences
- Friendly phrasing
- Avoid excessive formality or jargon

Preferred words and phrases:

- "Thanks for reaching out—here's what I can do for you."
- "I understand, and I'm going to help."
- "Here's the next step…"
- "To make this right…" (use carefully and only when appropriate)
- "If you prefer, we can…"
- "Missing detail:" (when you need information)

Words and phrases to avoid:

- "That's our policy" (without explanation)
- "You should have…"
- "Calm down" (never)
- Blame language: "you failed," "you didn't"
- Overpromises: "ASAP," "guarantee," "for sure" unless verified

Formatting preferences:

- Keep under 180–220 words when possible
- Use short paragraphs
- One question at a time when gathering info
- End with a clear next step

Proof and accuracy rules:

- Never guess timelines; verify or label Missing
- Never claim refunds, replacements, or outcomes unless authorized and confirmed
- Never include sensitive details in a way that could be forwarded publicly

Example closing lines:

- "If you confirm [detail], I'll take the next step immediately."
- "Thanks again—I'll follow up by [verified date/time] with an update."

Voice Card 3 — Marketing (Proof-Based, Benefit-Driven, No Hype)

Voice identity: Clear, grounded, benefit-driven, credible.

Tone:

- Confident, not exaggerated
- Helpful, not salesy
- Specific, not vague
- Values quality and trust

Default posture:

- Lead with the customer's intent and problem
- Offer a clear benefit
- Support with proof (features, process, examples)
- End with a simple call to action

Sentence style:

- Short to medium
- Avoid inflated adjectives
- Use concrete details (materials, process, lead times only if verified)

Preferred words and phrases:

- "Built for…"
- "Designed to…"
- "Made to last…" (if true and supportable)
- "Personalized with…"
- "Here's what you can choose…"
- "What to expect…"
- "Simple ordering steps…"

Words and phrases to avoid:

- "Best in the world"
- "Revolutionary"
- "Guaranteed perfect"
- "Instant results"
- "Game-changing" (unless you can support it)

Formatting preferences:

- Use scannable sections: benefits, options, what's included, how it works
- Keep calls to action simple: "Choose your option," "Request a proof," "Start customization"

Proof and accuracy rules:

- Avoid unverified claims (time, durability, comparisons)
- Avoid competitor bashing
- If describing materials or process, be accurate and consistent
- Include disclaimers when needed (e.g., "Lead times vary by customization")

Voice Card 4 — Create Your Own Voice Card (Fill-In Template)

Copy-paste and fill in:

Voice identity:

- [How you want to sound in one sentence]

Tone:

- [tone trait 1]
- [tone trait 2]
- [tone trait 3]

Default posture:

- [How you typically structure messages—what comes first]

Sentence style:

- [Short/medium/long, active voice, etc.]

Preferred phrases:

- [Fill in a preferred phrase]
- [Fill in a preferred phrase]

Phrases to avoid:

- [Fill in a phrase to avoid]
- [Fill in a phrase to avoid]

Formatting preferences:

- [Headings, bullets, length limits]

Proof and accuracy rules:

- [No invention, Missing label, scans, verification]

Examples of "good closings":

- [Provide an example or examples of "good closings"]

Appendix III: Ethical Use and Accuracy Guardrails (Printable Policy)

This appendix is a printable policy you can adopt personally or adapt for a team. It is written to be operational: clear rules, clear escalation points, and a standard process for verification.

It does not assume AI is an authority. It assumes AI is a drafting and structuring assistant that must be governed by human judgment and professional standards.

Purpose

This policy establishes guardrails for using ChatGPT (and similar AI assistants) in business and professional work.

It aims to:

- protect confidentiality
- prevent inaccurate or misleading outputs
- preserve trust with customers, stakeholders, and teams
- reduce rework through consistent verification habits
- provide a calm, repeatable standard of care

Core Principles

1. **Human judgment is responsible.**
   AI may support thinking and drafting. Final responsibility remains with the user.

2. **Truth comes from sources, not from fluency.**
   AI outputs can sound confident and still be wrong. Verification is required for meaningful claims.

3. **Confidentiality is non-negotiable.**
   Sensitive information must be sanitized or withheld unless the tool and context are approved.

4. **Risk level determines rigor.**
   Higher consequence requires higher verification and approvals.

5. **Transparency is professional.**
   When uncertainty exists, it must be labeled and managed, not hidden.

Definitions (Plain English)

Risk level

A three-level scale based on consequences if the output is wrong or disclosed.

- **Level 1:** low-risk internal work (drafts, organizing notes)
- **Level 2:** medium-risk or routine external work (customer emails, status updates, SOP drafts)
- **Level 3:** high-risk or sensitive work (legal/HR/medical/financial guidance, public statements with significant impact)

Claim

A factual statement that must be true (dates, numbers, policies, results, comparisons).

Commitment

A promise you make, explicit or implied (timelines, deliverables, guarantees, outcomes).

Verification

Checking claims against authoritative sources or trusted internal records.

Sanitization

Removing or abstracting sensitive details before using AI (replace names with roles, remove identifiers, remove confidential numbers).

Acceptable Use (What AI is Good For)

AI is appropriate for:

- structuring messy notes into decisions and action items
- drafting emails and memos from provided facts
- generating multiple wording options for tone and clarity
- creating checklists and SOP drafts from source notes
- summarizing internal content you provide (sanitized)
- brainstorming options and tradeoffs with assumptions labeled
- building templates and repeatable workflows

AI is most valuable when used as:

- a structuring tool
- a drafting assistant
- a review aid (commitment scan, claims scan, tone scan)

Prohibited Use (What Not to Do)

Do not use AI to:

1. **Invent facts or fill gaps silently.**
   If you don't know, label Missing and ask.

2. **Provide definitive legal, medical, or financial advice as authority.**
   AI can help draft questions, summarize known policies, or structure a memo, but it cannot replace professional counsel or authoritative references.

3. **Handle confidential or regulated information in unapproved tools.**
   Do not paste:

   - personal identifiers
   - protected health information
   - confidential customer data
   - internal legal strategy
   - sensitive HR performance details

   - proprietary numbers or contracts
     unless your organization explicitly approves the tool and context.

4. **Create deceptive communications.**
   Do not write messages that misrepresent what you know, what you verified, or what you can deliver.

5. **Overpromise outcomes.**
   Avoid guarantees unless verified and authorized.

Required Process (Standard of Care)

This is the minimum process for AI-assisted work.

Step 1 — Choose risk level

- Level 1: internal drafts/organization
- Level 2: routine external or meaningful internal work
- Level 3: high-stakes or sensitive work

Step 2 — Sanitize inputs (as needed)

- replace names with roles
- remove identifiers
- remove confidential numbers
- remove sensitive details

Step 3 — Provide source facts and constraints

- list facts as truth
- state constraints (tone, length, policies)
- specify output format (email, memo, checklist)

Step 4 — Draft with guardrails

Include these requirements in prompts:

- no invention
- label Missing information
- separate facts from assumptions
- keep plain English

Step 5 — Review scans before external use

- commitment scan: promises and implied promises
- claims scan: facts requiring verification
- tone scan: clarity, respect, neutrality

Step 6 — Verify

For Level 2–3:

- verify dates, numbers, policies, and material claims
- verify against authoritative sources (policy docs, contracts, system records, approved references)
- if verification is not possible, revise language to reflect uncertainty or delay sending

Step 7 — Approvals (Level 3)

For Level 3:

- obtain required review/approval
- save evidence trail (sources, decisions, approvals)

Step 8 — Save reusable assets

Save:

- final templates
- decision records
- context packets
- SOPs and checklists
  when they will be reused.

Verification Guidelines by Risk Level

Level 1 (low-risk internal)

- quick reasonableness check
- ensure no confidential details are included unnecessarily
- no external sending without Level 2 review

Level 2 (routine external / meaningful internal)

- run commitment scan
- run claims scan
- verify key claims (dates, numbers, policies, commitments)
- keep a record for reusable outputs

Level 3 (high-stakes)

- AI for structure and clarity only
- authoritative sources required
- expert review or formal approvals required
- documentation of verification required
- conservative language if uncertainty remains

Confidentiality and Data Handling Rules

Use this practical test:

If you would not paste it into an email to the wrong person, do not paste it into AI.

Sanitization checklist:

- replace names with roles (Customer, Vendor, Manager)
- remove personal identifiers (addresses, phone numbers, IDs)
- remove account numbers and contract numbers
- remove nonpublic financial figures
- remove internal legal strategy details
- remove HR performance specifics unless approved

When in doubt:

- summarize at a higher level
- ask the AI for structure and wording only
- keep sensitive facts in your own document and merge manually

Accountability And Transparency

When AI contributes to a deliverable:

- you remain accountable for accuracy and tone
- you must verify claims for Level 2–3
- you must not imply you verified something you did not verify
- if an error is discovered, correct it promptly and document the fix if appropriate

A professional correction is not a failure. It's a trust behavior.

Team Versioning and Template Governance (Optional)

If a team shares prompts:

- designate an owner for each template
- store templates in one location
- version templates (v1, v2, v3)
- require review for Level 3 templates
- keep a change log: what changed and why

- deprecate templates that cause errors or drift

This prevents prompt sprawl and inconsistent standards.

Quick Policy Summary (One Page)

AI Use Policy — Quick Summary

1. Choose risk level (1–3).
2. Sanitize inputs; protect confidentiality.
3. Provide facts and constraints; do not invite guessing.
4. Draft with guardrails: no invention, label Missing, plain English.
5. Before external use: commitment scan + claims scan + tone scan.
6. Verify key claims; use authoritative sources.
7. Level 3 requires approvals and documentation.
8. Save reusable assets; maintain templates monthly.

About the Author

Matthew J. Shively, MSc, is a senior leader with more than two decades of experience at the intersection of judicial operations, legal administration, federal compliance, HR strategy, and program transformation. He currently serves as a Court Reporter Program Administrator in Judicial Operations for the United States Air Force, where he supervises geographically dispersed teams across the U.S. and Europe and advises senior leaders on high-compliance, high-stakes mission requirements.

In his day-to-day work, Matthew is also an active practitioner of applied AI, using tools like ChatGPT to reduce cognitive load, accelerate drafting and analysis, strengthen decision-making, and standardize repeatable workflows (with verification and ethical guardrails). His approach emphasizes practical accuracy, clear communication, and human judgment as the final authority.

In addition to his federal service, Matthew is the Director of Digital Strategy & Business Development for Promethean Woodworks, L.L.C., where he leads growth-focused strategy across digital channels and customer experience, combining craftsmanship, operations discipline, and modern productivity systems to build a scalable, trustworthy brand.

Matthew holds a Master of Science in Organizational Leadership and maintains advanced professional credentials including the SPHR and Lean Six Sigma Green Belt.

www.ingramcontent.com/pod-product-compliance
Lightning Source LLC
Chambersburg PA
CBHW052340210326
41597CB00037B/6199